Electronic Literacies in the Workplace

Advances in Computers and Composition Studies

Series Editors:

Gail E. Hawisher
University of Illinois at Urbana-Champaign

Cynthia L. Selfe
Michigan Technological University

Series Design Editor:

James R. Kalmbach
Illinois State University

Creating a Computer-Supported Writing Facility:
A Blueprint for Action

Evolving Perspectives on Computers and Composition Studies:
Questions for the 1990s

Writing Teachers Writing Software:
Creating Our Place in the Electronic Age

Electronic Literacies in the Workplace:
Technologies of Writing

Electronic Literacies in the Workplace

Technologies of Writing

Edited by
Patricia Sullivan
Purdue University

Jennie Dautermann
Miami University

NCTE

Computers and Composition

NCTE Editorial Board: Colette Daiute, Hazel Davis, Bobbi Fisher, Keith Gilyard, Brenda Greene, Gail Hawisher, Ronald Jobe, Richard Luckert, Karen Smith, Chair, ex officio, Dawn Boyer, ex officio.

Manuscript Editors: Humanities & Sciences Associates

Production Editors: Michael Greer, Jamie Hutchinson

Interior Design: Adapted from James R. Kalmbach

Cover Design: Loren Kirkwood

NCTE Stock Number: 13079-3050

Library of Congress Cataloging-in-Publication Data

Electronic literacies in the workplace: technologies of writing/ edited by Patricia Sullivan, Jennie Dautermann.
    p. cm—(Advances in computers and composition studies)
    Includes bibliographical references and index.
    ISBN 0-8141-1307-9
    1. Business communication—Data processing. 2. Business writing—Data processing. 3. Computer literacy. 4. Workplace literacy. I. Sullivan, Patricia, 1951– . II. Dautermann, Jennie. III. Series.
HF5718.E42 1996
651.8—dc20
                            96–2657
                             CIP

Contents

Introduction

Issues of Written Literacy and Electronic Literacy in Workplace Settings

Jennie Dautermann
Miami University

Patricia Sullivan
Purdue University

Composition studies often links "computers and writing," "computers and literacy," "computers and workplaces," "writing and workplaces," or "literacy and workplaces." Seldom, though, do we simultaneously consider "computers," "literacy," "workplace," and "writing." Such a linking exposes a number of gaps in our thinking about how writing issues are constructed in working lives—gaps that we need to explore in order to build a set of issues that can drive the study of computers and writing in our workplaces. For example:

- *Workforce and Literacy:* At least since the publication of *Workforce 2000* in 1987, preparing workers for the vastly and rapidly changing workplace has spurred workplace literacy efforts. Yet, the resulting programs have been grounded in basic skills. Shouldn't our notions of workplace literacy also be tied to critical college literacies, since jobs requiring a college education (or more) are the ones that *Workforce 2000* predicts will increase?

- *Workplaces and Writing and Computers:* Writing-in-the-workplace research has helped us understand professional writing and rhetoric in workplace settings. Inquiries into how people write in particular workplaces have expanded our knowledge of the social factors in writing and have begun to change the writing instruction of future professionals. But, to date, how technology relates to workplace writing has not been central to this research. How can we find out the impact of technologies on writing in the workplace?

- *Computers and Writing and Literacy:* Computers have been theorized alternatively as neutral or as instruments of capitalist oppression or as opening spaces for democracy, with debates over the implications of each portrayal. Such debates have shown how writing at the machine challenges, seduces, and enriches our theories of writing and reading. But these discussions have focused on critical literacies in school settings. How will such discussions change in workplace settings?

- *Computers and Workplaces:* Workplaces are rapidly integrating a number of electronic media—electronic mail, voice mail, Internet communication, and faxes—into the fabric of communication at work. Research on communication in organizations, however, focuses on adoption and acceptance of media and not on issues of reading and composing in particular contexts. Thus, the questions that we would consider critical to written/electronic literacy in the workplace have not been asked about electronic media in the workplace. What is the nature of the computer's impact on workplaces as literate environments?

This collection aims to explore some of these gaps as a way to promote a fuller, more thoughtful approach to the uses of computers in the workplace. We contend that technology, especially when it networks writers to other writers, is more than a mere scribal tool. It offers—at the very least—a connection to new sources of information, a site for rethinking structures of texts, and an opportunity for interaction with co-writers. If we view technology as a mere scribal tool, it handicaps our efforts to understand workplace literacy in its fullest sense. What is needed, we think, is an interdisciplinary effort that combines and rethinks what we know about written literacy, about computers and writing, about writing practices in workplaces, and about computer use in workplaces. Thus, we intend for this collection to ignite interest in technology as one of the material conditions of workplace writing contexts, and we see this as an important move for the following reasons:

- Workplace literacy studies need to be informed by a broader view of the literate behavior demanded of citizens of modern democracies. With Heath (1990), we argue that most literacy work has focused on school literacies at the expense of very real needs in the areas of work, family, and community discourse.

- Workplace writing environments can be affected, in subtle and not so subtle ways, by the nature of the technological tools available there. We believe that exploring workplace cultures without understanding those effects can distort such research.

- Computers and composition researchers have found that computers may affect the very nature of writing activity in ways that extend well beyond mere text manipulation. That seems to be the case in our own work and in the experience of our students. We are curious if this holds true in the workplaces into which we send them.

- We believe that studying writing with technology in the workplace will bring attention to the complexity inherent in such activity—a result which is necessary if writing theorists and practitioners are to have any significant influence on the development of software and equipment intended for use by future writers.

Electronic Literacy and the Changing Nature of the Workforce

The significant employment report, *Workforce 2000* (Johnston & Packer, 1987), predicted that the overall growth in jobs in the next decade would "restructure U. S. occupational patterns . . . with most new jobs demanding more education and higher levels of language, math, and reasoning skills." It further predicted that the "number of jobs in the least-skilled job classes will disappear, while high-skilled professions will grow rapidly" (p. 97). More than half of the new jobs created will require some education beyond high school. That compares with the 22 percent of all occupations which currently require a college degree.

This forecast suggests that the coming workforce will need to know how to read and write and more. Businesses increasingly recognize critical thinking, an ability frequently associated with writing, as a marketable commodity. They further associate these skills with electronic literacy. *Business Week*'s report on recent trends in workplace technology articulates a business perspective on the need for workplace literacy by calling it "the ability to 'mine' information—the process of quickly gathering and analyzing the millions of bits of data that a business generates each day—and steer various pieces to the right people within the organization" (*Business Week,* 1994, p. 104).

Computer literacy demands on the American worker have already increased substantially since the *Workforce 2000* study was released in 1987. The 1990 census showed that 38.3 percent of American workers in all occupations used computers on the job. Among workers with some college education, that number was greater than 50 percent, and nearly 60 percent of workers who had completed a college education used computers at work. While these figures do not necessarily reflect the amount of *writing* done on those computers at work, 41.1 percent of people who reported using computers at work also reported using them for word processing (which we take to be an indicator of writing activity) (U.S. Bureau of Census, 1991, p. 412).

Educators have cited these workforce needs to argue for computers in education. Among students in American schools, access to computers in classrooms doubled between the years 1985 and 1989. Both public and private schools have continued to bring down the ratio of students per computer so that by 1993, government figures showed that there were fewer than 20 students per school-owned computer in the public as well as the private schools.

The U.S. Department of Education (1992) reported that by 1990 more than 95 percent of all public schools of any size offered their students some access to microcomputers. Instructional activities related to writing (word processing, keyboarding, learning English) were rivaled only by mathematics instruction in frequency of use.

Workplace literacy programs, though, have not responded by connecting writing, reading, and technology. Instead, they have focused on a basic skills set they identify as functional literacy, or "the level of proficiency necessary for effective performance in a range of settings and customary activities" (Scribner, 1988, p. 73). Thus, workplace literacy programs typically focus on basic reading, writing, and math—generally emphasizing forms, instructions (sometimes with graphics), and memos. When connected with schooling, workplace literacy efforts have led to secondary school curricular responses such as tech-prep programs, which link vocational and technical education in secondary schools with that in two-year colleges. In tech prep, students take some college courses while still in high school and earn an associate's degree in six years. English classes in these programs are often designed to fit with the work students are doing in their technical classes.

In a very real sense, workplace literacy efforts have existed separately from efforts to understand critical literacies. The "pragmatic" workplace focus—which too often stresses entering or fitting into a system rather than assessing and possibly resisting it—has fostered suspicion of writing that is connected with workplaces as being somehow "vocational" or "functional." Covino (1991), for example, is pointed in his negative portrait of functional literacy, connecting it with the magic of the *National Enquirer* and labeling it "uncritical literacy—the ability to read and write unreflectively that is often called functional literacy" (p. 34).

The unfortunate division between workplace literacy and academic literacy is maintained institutionally by connecting workplace literacy work with basic skills and/or vocational education rather than with critical skills, and it often limits university educators' understanding of workplace literacy issues even though some educators seem aware of this gap. As Heath points out in the closing essay of *The Right to Literacy* (Lunsford, Moglen, &

Slevin, 1990), "Perhaps the most important [notion] for direct effects on rethinking literate behaviors is the renewed interest in communication in the workplace" (p. 301).

Connecting higher education's view of literacy with workplace literacy issues and practices may be complicated by higher education's view of literacy learners as "students" who need improved "school skills," as Brandt (1990) suggests. A view of learning for its own sake, or for the sake of school success, may not be appropriate for the workplace. However, one complication may be easing. The long-espoused and mechanistic view of workplace literacy as a set of discrete skills is being challenged from within by research about the nature of work. Darrah (1994), for example, calls into question definitions of both the "workplace" and the "worker" that are based on a concept of discrete (and decomposable) skills. He posits a "heterogeneous workplace held together by networks of assistance with expertise distributed throughout," which simultaneously "challenges the assumption that workers holding the same jobs need the same skills, and points to the importance of various social skills and organizational structures to coordinate this distributed expertise" (p. 66). In such a place, adaptability may be one's primary survival skill.

Electronic literacy, too, has to contend with the problem of change, particularly as it impacts on habits learned in one environment which must be made to work in another. Whether workers face fancy new equipment or use old survivors of make-do equipment policies, they often must learn unfamiliar technology as they are pressured to keep up with their usual work load. To survive, workers must develop flexibility, creative approaches to problems, and a spirit of tolerance for learning under pressure. Forman (1994) calls this learning "the ability . . . to make intelligent choices and uses of [composing] technology" (p. 132). Scribner further acknowledges this quality as she names one of her metaphors for literacy "adaptation" because it focuses on this changing set of circumstances and on enabling people to contribute to economic growth and stability. As Scribner (1988) examines this changing nature of the literacy normally labeled "functional," she argues that new technologies are not reducing literacy requirements, as some have argued, but are adding new literacies to those derived from natural language literacies—implying that these new technologies require reading and writing to move into new settings and to respond to these electronic settings.

Thus, we approach this collection with a conception of *workplace electronic literacy* that includes dexterity and critical rhetorical skill with texts, as well as flexible use of electronic sources, storage media, and word-processing programs. In this sense, workplace literacy affects all people in an organization who read, write, produce, reproduce, and edit the texts and other information sources. We also see electronic literacy as moving beyond the traditional label of "functional literacy" and aiming to include more than one of the metaphors that Scribner associates with the types of literacy studies. Like Scribner, we find each of the traditional metaphors—adaptation, power, and state of grace—far too limited to explain the literacies we need to develop.

Writing in the Workplace and the Technologies of the Workplace

It has been more than a decade since Odell and Goswami (1985) edited *Writing in Nonacademic Settings,* a pioneering collection about nonacademic writing that grew out of their study of social workers in New York. Since then, composition researchers in professional and technical writing have investigated a broad range of writing that professionals perform in the workplace. But even though Odell and Goswami's collection had two articles which focused on technology's roles in workplace writing, few subsequent studies have developed the issues related to how technology shapes, and is shaped by, writing practices in actual workplaces. Much of the research has focused on identifying the social fabric out of which writing and communication arises and has produced insights into the practical conditions of writing at work. As a way of establishing the importance of the social fabric to the construction of writing, researchers have contributed evidence that collaboration is important in workplace writing contexts (Doheny-Farina, 1984; Couture & Rymer, 1989; Simpson, 1989; Ede & Lunsford, 1990); that organizational hierarchies can have negative effects on the writing of working professionals (Cross, 1990;

Dautermann, 1991); that audience concerns can moderate the power of previous texts (Huettman, 1990); that oral and written composing overlap and complicate one another (Spilka, 1993); and that writing-quality questions in a work culture can be quite different from those in classrooms or on the literary page (Brown & Herndl, 1986; Barabas, 1990). Removed from composition classrooms, these researchers have studied engineering (Selzer, 1983; Spilka, 1988; Winsor, 1989), journalism (Kelvin, 1993), computer science and documentation (Doheny-Farina, 1984; Mirel, 1993; Hovde, 1994), banking (Smart, 1993), government (Kleimann, 1989; Griggs, 1994), and so on. Certainly, this work has prepared us for considering the social dimensions of how computers and writing inhabit the workplace in more sophisticated ways. But, curiously enough, workplace researchers have yet to develop a coherent relationship for computing and writing in workplace settings.

Perhaps technology has been little noticed in workplace writing research because of the primarily print-based perspectives on the nature of writing that are our heritage. Only recently have we begun to systematically address visual literacy in texts. Although writers, advertisers, graphic designers, and many others acknowledge forms of rhetorics that are not based solely on printed texts (see Bernhardt, 1993; Barton & Barton, 1993; Mirel, 1993; Sullivan, 1991), we have been slow to recognize that these rhetorics are in some way shaped by the various technologies that house them. Computers contribute to the blurring of graphical and textual information and can also offer radical ways of reconceiving the structures of extended text. Consider, as an example, the enthusiastic discussions of electronic texts as a new way of composing, reading, and even thinking (Bolter, 1991; Tuman, 1992; Porter, 1993; Heim, 1993; Johnson-Eilola, 1994). When writing is defined to include issues such as visual rhetoric, online writing, hypertext design, or database reporting, the computer's importance to workplace writers is more noticeable. And once noticed, such issues as collaboration, invention, and drafting and revising strategies change as they inhabit new electronic spaces.

Whatever the reason for downplaying technology, workplace writing research needs to account for electronic media because of the increasing pervasiveness of computers in workplace settings. Standard and Poor (1993) estimates that current sales of PCs and workstations amount to more than 25 million units per year (p. c-84) and that more than 40 percent of all software sales are for writing-related applications such as word processing, spreadsheets, desktop publishing, and graphics (p. c-108). Such equipment is no longer exclusively distributed by knowledgeable sales representatives and supported by large training staffs; it is often marketed to ordinary businesses by mail-order houses or retailers whose commitment to end-users may be minimal.

Networked communication also looms large as a work environment. Standard and Poor estimated that by 1995, more than 69 percent of all business PCs would be connected to networks. That number is closer to 90 percent in "leading-edge" companies (p. c-97), and the number of electronic mailboxes will reach 35 million (p. c-117). So even ordinary businesses are beginning to travel the information superhighway. These projections match Lawrence Tesler's conception of the 1990s as the decade of networked computing. "It is believed," Tesler (1991) predicted, "that the computer will come to play a much more active role by collaborating with the user" (p. 86) as the computer changes roles from "cloistered oracle to personal implement to active assistant" (p. 87). The paradigm shift Tesler envisioned is one where the desktop metaphor (that treated users as individuals) yields to a network metaphor (that deals with users as groups). Already we have seen some evidence of an increased public consciousness of networking: What newsstand lacks a magazine article focusing on the information superhighway, the Internet, virtual corporations, or cyberspace? Even David Letterman, our ignorant Everyman, jokes about not understanding the information superhighway.

However, we are also dealing, as government statistics show, with environments where the state-of-the-art is not in force. Even though work at the technological edge is valuable, we see the present collection as important to the study of writers' interactions with whatever technology they live with on the job. We consider it important here to understand the ways in which equipment functions in connection with writing tasks as they occur in working organizations. For that reason, linking computers in the workplace to workplace writing research that is already yielding impressive results can portend a profitable alliance.

Computers and Composition and
Electronic Media in the Workplace

Two other research communities, computers and composition and organizational communication, help to articulate certain aspects of electronic workplace literacy. At the very least, computers and composition researchers share an excitement about the ways in which electronic media have created new possibilities for communication and community with those researchers in organizational communication who study the uses of electronic media in workplaces. They also share a realization that as each new technology is added to the mix of communication alternatives, its addition exposes some of our deep-seated assumptions about how communication works or "ought" to work. Though most research in both areas focuses on technological possibilities brought about by each change rather than focusing on the accompanying denouements (or the losses of jobs and skills to automation, as some would argue), researchers from both communities understand the instability of communication patterns wrought by technological change.

Yet the two groups are quite different in the ways they frame their studies, with computers and composition researchers focused on the study of college writing (often to the exclusion of writing outside of academic settings) while electronic media researchers explore choice, acceptance, and integration of new media into organizations. As we see it, the computers and composition group is sensitive to learning, people, and the nature of writing. Meanwhile, the electronic-media-in-the-workplace group (usually performed in organizational communication settings and called computer-mediated communication or technology research) is sensitive to the larger shifts in the ways work is organized, the roles people play in organizations, and the selection of communication media to support those roles. In our quest to examine issues of computers and writing in the workplace, we hope for better communication among these groups about the nature of electronic writing in workplace settings. Yet we also recognize that, because the computers and composition group normally identifies with students and learning while the electronic-media-in-the-workplace group usually identifies with information flow and with the leadership in organizations, their interests may be divergent enough to inhibit such communication.

In the past decade, in part because of the explosion of the microcomputing age, we have seen a tremendous growth in the study of computers and composition inside the broader field of rhetoric and composition. Since computers were often introduced into writing education as instruments of remediation (Schwartz, 1982), they were originally metaphorized as assistants, as instruments, as tools, as facilitators of instruction. Thus, much early debate centered on their effectiveness in writing instruction (see Atkinson, 1993, for evidence of that effectiveness). As the use of computers in writing instruction became more widespread (see Becker & Sterling, 1987, and U.S. Bureau of Census, 1993, for statistics on K–12 computer use; college-use statistics are not available), both the uses of computers in writing classes and also the theorizing about computers and writing have become more diverse. Researchers and theorists have become more willing to consider the computer as more than a tool (see Bolter, 1991; Barker & Kemp, 1990; Kaplan, 1991; Hawisher, 1992; Moran, 1992; Eldred & Fortune, 1992; Haas & Neuwirth, 1994) and to critique various positions the computer might be given in reading and writing.

A number of essays have pointed to the ways in which new technologies complicate both writing processes and theories of writing processes. In *Evolving Perspectives on Computers and Composition Studies* (Hawisher & Selfe, 1991), several essays clarify issues of hypertext and writing. Moulthrop, for example, discusses the theoretical problems attending the description of the reading process used with hypertext, while Smith articulates the ways in which hypertext makes composing a social activity. In *Computers and Community* (Handa, 1990), a number of essays explore issues of networking and writing. Barker and Kemp, for example, discuss ways in which networked classrooms can enact postmodern pedagogies, while Langston and Batson describe the ways in which ENFI classes create such social shifts in composing processes that they invite collaboration.

These discussions have aided the growth of "electronic literacy" as a topic of substance. In Hawisher and Selfe's *Critical Perspectives on Computers and Composition Instruction* (1989), Selfe contends that electronic literacy is a collection of multilayered literacies that allow people to move back and forth between print and electronic media in their efforts to read and write in the emerging electronic culture. She further contends that a sensitivity to the differences between page and screen must inform our notions of computers and writing instruction. Selfe and Hilligoss's *Literacy and Computers: The Complications of Teaching and Learning with Technology* (1994) focuses on some of those literacies by considering how schoolrooms provide contexts for electronic literacy, how networks extend our notions of literacy, and how reading and writing in hypertext challenge our notions of those skills.

These developments point to how new technology challenges contemporary rhetorical theories of writing and the teaching of writing. But much of the computers and composition research also focuses on the experience of students isolated from workplace conditions. While computers and composition scholars, teachers, and researchers are making strides toward understanding more about how computers can be used in the service of learning to write, they have not yet spent considerable energy on how electronic writing operates in settings other than the academy. As such, this work can carry baggage about "creativity," "learning as a timeless or leisure pursuit," and "breadth as a goal" that comes from thinking of students as apprenticed to literacy learning rather than as workers (Sullivan and Beason, 1994, argue the implications of seeing students as workers). The very important issues addressed in computers and composition, therefore, have to do more with intellectual and cultural capital than with the issues of value and production.

Simultaneously, researchers in organizational communication have studied how computers are used for communication in workplace settings. Focusing on how new communication media are selected and integrated into organizations, these researchers have extensively studied electronic mail in a variety of workplaces (for reviews of this work, see Allen, Gotcher, & Seibert, 1994; Fulk & Boyd, 1991). By and large, they have tried to build models of acceptance, motivation, or use that explain questions about media use in organizations: Why do people use e-mail in some circumstances and voice mail in others? Which of the media are richer forms of communication? What are the various media's strengths for supporting communication tasks?

This work is just beginning to mature. Allen, Gotcher, and Seibert (1994), in their review of organizational communication research published in the 1980s, contend that organizational communication needs to invest more research in the actual content of communication on the networks. They call for work that explores the richness and cues (or lack of cues) in electronic communication and that identifies the communication processes associated with acceptance and use of new technologies. They go on to point out that interest in networks and communication grew during the 1980s, with networks and technology blossoming suddenly at the end of the decade. Changes in technology, they claim, have been shown to alter organizational structure (Allen & Hauptman, 1987), network roles (Barley, 1990), and network power (Sproull & Kiesler, 1991). But network processes have also been influenced by technology use (Papa, 1990; Schmitz & Fulk, 1991; Rice, 1993) and by patterns of social organization (Fulk, 1993). The research concerns they identify as central to organizational communication are (a) acceptance of new technologies, (b) technology's impact on organizational practices, and (c) technology's effect on interpersonal interactions (p. 279).

Obviously, this research has focused more on equipment—its introduction, acceptance, and use—and on management of workers. Thus, it holds no easy answers for us about *how people in organizations use computers to write and communicate.* Still, despite differences in aim and approach from computers and writing, these studies give us considerable information about actual use of computers and networks in particular workplaces. What the electronic media research tends to underplay are the organizational contexts—a strength of the workplace writing research discussed above—and the activity of *communication* of groups via electronic media—a strength of computers and writing. Thus, we hope for the connection of (1) research in computers and composition that probes the nature of writing and writers in electronic environments, and (2) research in workplace writing that probes how various types of communication shape and are shaped by organizations, with (3) research on electronic media in the workplace.

Taken together within the framework of electronic literacy, these literatures can help us better understand the issues that need to emerge as we try to understand the uses of computers for writing in particular workplaces.

Computers and Writing in the Workplace: Opening Spaces

This collection aims to open spaces for new conceptions of electronic literacy in the workplace by exploring how computers and literacy operate outside classrooms, by examining what potential bridges might be built between workplaces and classrooms, and then by considering how to build theory and conduct research about computers and writing in the workplace. We've arranged the chapters around themes that seem to be focal, but we do not mean to imply that they speak only to the themes we highlight. Rather, we hope that readers see these discussions as related in ways beyond the ones we suggest here.

Workplace Cultures as Contexts for Technology and Writing

The first group of chapters in this volume begins to detail a number of ways that computers fit into workplace writing environments. The common thread is not a specific text, activity, or computer system, but rather the everyday act of writing in some form of a computer environment. Whether the computer has a central focus in the mission of the organization, as is the case with the MIT Athena network, or is thought of as an "electronic pencil," as Powell Henderson's colleagues do, the writing climate in all of these organizations bears the mark of technology. We assemble these examples of computer-assisted writing so that readers (particularly those unfamiliar with writing in the workplace research) might see some of the ways that computers can be conceived of, integrated into work patterns, and perhaps forgotten as transparent instruments of communication.

As the chapters indicate, these workplace writing cultures have been changed by technology's presence in some fundamental and some very mundane ways. In fact, the sites and writers discussed here were not selected for their salient innovations but for their variety. They include a range of American business contexts: high technology sites such as a nuclear power plant, a missile test range, and a computer network support facility; several manufacturing firms; and everyday businesses such as a bank, an accounting firm, a department store, a hospital, and a not-for-profit charity. Through this range of descriptions, we hope to show that questions about electronic workplace literacies are not exclusive to state-of-the-art installations or to professional technical writers. Some of the writers are professional writers or interns, but there are also workers in other professions (e.g., personnel, sales, architecture, accounting, and management) for whom writing is one part of their jobs.

Taken together, these articles inspire questions such as these:

- How does writing technology respond to and affect *material conditions of writing within particular corporate cultures?* What writing conditions does the technology improve? Complicate? How does the presence of electronic media affect a company's writing environment? What social, financial, or physical conditions of the writing environment are also affected? The chapters in this section suggest that these questions are important to understanding computers and writing in the workplace.

- How are *innovations enacted in the practical realities of the working world?* How do writers work in the elastic gap between the state-of-the-art and their actual working conditions? Is it always important or necessary to keep up with new technology as a practitioner or as an organization? What are the consequences of either choice? Susan Jones's recounting of interface development with MIT's Athena network shows how choice of language is focal to the dynamics of innovation in product development, while Jennie Dautermann's interviews with a variety of writers point to the dynamics of innovation in everyday writing practices. Powell Henderson, by contrast, depicts an organization whose writing practices, notably its use of the carbon form, militate against innovation.

- What about *questions of access?* Increasingly, computers are necessary to office work; advertisements for support staff routinely require word-processing software experience. Further, the personal computer no longer is sold exclusively in specialty shops, where high customer service and expertise are assumed, but in discount stores of all kinds. Does the popularizing of computers bring expectations that all citizens can easily access them? Both Henderson and Dautermann speak to working with older technology as one dimension of access. Jones examines arcane system language as another aspect. Brenda Sims further explores some contours of access as she contrasts the electronic mail systems at work in a bank and in a computer firm. As her examples show, all electronic mail systems are not the same. Later in the collection, Selfe examines the politics of e-mail access with a broader brush, and Johnson relates interns' access adventures.

- How does *technology relate to social roles* in organizations? How are jobs changed, added, lost? What pressures on individuals' writing skills result from such shifts? Is gender a factor? Do people connect with each other in different ways when the medium is electronic? Sims explores these questions from the angle of textual markers that give us information about the social roles in two organizations. Later, Selfe, Johnson-Eilola and Selber, and Wieringa et al. speak of the power exerted over new technologies by organizations' previous conceptions of how writing functions.

- We suspect that the growth of *virtual offices* may move the corporate culture into a new space in our lives. What happens to the nature of a writer's work when it is accomplished via networked connections to home or other distant sites? Is the distinction between work and the other parts of people's lives being muddied? What effects will these virtual offices have on the status of writers and their ability to write successfully within a possibly "invisible" culture?

Electronic Literacy as It Challenges
Traditional Views of Writing

The second group of chapters pushes at the definitions of writing in interesting ways. Two chapters examine new meanings for writing: first, the questions surrounding ownership; and second, the potential effects of automation on writing processes. Barbara Mirel connects database report writing, an activity that is growing quickly in many businesses because of their ever-expanding data needs. In a number of views of rhetoric, database report writing would not be considered writing; yet, as Mirel shows, it clearly is saturated with rhetoric. Johndan Johnson-Eilola and Stuart Selber, on the other hand, show how difficult it is to develop new meanings for writing inside corporate settings as they argue that commercial conceptions of hypertext (perhaps, because they align themselves with corporate values) can lead to impoverished meanings for hypertext readers and writers. Addressing who owns electronic texts, Tharon Howard examines questions of "authorship," "ownership," and "ethics" for electronically produced texts as he considers a number of cases where these three concepts intersect and clash. Both Farkas and Poltrock and Wieringa et al. present developments in automation of text production as a way to consider how the computer is further entering the activity of authorship. David Farkas and Steven Poltrock review the software tools being developed for online editing from the perspectives of the models for editing that they project as a way to facilitate collaboration between authors or between author and editor. Douglas Wieringa, Marvin McCallum, Jennifer Morgan, Joseph Yasutake, Hachiro Isoda, and Robert Schumacher describe the online system for managing documentation updates that they have been designing for a nuclear power plant. Their story underlines the resistance that occurred in a situation where people in the organization feared the computer becoming an author.

These articles suggest questions such as the following:

- How may we need to *redefine writing* in light of activities writers do with computer tools such as hypertext, databases, and online information sources? Is production of a database

report a writing act? Is revising your own previously written letter? If these are *not* writing acts, and people are doing
all of them at their desks, then what happens to specialty
groups where these activities are clearly divided? Mirel examines several of these questions.

- What types of *organizational resistance* are actively combat-
  ing new notions of reading and writing online? Are potential expansions of writing and reading sometimes limited by
  organizational conventions, essentially negating some of the
  possibilities of the new technology? Johnson-Eilola and Selber
  examine how corporate cultures can limit an innovation.

- How much of writing can we *automate?* What happens when
  we try to give the computer some of the scribal authority
  that we have previously reserved for people? Wieringa et al.
  offer evidence of a company's resistance to seeing the computer as an author.

- *Collaboration* among co-authors can also occur when interaction is largely mediated by electronic means. What happens
  to writing processes spread out across space and time? Are
  precedents in evidence in the work of annotators or editors
  in other centuries, or is this interaction something quite new?
  Farkas and Poltrock focus on *electronic editing and the special
  tools being developed for these tasks.*

- What bearing do electronic literacies have on the ethics of
  intellectual property? Some electronic media force us to find
  new ways of viewing writing resources and rhetors. Who
  owns, controls, distributes, and co-authors text, and on what
  medium? Howard's discussion of copyright law reflects the
  discussions going on elsewhere in which scholars, legal experts, and authors alike struggle to address postmodern ideas
  of authorship within a capitalist system of intellectual property.

- To what extent are the technologies a person uses to write
  and communicate in the workplace marking the status that
  person holds within the organization? How is a person's organizational role (engineer, secretary, accountant, and so on)
  reflected in the equipment used for writing?

Intersections between School and Workplace Electronic Literacies

The third section examines ways in which we might link work-places with the academy, cautioning that the setting for technology and the purposes for which it is used affect the possibilities for crossovers between school and work. In their discussions, Craig Hansen, Nancy Allen, and Robert Johnson do not embrace technology uncritically; instead, they share experiences designed to help us move carefully into the arena of thinking about how to act as teachers who must prepare students to become workers in electronic workplaces:

- *What if the technologies of school and work do not intersect?* Are we approaching the same technology from such different perspectives in school and at work that the experience of that technology for writing is fundamentally different? Both Hansen and Allen explore these possibilities.

- In what ways do the technologies connect with *socialization* of people in their writing classes and in their jobs? Johnson's report of his interns' work experiences shares some insight into the kinds of initial experiences students are likely to have with computers in the workplace.

- Given the tremendous growth of networked communication, what should we expect in the way of *surveillance* of work activities? What limits to writers' privacy and institutional oversight are proper, necessary, or even possible when writing inhabits electronic spaces? How should we prepare students to cope with the surveillance they will encounter online? Both Hansen and Howard offer considerations relevant to our thinking.

- How does a *computer-literate writer* behave? Beyond the keyboard, what knowledge is helpful/useful/necessary for a writer working in an electronically enriched (or impoverished) environment? How do people *achieve and extend their electronic literacies?* Where and how do people learn these literacies? To some extent, all the chapters in the first three sections explore dimensions of these questions.

Approaches to the Study of Technology and Writing in the Workplace

The final section of this collection probes how we can theorize and research computers and writing in organizational settings; the authors argue that theory and method help us bootstrap ourselves to better understandings. Cynthia Selfe theorizes electronic mail—a key technology for understanding electronic literacy in homes, schools, and workplaces—within its broader cultural framework and begins to build a postmodern understanding of how this technology operates inside various social settings. James Porter and Patricia Sullivan examine the framing of research, demonstrating how constructing competing maps can contribute to the more complex understandings necessary for interdisciplinary areas such as computers and writing in the workplace:

- How do we develop a theoretically driven understanding of how the *cultural contexts of technology* affect our understanding of that technology's identity? Selfe begins that process as she theorizes electronic mail from a cultural-critique perspective.

- *What methodologies are needed* for conducting research into the uses of computers and writing in particular workplaces and the natures of electronic literacy at work? Porter and Sullivan argue that descriptions of existing methods (case study, survey, ethnography, etc.) do not yield sufficient discussions of methodology for interdisciplinary study.

- Given that many researchers embrace many tenets of *postmodernism*, how can those tenets be actualized in our research? Both Selfe's and Porter and Sullivan's chapters address this question as they explore *how* theory and research in this area can be performed.

New Spaces, New Questions

As we complete this volume, we find that we have more questions about computers and writing in the workplace than we had at the start of the project. Then, we sensed a gap and searched for authors who could thoughtfully guide us toward some closure. Now, we realize that the gaps are not so easily filled, that our collection raises questions in a variety of areas:

- Our chapters imply a *social and cultural capital* which accrues to people who are successful with school literacy. What sort of social and/or cultural capital accrues to computer-literate writers? Does the computer perhaps invite more sloppiness, for example, or does using a particular computer technology offer some local institutional edge?

- Do computers really offer a new version of *empowerment* and voice? Or do they provide new ways of enacting the old institutional roles? If the technologies introduce potentials for challenging established hierarchies at work and elsewhere, how do we engage those potentials? What are the effects of electronic literacies on social/cultural structures, gender, power structures, and access?

- Does electronic literacy in the workplace require a *new rhetoric?* Some sort of sophism in an electronic realm—is a relativistic rhetoric enough? Is a socially constructed one adequate? Is a traditional one even possible?

- Is it likely that we will need to *rethink language* itself in the face of emerging computer technologies? If so, what does that mean for writers and readers?

It is true that research in the areas of literacy, writing in the workplace, computers and composition, and electronic media in the workplace are all grounded in different focal issues, disciplinary frameworks, and methodologies. Yet, it is also possible that the intersections of these literatures offer ways to think across these traditional categories. We intend this book to open a dialogue that explores the intersections among these research strands and that promises to enrich each of them. Our expectation is that readers of this collection will find, as we have, that observing the nature and extent of the computer's influence on workplace writing cultures can be, to varying degrees, complex, puzzling, or liberating, and sometimes all of these together. We hope that an examination of the ideas represented in these chapters will be provocative of new research questions into the nature, direction, and conduct of workplace writing.

References

Allen, M.W., Gotcher, J.M., & Seibert, J.H. (1994). A decade of organizational research: Journal articles from 1980–1991. *Communication Yearbook, 16,* 252–330.

Allen, T.J., & Hauptman, O. (1987). The influence of communication technologies on organizational structure: A conceptual model for future research. *Communication Research, 14*(5), 575–585.

Atkinson, D.L. (1993). A meta-analysis of recent research in teaching of writing: Workshops, computer applications, and inquiry. Unpublished doctoral dissertation, Purdue University, West Lafayette, IN.

Barabas, C. (1990). *Technical writing in a corporate culture: A study of the nature of information.* Norwood, NJ: Ablex.

Barker, T.T., & Kemp, F.O. (1990). Network theory: A postmodern pedagogy for the writing classroom. In C. Handa (Ed.), *Computers and community: Teaching composition in the twenty-first century* (pp. 1–27). Portsmouth, NH: Boynton/Cook-Heinemann.

Barley, S.R. (1990). The alignment of technology and structure through roles and networks. *Administrative Science Quarterly, 35,* 61–103.

Barton, B.F., & Barton, M.S. (1993). Ideology and the map: Toward a postmodern visual design practice. In N.R. Blyler & C. Thralls (Eds.), *Professional communication: The social perspective* (pp. 49–78). Newbury Park, CA: Sage.

Becker, H.J., & Sterling, C.W. (1987). Equity in school computer use: National data and neglected considerations. *Journal of Educational Computing Research, 3,* 289–311.

Bernhardt, S.A. (1993). The shape of text to come: The texture of print on screens. *College Composition and Communication, 44*(2), 151–175.

Bolter, J.D. (1991). *Writing space: The computer, hypertext, and the history of writing.* Hillsdale, NJ: Erlbaum.

Brandt, D. (1990). Literacy and knowledge. In A. Lunsford, H. Moglen, & J. Slevin (Eds.), *The right to literacy* (pp. 189–196). New York: Modern Language Association of America.

Brown, R.L., & Herndl, C.G. (1986). An ethnographic study of corporate writing: Job status as reflected in written text. In B. Couture (Ed.), *Functional approaches to writing: Research perspectives* (pp. 11–28). Norwood, NJ: Ablex.

Business Week. (1994, July). The information revolution: How digital technology is changing the way we work and live. *Business Week.* [Special 1994 bonus issue.]

Couture, B., & Rymer, J. (1989). Interactive writing on the job: Definitions and implications of "collaboration." In M. Kogen (Ed.), *Writing in the business professions* (pp. 73–93). Urbana, IL: National Council of Teachers of English and Association for Business Communication.

Covino, W. (1991). Magic, literacy, and the *National Enquirer.* In P. Harkin & J. Schilb (Eds.), *Contending with words: Composition and rhetoric in a postmodern age* (pp. 23–37). New York: Modern Language Association of America.

Cross, G.A. (1990). A Bakhtinian exploration of factors affecting the collaborative writing of an executive letter of an annual report. *Research in the Teaching of English, 24*(2), 173–203.

Darrah, C. (1994). Skill requirements at work: Rhetoric versus reality. *Work and Occupations, 21*(1), 64–84.

Dautermann, J. (1991). Writing at Good Hope Hospital: A study of negotiated discourse in the workplace. Unpublished doctoral dissertation, Purdue University, West Lafayette, IN.

Doheny-Farina, S. (1984). Writing in an emergent business organization: An ethnographic study. Unpublished doctoral dissertation, Rensselaer Polytechnic Institute, Troy, NY.

Ede, L., & Lunsford, A.A. (1990). *Singular tests/plural authors: Perspectives on collaborative writing.* Carbondale: Southern Illinois University Press.

Eldred, J.C., & Fortune, R. (1992). Exploring the implications of metaphors for computer networks and hypermedia. In G.E. Hawisher & P. LeBlanc (Eds.), *Re-imagining computers and composition: Teaching and research in the virtual age* (pp. 58–73). Portsmouth, NH: Boynton/Cook-Heinemann.

Forman, J. (1994). Literacy, collaboration, and technology: New connections and challenges. In C.L. Selfe & S. Hilligoss (Eds.), *Literacy and computers: The complications of teaching and learning with technology* (pp. 130–143). New York: Modern Language Association of America.

Fulk, J. (1993). Social construction of communication technology. *Academy of Management Journal, 36*(5), 921–950.

Fulk, J., & Boyd, B. (1991). Emerging theories of communication in organizations. *Journal of Management, 11,* 407–446.

Griggs, K. (1994). Writing in the public sector: An historical case study of a water quality law. Unpublished doctoral dissertation, Purdue University, West Lafayette, IN.

Haas, C., & Neuwirth, C.M. (1994). Writing the technology that writes us: Research on literacy and the shape of technology. In C.L. Selfe & S. Hilligoss (Eds.), *Literacy and computers: The complications of teaching and learning with technology* (pp. 319–335). New York: Modern Language Association of America.

Handa, C. (Ed.). (1990). *Computers and community: Teaching composition in the twenty-first century.* Portsmouth, NH: Boynton/Cook-Heinemann.

Hawisher, G.E. (1992). Electronic meetings of the minds: Research, electronic conferences, and composition studies. In G.E. Hawisher & P. LeBlanc (Eds.), *Re-imagining computers and composition: Teaching and research in the virtual age* (pp. 81–101). Portsmouth, NH: Boynton/Cook-Heinemann.

Hawisher, G.E., & Selfe, C.L. (Eds.). (1989). *Critical perspectives on computers and composition instruction.* New York: Teachers College Press.

Hawisher, G.E., & Selfe, C.L. (Eds.). (1991). *Evolving perspectives on computers and composition studies: Questions for the 1990s.* Urbana, IL: National Council of Teachers of English; Houghton, MI: *Computers and Composition.*

Heath, S.B. (1990). The fourth vision: Literate language at work. In A. Lunsford, H. Moglen, & J. Slevin (Eds.), *The right to literacy* (pp. 289–306). New York: Modern Language Association of America.

Heim, M. (1993). *The metaphysics of virtual reality.* New York: Oxford University Press.

Hovde, M.R. (1994). The knowledgeable practice of computer documentation writers: Tactics for constructing user and software images and for negotiating organizational boundaries. Unpublished doctoral dissertation, Purdue University, West Lafayette, IN.

Huettman, E. (1990). Writing for the unknown reader: An ethnographic case study in a business setting. Unpublished doctoral dissertation, Purdue University, West Lafayette, IN.

Johnson-Eilola, J. (1994). Reading and writing in hypertext: Vertigo and euphoria. In C.L. Selfe & S. Hilligoss (Eds.), *Literacy and computers:*

The complications of teaching and learning with technology (pp. 195–219). New York: Modern Language Association of America.

Johnston, W.B., & Packer, A.E. (1987). *Workforce 2000: Work and workers for the 21st century.* Indianapolis, IN: Hudson Institute.

Kaplan, N. (1991). Ideology, technology, and the future of writing instruction. In G.E. Hawisher & C.L. Selfe (Eds.), *Evolving perspectives on computers and composition studies: Questions for the 1990s* (pp. 11–42). Urbana, IL: National Council of Teachers of English; Houghton, MI: *Computers and Composition.*

Kelvin, P. (1993). Classical rhetoric and contemporary composition at work: A study of editorialists and their writing. Unpublished doctoral dissertation, Ohio State University, Columbus, OH.

Kintgen, E.R., Kroll, B.M., & Rose, M. (Eds.). (1988). *Perspectives on literacy.* Carbondale: Southern Illinois University Press.

Kleimann, S.D. (1989). Vertical collaboration and the report review process at the United States General Accounting Office. Unpublished doctoral dissertation, University of Maryland, College Park, MD.

Langston, M.D., & Batson, T. (1990). The social shifts invited by working collaboratively on computer networks: The ENFI project. In C. Handa (Ed.), *Computers and community: Teaching composition in the twenty-first century* (pp. 140–159). Portsmouth, NH: Boynton/Cook-Heinemann.

Lunsford, A., Moglen, H., & Slevin, J. (Eds.). (1990). *The right to literacy.* New York: Modern Language Association of America.

Mirel, B. (1993). Beyond the monkey house: Audience analyses in computerized workplaces. In R. Spilka (Ed.), *Writing in the workplace: New research perspectives* (pp. 21–40). Carbondale: Southern Illinois University Press.

Moran, C. (1992). Computers and the writing classroom: A look into the future. In G.E. Hawisher & P. LeBlanc (Eds.), *Re-imagining computers and composition: Teaching and research in the virtual age* (pp. 7–23). Portsmouth, NH: Boynton/Cook-Heinemann.

Moulthrop, S. (1991). The politics of hypertext. In G.E. Hawisher & C.L. Selfe (Eds.), *Evolving perspectives on computers and composition studies: Questions for the 1990s* (pp. 253–271). Urbana, IL: National Council of Teachers of English; Houghton, MI: *Computers and Composition.*

Odell, L., & Goswami, D. (Eds.). (1985). *Writing in nonacademic settings.* New York: Guilford.

Papa, M.J. (1990). Communication network patterns and employee performance with new technology. *Communication Research, 17*(3), 344–368.

Porter, J.E. (1993, May). *Rhetorics of electronic writing.* Paper presented at the Ninth Conference on Computers and Writing, Ann Arbor, MI.

Rice, R.E. (1993). Media appropriateness: Using social presence theory to compare traditional and new organizational media. *Human Communication Research, 19*(3), 451–484.

Schmitz, J., & Fulk, J. (1991). Organizational colleagues, media richness, and electronic mail: A test of the social influence model of technology use. *Communication Research, 18*(4), 487–523.

Schwartz, H. (1982). Monsters and mentors: Computer applications for humanistic education. *College English, 44,* 141–152.

Scribner, S. (1988). Literacy in three metaphors. In E.R. Kintgen, B.M. Kroll, & M. Rose (Eds.), *Perspectives on literacy* (pp. 71–81). Carbondale: Southern Illinois University Press.

Selfe, C.L. (1989). Redefining literacy: The multi-layered grammars of computers. In G.E. Hawisher & C.L. Selfe (Eds.), *Critical perspectives on computers and composition instruction* (pp. 3–15). New York: Teachers College Press.

Selfe, C.L., & Hilligoss, S. (Eds.). (1994). *Literacy and computers: The complications of teaching and learning with technology.* New York: Modern Language Association of America.

Selzer, J. (1983). Composing processes of an engineer. *College Composition and Communication, 34,* 178–187.

Simpson, M. (1989). Shaping computer documentation for multiple audiences: An ethnographic study. Unpublished doctoral dissertation, Purdue University, West Lafayette, IN.

Smart, G. (1993). Genre as community invention: A central bank's response to its executives' expectations as readers. In R. Spilka (Ed.), *Writing in the workplace: New research perspectives* (pp. 124–140). Carbondale: Southern Illinois University Press.

Smith, C.F. (1991). Reconceiving hypertext. In G.E. Hawisher & C.L. Selfe (Eds.), *Evolving perspectives on computers and composition studies: Questions for the 1990s* (pp. 224–252). Urbana, IL: National Council of Teachers of English; Houghton, MI: *Computers and Composition.*

Spilka, R. (1988). Adapting discourse to multiple audiences: Invention strategies of seven corporate engineers. Unpublished doctoral dissertation, Carnegie Mellon University, Pittsburgh, PA.

Spilka, R. (1993). Moving between oral and written discourse to fulfill rhetorical and social goals. In R. Spilka (Ed.), *Writing in the workplace: New research perspectives* (pp. 71–83). Carbondale: Southern Illinois University Press.

Sproull, L., & Kiesler, S. (1991). *Connections: New ways of working in the networked organization.* Cambridge, MA: MIT Press.

Standard & Poor. (1993, October 7). Computers. *Standard and Poor's Industry Surveys, 161*(40), c75–c122.

Sullivan, P. (1991). Taking control of the page: Electronic writing and word publishing. In G.E. Hawisher & C.L. Selfe (Eds.), *Evolving perspectives on computers and composition studies: Questions for the 1990s* (pp. 43–64). Urbana, IL: National Council of Teachers of English; Houghton, MI: *Computers and Composition.*

Sullivan, P., & Beason, G. (1994, May). *Methodology as heuristic: Maps and disruptions as devices for opening research spaces in computers and composition.* Paper presented at the Tenth Conference on Computers and Writing. Columbia, MO.

Tesler, L.G. (1991, September). Networked computing in the 1990s. *Scientific American, 265*(3), 86–93.

Tuman, M.C. (1992). *Word perfect: Literacy in the computer age.* Pittsburgh: University of Pittsburgh Press.

U.S. Bureau of the Census. (1991). *Statistical abstract of the United States, 1991.* 111th edition. Washington, D.C.: Government Printing Office.

U.S. Bureau of the Census. (1993). *Statistical abstract of the United States, 1993.* 113th edition. Washington, D.C.: Government Printing Office.

U.S. Department of Education. (1992). *Digest of education statistics, 1992.* Washington, D.C.: Government Printing Office.

Winsor, D.A. (1989). An engineer's writing and the corporate construction of knowledge. *Written Communication, 6,* 270–285.

Part One

Workplace Cultures as Contexts for Technology and Writing

Chapter 1

Writing with Electronic Tools in Midwestern Businesses

Jennie Dautermann
Miami University

*The growing acceptance of personal computers as office equip-
ment assumes certain electronic literacies among modern workers.
Drawing on interviews with employees of Midwestern businesses,
this study highlights the influence of computer technology on the
everyday writing activity of working professionals. The author
shows how workplace writing strategies may fail to use the equipment to its fullest advantage by merely adding electronic techniques
to more familiar approaches. Meanwhile, differences in the electronic
resources available to various functional groups may serve to reinforce existing organizational hierarchies.*

Recent studies of workplace writing have offered important perspectives on the social conditions that affect writing in professional settings. We have seen the extent to which collaborative
efforts seem to be increasing among workplace writers (Ede &
Lunsford, 1990) and how engineers and others reuse their work
with "boilerplate" techniques (Selzer, 1983). We also are beginning to understand the many ways that the social fabric of an
organization's corporate culture is embedded in the texts produced
there (see, for instance, Cross, 1990; Dautermann, 1993; Simpson,
1989; Spilka, 1993). But in a world where the desktop computer is
becoming standard office furniture and where exchange of electronic information has the popular status of a "superhighway,"
studies of writing in the workplace have seemed surprisingly reluctant to account for the influence of electronic devices on workplace composing.

Even workplace researchers whose observations have brought them into close contact with the writing activity of their informants generally fail to account for the electronic tools used by writers, thereby treating electronic media as somehow transparent in the same way as a pencil, or a secretary taking dictation, sometimes is. Of course, the pencil is a relatively simple technology, but creation of text via dictation has quite a decided impact on the types of strategies used by a writer and represents significant patterns in the institutional culture (see Pringle, 1988, on the evolution of the technologies of dictation and its connection to gender roles). In the same way, electronic environments are not likely to be either transparent or innocent of effects on workplace writing.

In contrast to workplace studies, research into the relationship of computers to the writing (and learning) of composition students has been extensively examined. Selfe and Hilligoss's (1994) collection on technology and literacy is a recent example. Such work has taken on the stature of a subdiscipline in composition studies, with its own annual conference, electronic communication network, scholarly journal, and significant body of literature. Its research suggests that user interfaces, prior knowledge of the computer, available hardware and software, and even the arrangement of computer classrooms may have significant effects on student writers. Therefore, NCTE's sponsorship of the present collection, which investigates computer use among workplace writers, seems particularly appropriate.

In the study reported here, I examined the influence of computers and other electronic tools on the writing environments of fifteen working professionals in the Cincinnati metropolitan area. Contacted in the summer of 1993 as alumni and friends of my university's school of business, the fifteen participants represented a variety of professional fields. All were college graduates; seven were women; nine were recent graduates in entry-level positions; six were midcareer professionals. They worked in companies that ranged from small, entrepreneurial firms to multinational corporations. Table 1 summarizes the participant pool.

The interviews were originally designed to explore the preparation needs of students in business and technical writing courses and focused on the types of writing people do at work and the

Table 1. Summary of participants interviewed, July 1993.

Position	Work Experience	Size of Company	Type of Company
Accounting supervisor	Recent graduate	National company	Manufacturer of paper products
Assistant production manager	Recent graduate	Small local plant for national company, 20 employees on site.	Manufacturer of office paper
Executive vice president, regional chapter	Midcareer	International not-for-profit organization	Education, disaster relief, charity
Loan officer	Recent graduate	Regional bank	Financial services
Owner	Midcareer	Small local firm, 5 employees	Medical records services
Partner/ General manager	Midcareer	Small local firm, about 20 employees	Architectural services
Partner/ Office manager	Midcareer	Small local firm, about 20 employees	Accounting services
Personnel manager	Recent graduate	Regional retailer	Department stores
Personnel manager	Recent graduate	Regional hospital	Health services
President, CEO	Midcareer	Local company, 70 employees	Lumber wholesaler
Regional sales manager	Midcareer	International corporation	Manufacturer of consumer products
Salesperson	Recent graduate	National company	Printing/Distributing data forms
Salesperson	Recent graduate	National company	Manufacturer of pharmaceuticals
Systems developer/ Management trainee	Recent graduate	International corporation	Manufacturer of airplane components
Underwriter	Recent graduate	National company	Insurance services

strategies they use as they compose. A few questions about computer use were included in the original interview plans, but as the interviews progressed, I began to notice the nearly inevitable presence of a computer of some sort in each office. As I asked important questions about their writing strategies, the sort of preparation each person had experienced, and issues they thought important for current students, each respondent, in some way, brought the conversation around to the computer equipment and the skills he or she needed for writing. In keeping with the theme of this collection of essays, I will deal here specifically with the question of how electronic equipment appeared to affect the nature of writing in these organizations.

Computers and Writing Practices at Work

Except for one person, each of the fifteen interviewees had a personal computer or a networked terminal in his or her office. The one person whose office equipment did not include a computer (a recently graduated hospital human resources manager) told me that she used her own computer at home to work on projects for her job and that she had recently requested a personal computer for her office use. Thus, every individual in the study had (or would soon have) office access to a personal computer or a networked terminal right at his or her desk. Of course, there are still many offices where computers are not nearly so available, but it seems significant that in this sample of college graduates, which represented a wide variety of fields and a broad range of experience and responsibilities, the computer was considered something of an office necessity.

Most people told me their writing strategies had changed when they started using computers, particularly their method of drafting as it related to keyboard use. Most people had learned to compose at the keyboard, a complicated act for those more experienced professionals who had few keyboarding skills. But a few still found it more comfortable to draft on paper and then enter the text into a word processor for editing later. Of course, as in the case of meeting notes, some texts were written by hand first because the computer was not available during the composing stages. But my respondents also told me about ways computers enhanced their invention or prewriting activity and allowed for more efficient revision and proofreading. Table 2 was developed by inferring writing activities from comments made during the interviews about the advantages of electronic writing environments. Some of the items (especially those in the last section) are particularly related to distributing texts or connecting them to specific actions. These action contexts were frequently mentioned in connection with respondents' writing activity.

When important documents and working decisions depended on complex information, generally that information had been developed electronically. Databases were searched for specific information or mined to produce detailed reports. Occasionally, databases were created to house complex information and to sort or organize it. Though some of the writers did not think of this activity as writing, when asked what eventually happened to such information, they agreed that most of it became embedded in or formed the source of some informational text. Mirel (this volume) explores the rhetorical elements of creating reports from databases.

Each of these writers was directly involved in producing, in some form, electronic versions of his or her own writing. Their responses represent a significant change in that at least a part of the production technology, once done mostly by typists and transcribers, has been moved directly onto the desk of the professional worker. Even the highest-level executives I met generally composed their own rough drafts on their own desktop computers. This move has brought with it more opportunity for writers to reuse the texts they have previously produced. Everyone told me about some use of a boilerplate or adaptation of old texts for new purposes. The architects, for instance, use formal boilerplate contracts purchased from their professional society. Their clerical staff has developed a way to print details of specific agreements directly onto copies of these forms by adjusting their printer output to fall into the appropriate blank areas. The accounting firm, as another example, incorporates standardized accounting explanations into its reports to customers. Although these paragraph-length explanations have also been developed by a professional accounting society, the clerical staff in this office retypes these

Table 2. Advantages of writing with computers named or implied by respondents in the interviews.

Enhances Invention	Provides for synthesizing or combining information from multiple sources (production statistics, database reports).
	Provides ways to manage complex information (for storing, organizing, and thinking through relationships within data).
	Provides for direct links between professional activity and texts: accounting results, computed or sorted data can be dumped directly into rough drafts.
	Makes collaboration over long periods of time more convenient by preserving the negotiated results and making them easily revisable.
Simplifies Drafting and Revision	Streamlines production of drafts later sent to clerical staff.
	Saves time over dictation (sometimes replaces it).
	Preserves reusable text (that which is difficult to produce, standardized, successful, appropriate for recurring situations, professionally developed boilerplate).
	Streamlines adaptation of previously successful texts.
	Enhances spell checking and proofreading by others.
Converts Text to Action and Facilitates Distribution	Keeps one's day organized (meeting notes, phone notes, calendars, negotiations with co-workers…). List making, contextualized self-reference.
	Eliminates paper delays (online billing) and transfers information more quickly.
	Makes collegial contact more efficient and records those conversations (especially with e-mail, but also with phone mail).

paragraphs into company documents even though they can be obtained in electronic form.

Most of these workers adapt old letters for new contexts. Some ghostwrite them for their bosses and spend as much time as possible working from previously successful models. Of course, drafting activity is more complex when the situation seems to have no adequate text precedent. Also, some adaptations are so extensive that the original is not much recognized in the resulting text, but the timesaving benefits of electronic text production and reuse were mentioned by nearly all of my respondents. Several people also mentioned the advantages of spelling and grammar checkers to increase their confidence in the products.

Some people told me of converting electronic messages to hard copy for their files, and one person discussed with me the style difference she had noticed when electronic mail was converted into hard-copy memos. Levels of informality perfectly acceptable in the electronic environment had seemed odd to her when they appeared in printed-out memos.

The use of dictation, though declining, still appeared in this sample. A few people told me that such practices were quite wasteful of company time, given the need for two people to devote time to producing a draft this way. However, one person described an experience with a typing pool where he had dictated every detail (even punctuation) to his typing staff, who then transcribed his instructions quite literally. One other user of extensive boilerplate was required by her office situation to read altered boilerplate into a tape recorder so that it could be transcribed as a new text. This second example came from a medical environment where dictation is still quite commonly used.

Electronic Equipment and Collaboration

One of the great hopes for computer use in writing classrooms is that students will find collaborative writing more productive and efficient (Batson, 1989). In this sample of business professionals, the use of computer equipment to facilitate collaborative writing seems mixed. The businesspersons interviewed here showed how texts may be subject to increasing levels of shared author-ship in the form of editing, revising, and proofreading help. As a way of exposing emerging texts to more office employees, the use of computer disks, networked or e-mailed letters between super-visors and their staff, or between primary writers and their advi-sors, seemed well developed in this sample. People also frequently told me, as did the lumber company executive, that this sort of shared writing via computer had greatly increased the efficiency of their offices.

But if we discount editing, clerical involvement, and writing from templates, collaborative writing in its fullest sense (where a text is developed over time by an ongoing group) happened only occasionally in this sample. Generally citing the need for efficient use of time, most of these respondents claimed to write with oth-ers only rarely, and then, primarily in the service of large policymaking projects, such as employee manuals or policy and procedural documents.

The lumber company executive, for instance, described a year-long effort to coordinate sales procedures with the accounting department's need to use sales documents for recordkeeping. A committee representing both of these company groups met regu-larly with management to design new forms and to spell out spe-cific procedures for sharing information between these two im-portant elements of the company's business. After some major compromise, a procedure manual was developed that described the way sales were to be recorded in the lumberyard and inter-preted in the accounting office.

The executive was particularly sensitive to the amount of time such work required and described his company as having grown to a size that required documentation of procedures they had al-ways taken for granted when the company was smaller. This project, he told me, was necessarily completed in a collaborative group in which the interests of each member could be negotiated without losing the support of the other users. Of course, these documents were designed, recorded, and eventually produced on the local computers, but the composing was, for the most part, conducted orally in committee work. This company does not have enough physical space to require or use networking, and, consequently, uses the disk-to-hand system of file exchange. But I suspect that the collaborative writing project he described would not have been conducted via network even if the company had one.

In contrast to the lumber sales project, the system developer for an airplane manufacturer described her work on a major software project as having been almost completely mediated by computer interaction. But she was frustrated with the way the computer facilities used by her group served to separate rather than unite the collaborators. She spoke of the distance this computer interaction had introduced between herself and her colleagues. She remarked that her projects sometimes felt as if they were "thrown over the wall" to her collaborators, who rarely met together to discuss their common projects. This work group did not function together effectively enough to find a system for preventing undocumented changes in a common project. Those changes could cause their emerging software product to react differently when opened a few days later, a process which produced considerable repeated work and frustration. It's quite possible that her experience was as much a function of poor group coordination as of computer intervention, but nevertheless, both of these examples point to a felt need for more contact among collaborators than could be achieved through exclusively electronic interaction. Two things that might improve such work, however, are better editing tools (see Farkas and Poltrock in this volume) and greater network transparency for word-processing formats.

Networks and Corporate Writing Contexts

Most of the machines used by my respondents were desktop personal computers, but some served as dedicated terminals connected to larger machines elsewhere, and a few were connected to local-area networks serving a specific work group or office complex. Some of the larger companies used a wide-area network to connect geographically distributed sites to a national headquarters and to each other. However, only one person spoke of a connection to the Internet or other public-access sites, and that was in terms of preparation he encouraged for students.

Many of the companies owned more than one computer system, each dedicated to a separate purpose. Word processing was most likely to be separated from other professional activity (architecture, accounting, hospital records, engineering, manufacturing controls) on different computer systems. As Brenda Sims's article in this collection points out, companies in which different work groups do not use the same equipment may face special barriers to local networking and widespread participation in internal electronic mail. The system developer whose collaborative project is discussed above spoke of frequent e-mail use in a special-purpose network among computer professionals in her very large company, but she indicated that other departments had much less convenient access to company-wide e-mail. As will be discussed later, this tendency toward purchasing special equipment for specific tasks is sometimes related to organizational role and status.

These interviews provided evidence that incompatibility between an organization's computer equipment may emerge from the introduction of computers into different departments over time, from differences in training, from personal preference, or from the tendency of individual offices to avoid the disruptions of upgrades. Such conditions can complicate maintenance and text transfer; they can also present complex barriers to standardization. Most systems in the smaller companies in my sample were not networked beyond simple printer sharing. I even saw several instances of dedicated systems side-by-side with other dedicated systems where the two were not connected (or even thought of as compatible in any significant way).

Among companies with widely distributed sites, or people with an interest in sales, electronic contacts at some distance were becoming essential. The insurance underwriter, in particular, used electronic mail primarily to contact sales offices in small towns where employees did not have voice-mail systems. However, he told me that his contacts in larger installations generally preferred messages left with the receptionist staff, since e-mail-equipped terminals were housed elsewhere in the building and were difficult to reach. One respondent used dial-up modem facilities, but only to connect to the online billing facilities of Medicare.

In one case, computer network technology was becoming a major factor in a respondent's writing activity. An accountant for a paper manufacturer was working on a project intended to access accounting information directly from electronic input generated by computers on the manufacturing floor. Intended to reduce error and information transfer time, this project provided the potential for entering electronic production information directly into her written reports. It also frequently took her to the production floor, where she was becoming more directly aware of the production processes themselves. Eventually, this network contact with the production floor produced accounting data which became the basis for her accounting reports. It also prompted several elaborate project reports which evaluated this electronic production-to-accounting link.

One or two respondents mentioned that their companies were consciously moving away from the use of paper forms toward electronic means for exchanging information between major areas of the organization and were consciously incorporating networking into their communications patterns. Computer links between production and management appeared both in the accounting project mentioned above and in the office paper-distribution center, which employs fewer than twenty people. Note, however, that such a pattern of reducing paperwork via electronic tools did not seem to be occurring in the much larger, military-influenced context Henderson describes in his chapter in this volume.

Electronic Writing Equipment and Office Role

My own observations correspond to those of Peters (1992), who suggests that networking and information technologies may remake business environments and challenge traditional management structures in a number of ways. Sometimes electronic environments can offer ways in which the traditional writing roles in a company are extended or altered. Most commonly, the businesspersons interviewed referred to generating first drafts on a computer and then handing the disk to a secretary who "cleaned it up" before it was sent out. Thus, clerical personnel were no longer considered primarily typists; the businesspersons in this sample saw their secretaries in various roles, such as editors, proofreaders, data-entry personnel, or ghostwriters. Secretaries also altered previously stored letters, submitted their own work to a supervisor's editing, and composed master texts for mass mailings, newsletter copy, and other materials. Computers sometimes extended the involvement of clerical personnel into such work as page design, report generation from databases, and database management for mailing lists or client records. Some of the professionals took on such roles in the production of community texts as well. The executive vice president of the not-for-profit organization reversed this pattern by editing a good deal of the material her subordinates produced and gave her on floppy disk.

In some organizations, equipment designated for special purposes also seemed to exaggerate the differences between traditional functional roles. In many places, secretaries' machines had only word-processing capability, while the professional mission of the office was carried out by others on different machines. Thus, the equipment available reflected expectations for certain employees, a condition also noted by Pringle (1988) in her work on technology and the role of the secretary.

One indication of role distinctions being reinforced by computer use appeared in the architect's office, where the partner I met refused to learn his firm's new computer-aided drawing (CAD) system in order to avoid drafting with the new equipment—a function often done by special drafting personnel in large firms. "Most people resist [learning the CAD system]," he explained, "because they're concerned that if they become operators, [they'll] get trapped in that role."

It is possible that some of this connection between role identity and computer use results from new equipment being brought into offices where those roles had previously been well defined, but it appears that the computer can reinforce those roles while possibly closing off certain pathways between them. It seems more difficult somehow for a person to grow into a new role in an office if the shift is complicated by computer-skill barriers in addition to those already inherent in the office culture. When viewed through the lens of workplace computer literacy, this tendency toward specialization may reinforce certain electronic literacies in specific organizational groups and potentially discourage them in others. In one extreme example, data generated by a separate "accounting system" was reentered and edited with completely different equipment when clerical staff incorporated that data into word-processed reports. Of course, after retyping enough balance sheets, the clerical staff in an accounting office may eventually learn to operate the accounting system and become motivated to look for electronic transfer potential, but such changes demand time, curiosity, and the opportunity to explore the capacity of existing equipment well beyond its daily use. Henderson's chapter in this collection suggests that these opportunities are not always apparent in organizations and that historical patterns of computer use tend to make some employees relatively conservative about exploring new software.

Using the Available Electronic Tools

Several of the respondents mentioned underuse of the equipment they had available and were somewhat aware that the equipment had many features they had not taken time to learn. Others discussed their own computer use in terms that led me to believe that they had developed little competence beyond their own current needs.

Indeed, most of the respondents here seemed happy enough with their current equipment and expressed their need for more competence mainly in terms of using their existing equipment more extensively. This finding also agrees with Henderson's survey (in this volume) in which employees expressed widespread satisfaction with their current equipment even when it did not conform to the standard being advocated by the computer services directorate. Few of my respondents seemed to be pushing hard for better and more advanced systems on their desks; rather, most were struggling to find ways to achieve the tasks they understood the equipment to be capable of doing.

A pattern that cut across all the interviews was a pragmatic view of computers as one tool among a larger set of available writing resources, which might include typewriters, copying machines, handwritten notes, drafts, boilerplate, and dictation. Given the variety of computer equipment (some of it relatively outdated) being used in these organizations, there remained a number of tasks people chose (or felt forced) to do by other means. Sometimes a hybrid mix of computer and hand strategies was integrated to achieve specific results in organizational texts.

Besides the accounting office described earlier, where output from accounting software was retyped into a word processor by the clerical staff, other respondents spoke of retyping, generally in the context of frustrations with incompatible software or hardware. Occasionally, a person with good typing skills or ample secretarial help would retype a short piece to avoid the hassles of file transfer or messed-up formatting. A related strategy was to print out material from two different computer-system sources and use cut-and-paste layout techniques to put the material into a single document. With copier technology, this produces relatively clean-looking documents but requires quite a bit of concentration if the document is to look professional.

Most preprinted paper forms were completed by hand. The insurance forms and employee documents that dominated the work of the two personnel managers I interviewed highlighted this problem. Most of their forms were filled out with pen or pencil unless the level of formality required typing, in which case a secretary generally used a typewriter to insert the information.

Some persons quite expert at using word processing were unable to produce complex formats such as tables with their equipment. Thus, I was told of several projects in which page layouts of complex lists or tables were produced using typewriters and rulers, then photocopied for distribution. One rather expert computer user kept his work calendar on a computer, but his secretary carefully retyped it onto daily pages for his pocket calendar. This same manager traced intersections among a series of interrelated procedural documents with a hand-drawn flowchart.

There are widely available tools to do all the tasks I describe here as hybrid computer/hand processes. Many of these tools appear in the directories of the people who described them. This discussion is not meant to point to the lack of expertise evident in this group of respondents, but to illustrate that, frequently, when a familiar task can be achieved without the use of a computer tool (even one which the user has available), that task is not necessarily converted to the computer. I suspect that most of these hand-generated processes remain outside the electronic media because of the amount of time these users expect to devote to mastering the new techniques necessary to accomplish them. In a busy office, the investment may not seem worth the long-term payoff. Indeed, some people may not even be aware of the payoff at all.

Of course, there are cases in which genuine incompatibility between 1980s vintage software and hardware platforms can only be circumvented by human interventions like those mentioned here. I suspect that despite the growth of networking and transferability, such problems will persist in organizations where computers are brought into offices at different times for different purposes and are used by people with a variety of office roles.

Essentially, this picture reflects the tendency of working professionals in everyday offices to learn to use their electronic equipment in task-specific ways. This attitude would seem to have a direct bearing on the development of new computer literacies among working professionals.

Acquiring the Skills to Use Electronic Tools (Achieving Electronic Writing Literacy)

All the working professionals interviewed for this study had graduated from college, many from the same university's school of business. However, their experience with computers varied considerably if their college experience was more than fifteen years old. The group who had been out of school for fifteen or more years had not generally been exposed to computers in college, but the more recent graduates all had some experience writing with computers in their college work. One person who had received her degree about fifteen years earlier had programmed computers using punch cards during her college study, but she had not experienced word processing with computers until her first job. This evidence seems consistent with the rise of word-processing software, which began to be widely available in the early 1980s. (Note: Some of the equipment in these offices was purchased at that time.)

In the sense that producing college papers is preparation for workplace writing, college computer experience seemed to have been helpful for those respondents who had it. However, in many cases, such experience did not seem to determine the attitudes people held about computers. Some of the older respondents who had learned their computer skills on the job expressed inhibitions about exploring the writing potential of computers beyond using them as fancy typewriters. But several of the older employees interviewed had developed extensive computer expertise, particularly when their company role involved computer use in some professional area. The architect, the accountant, and the document-writing entrepreneur all seemed more comfortable with computers in general and therefore with writing with one. Others, such as the regional sales manager, were less comfortable. When asked about electronic tools, this otherwise confident woman told of using her local electronic mail editor exclusively as her word-processing software. She used its editor to produce all her texts, which were then converted to other formats by her secretary in the next room. Sensitive to her limitations in this area, she spoke of wanting to find time to "get through the training tapes" and learn the word-processing software used by her secretary.

Among the respondents who had used word-processing programs in college, most had written papers, developed spreadsheets, and sometimes performed statistical analyses using computer tools. Some mentioned specific assignments which required Lotus 1-2-3 or DBIII. Two of them recalled high school classes (programming in BASIC) that they thought of as preparation for writing on computers at work. All the graduates who had been out of school less than fifteen years had used computers to write some papers in their college work. One claimed to have done every paper on an Atari, while others referred to computers owned by their fraternities, dorms, or their home departments.

All the respondents had learned some (if not all) of their computer skills through on-the-job experience. But that learning seems to have been directly related to completion of immediate tasks.

When those tasks are routine and fit well with the employee's vision of the computer's capabilities, the learning seems thorough and effective, whether achieved by trial and error (a commonly expressed method), training workshops, or individual instruction such as tutorials or videotapes. One person did mention that she read manuals to learn about new system features. What seems significant is that the level at which this learning seemed to stop correlates to the skill requirements of the current task.

One or two people were curious about the unused potential of their equipment, but more often, discussion of that unused potential elicited apologies or troubled reactions: "We have a word-processing program in here, and I have to admit I haven't mastered it yet." But curiosity and adventure, two proven motivations used by experienced educators in school settings, were not as frequently expressed. Pressure to achieve a specific task seemed to be a frequent motivator, as was the need to cope with some new feature, equipment change, or expanding task. Thus, the two people with the fewest computer-related tasks and the best access to secretarial help for those tasks appeared to be the weakest computer users. They both also resisted writing in some way. In one case, the respondent seemed to see little need for much writing beyond simple letter writing or performance reviews. In the other case, the respondent actively criticized the paper explosion and waste of resources devoted to documenting work in her company. Both, however, expressed confidence that they could deal with the computer if they had more time to explore its uses.

One mature respondent, on the other hand, behaves more like the early adopters observed in some studies. He has made a career of getting the most out of his computer equipment for his medical service organization. Handling arrangements between mobile dental units and nursing homes, this entrepreneur creates policy documents, procedural forms, reports to insurance companies and regulatory agencies with the four desktop computers in his small office. He also manages all office scheduling and billing on them as well. Together with his four employees, he submits billing to Medicaid and Medicare via modem and a dedicated phone line. However, he has never used e-mail and touted instead the virtues of phone mail, where he could sort, review, and store messages in ways that actual telephone contact could not provide. Indeed, he uses phone mail for many of the same advantages that others value in e-mail and often has his secretary transcribe it. But, given the much more extensive telephone availability among his business contacts, telephone technology is likely to be more efficient for him until e-mail becomes as common in offices as a telephone.

In another, much smaller organization, a production manager worked with production personnel to design manufacturing updates to be entered on networked PCs that had been placed on the operations floor. While soliciting repeated input from the production employees on the screen layouts for the PCs, she used an interesting strategy for increasing their overall computer literacy. Early in the project, she brought the production employees into the office, where she taught them the basics of the office word-processing software and asked them to prepare their regular reports on the office computers. She found this transfer of computer skills from the office work to the production interface tasks to be quite successful in enhancing her employees' understanding of the issues at stake and improving their keyboarding skills. Other respondents whose enthusiasm matched hers seemed to thrive on teaching what they knew to others, thus reinforcing their own learning.

In general, motives for exploring the equipment's capacity tended to come from task-related requirements as well. People respond to neat tricks they see others do (or from advice from sponsors/consultants). They may find a need for increased efficiency for old tasks, and they need to have some previous success with using a computer. The people who were involved in teaching others in their office about computers also mentioned that they tried to help people have confidence that the computer was not a threat.

Conclusion

Rather than attempting to be exhaustive or complete, this study has described a small group of working professionals whose office standing was generally high and whose educational background gave them confidence that they could learn complex ideas. Most held supervisory responsibilities in their organizations. However, certain patterns related to writing with computers in the workplace can be posited from summarizing their experiences and the ways they discussed writing in their jobs.

The writers in this study saw significant benefits to their writing that were attributable to the use of computers. They found the storage of text for reuse to be possibly its most important contribution, although its data-manipulation functions were found to be valuable for adding specific detail to informational text. They also found the potential for revision and shared texts to be useful.

It seems apparent from this study that writers in ordinary workplaces have accepted the computer as a business resource even though some individuals seriously underuse them and mix them together with hand techniques or other inefficient patterns of use. Moreover, even when their equipment is quite new, writers often do not function at state-of-the-art levels. Apprehension, underuse, incompatibility with older equipment, and concentration on specific tasks complicate their ability to even comprehend what is the "state of the art."

Those people in this study who seemed the most open and flexible in the face of learning had some interest in teaching computer features to others, and even though they learned specific tasks primarily, they possessed some vision for seeing additional writing tasks that could be managed with computers. On the other hand, those people in this study who seemed the most significant underusers of computers for their writing had less extensive writing demands in their jobs and may have devalued writing in general; they may have had equipment on their desks which was inappropriately used or not specifically appropriate to their own jobs.

Conditions of corporate culture reported in these interviews also suggest that computer equipment can reinforce office roles and perpetuate power relationships, especially between professional and clerical personnel. Despite requiring clerical staff members to be involved in more direct ways with text production, separating word-processing software from professional computer systems can often reinforce inequalities in the modern office.

References

Batson, T. (1989). Teaching in networked classrooms. In C.L. Selfe, D. Rodrigues, & W.R. Oates (Eds.), *Computers in English and the language arts: The challenge of teacher education* (pp. 247–255). Urbana, IL: National Council of Teachers of English.

Cross, G.A. (1990). A Bakhtinian exploration of factors affecting the collaborative writing of an executive letter of an annual report. *Research in the Teaching of English, 24*(2), 173–203.

Dautermann, J. (1993). Negotiating discourse in a hospital nursing community. In R. Spilka (Ed.), *Writing in the workplace: New research perspectives* (pp. 98–110). Carbondale: Southern Illinois University Press.

Ede, L., & Lunsford, A. (1990). *Singular texts/plural authors: Perspectives on collaborative writing.* Carbondale: Southern Illinois University Press.

Peters, T. (1992). *Liberation management: Necessary disorganization for the nanosecond nineties.* New York: Fawcett/Columbine.

Pringle, R. (1988). *Secretaries talk: Sexuality, power and work.* New York: Verso.

Selfe, C.L., & Hilligoss, S. (Eds.). (1994). *Literacy and computers: The complications of teaching and learning with technology.* New York: Modern Language Association of America.

Selzer, J. (1983). Composing processes of an engineer. *College Composition and Communication, 34,* 178–187.

Simpson, M. (1989). Shaping computer documentation for multiple audiences: An ethnographic study. Unpublished doctoral dissertation, Purdue University, West Lafayette, IN.

Spilka, R. (Ed.). (1993). *Writing in the workplace: New research perspectives.* Carbondale: Southern Illinois University Press.

Zuboff, S. (1988). *In the age of the smart machine: The future of work and power.* New York: Basic Books.

Chapter 2

Specialized Language as a Barrier to Automated Information Technologies

Susan B. Jones
Massachusetts Institute of Technology

Sometimes language choices can erect unnecessary literacy barriers for computer users. This chapter discusses the MIT Athena network, which uses terms that mix classic Greek names with other jargon rooted in MIT's local institutional history. Difficult and time-consuming to learn, these metaphors do not always map obviously to their referents. The author describes the need to distinguish between user problems with complex tasks and difficulties created by this complex (and, thus, exclusive) language. She also describes current efforts at MIT which seek to avoid transporting the Athena jargon into an emerging Macintosh network.

This chapter explores how language can erect literacy barriers for computer users and discusses ways that technical writers can participate in bringing down those barriers. When I submitted the first draft of this chapter to the editors of this book, my mood was rather bleak. I had to settle in my conclusion for admitting to small gains.

Since that time, much has happened in our department at MIT, and many of the complaints that I have made in this chapter have been addressed. Because I believe that the original draft of this chapter, which was reviewed by members of all the parties discussed here, played a role in the changes both to software and attitude, I am leaving the original draft for you to read. Where I feel there has been a response to my complaints, I have included an update.

Introduction

Language is power and language divides. Remember Professor Henry Higgins discoursing on the language of the "guttersnipe" Eliza Doolittle? Eliza's mastery of her Cockney argot made her a recognizable member of her society, while her failure to speak cultured "standard" English kept her out of refined society.

Remember how language is used in partisan politics to deliver coded messages about ourselves and "them"? In the 1992 U.S. election campaign, "family values" was used by the Republicans as just such a code in order to divide and morally define "the good"—those who supported the issues of the Republican campaign—from "the bad"—those who didn't. In 1992, that message lost, which was a surprise to many because very much the same message had won in three previous elections.

Language Is Power and Language Divides

In the world of computing, it is also true that language can exclude and divide the knowing from the newcomer. The ability to understand the commands and command syntax of a system is a step toward being able to use that system. So why do software developers, computer gurus, and wizards construct command structures and syntaxes that exclude people from using the systems they develop? Do writers have a role in ensuring that users will be able to use applications and systems? Where does that role start? As the last step before a product goes out the door or as part of the development process itself? When writers are added to the roster of attendees at developers' meetings, what is the writer's role? Is she there to learn the new application from the bottom up so as to be able to interpret and diffuse the product's complexities for users? Or is she there to help avoid pitfalls and unnecessary levels of complexity in the development stage so that she won't have to document these "features" later?

For several years now, I have been trying to address the question of how the role of technical writers is and should be changing with the growth of distributed and networked computing environments. It has been and continues to be my belief that the role of the technical writer is critically affected by this expansion of computer access. I believe that, among other things, distributed computing stretches the writer's role to a more general role as "communicator." The output of the writer should be focused more on screen and interface design and online help than on the production of paper documentation. Some changes are beginning to happen, particularly the electronic distribution of documentation. But some, particularly the use of technical writers for interface design, are slow to come. The problem, I fear, is territorial. Developers and programmers feel total ownership of their products, right up to the end-user. They do not really see a role for writers and trainers, except as an afterthought. But I think that the writer's role begins with the design of the interface—how the user figures out how to use the program.

A Warning

Although the remainder of this chapter is about the relationship of developers and writers at MIT, MIT is only an example. Software developers at MIT are no worse than developers anywhere. And MIT technical writers are no more an afterthought than they are elsewhere. I've used a specific group of MIT developers as my "whipping boys" only because they are the ones I know best. The people who were good enough to review this piece cautioned me to make sure that you, the reader, understand that the problems described here are not peculiar to MIT.

I am a technical writer at MIT in the central computing department of the institute. My job, nominally, is to write end-user documentation for microcomputer users at MIT. In fact, my job is much more varied and interesting than its description. I also write articles on network use for a campus newsletter, edit and produce an informal department newsletter, create posters on a variety of subjects from software piracy to harassment, write and design brochures, and carry on a low-key usability campaign. What I try not to do is to write any documentation that exceeds twenty pages. My document size of choice is whatever fits on a folded letter- or legal-size page. I prefer reading novels to documentation, and so, I assume, do most users. In this I have sometimes been proven wrong, but so it goes.

My particular interest in computers is the ability the computer confers on us to communicate across and explore among the rapidly growing networks and network resources. At MIT, we are actively involved in networking as much of the campus and as many of the people as possible. This is not a simple task at an institution with no official computer platform. Our users compute on Athena workstations, Macintoshes, DOS-based systems of many flavors, a variety of UNIX workstations, IBM mainframes, and even supercomputers. Each of us has an operating system of choice—or one that has been chosen for us by circumstance. Everyone on campus has or can have access to the Athena Computing Environment, that is, free accounts for all. But Macintoshes and DOS machines can also get (for a price) ethernet connections to the campus network, MITnet. And, of course, dial-up connections to e-mail, the network, and various mainframes are also available.

At MIT, working across the network is part of our everyday life. The adoption in 1991 of Athena as MIT's academic computing infrastructure has much to do with this. In the years since its inception to 1995, Athena has grown from a system built on time-shared minicomputers to a client-/server-distributed system with more than 600 public-accessible workstations across campus, in both public and departmental clusters, that are open to students and faculty 24 hours a day, 365 days a year, for coursework, writing papers, doing personal work, or even playing games.

In terms of Athena, the client/server model means that individual end-user workstations, called *clients,* can access services from other machines, called *servers,* that are located elsewhere on the network. In terms of Athena, this also means that while computation, word processing, and the like are handled at the user's workstation, files and applications are stored elsewhere on the network. For users of Athena services, this means that they can sit down at any Athena workstation on the network and have access to their personal files and all of Athena's services. Although, in many ways, it doesn't feel all that different to the user from using a time-shared computer, the network creates a far more powerful computing environment.

In 1991, Athena officially merged with MIT's central computing department, Information Systems. This is the department for which I work. A result of this merger is that some of the distributed network services developed for Athena are being ported to lower-end platforms, including Macintosh computers.

To this end, special Macintosh, DOS, and Windows™ programs are being created to give users of these platforms access to some Athena services. And some new services are being developed that will originate with three distinct programs for each platform. In the past year, Macs with MITnet/Internet connections have been able to use a real-time messaging system, an online bulletin board, and a group scheduling system. And this is only the beginning. More applications will come, and all of them will be ported to the DOS and Windows™ environments as well. This is the good news.

One of the missions of Information Systems is to create a seamless, ubiquitously distributed environment. In simple terms, this means that everyone should be able to have access to the network from the environment from which she or he is most familiar. My access to MITnet should look like a Mac; from a DOS machine it should look and feel and act like the DOS or Windows™ environment; and so on.

The Problem

The bad news is that when we port applications developed for Athena to the Macintosh and DOS environments, we're porting the language of Athena as well as the tools. The Athena operating systems are UNIX and X-Windows. The language of Athena is UNIX with an overlay of classic Greek names that do not always map obviously to their referents. It is a fun language, but it is not, strictly speaking, English. It is jargon, rooted in its own local history. It is my contention that this mixture makes it more difficult to penetrate the system it describes than a system, such as the Macintosh OS, that uses a more universal language, based on a simpler metaphor. Although the Macintosh OS uses the desktop as its primary metaphor, it is not an overwhelming metaphor, and I do not have to bear it in mind as I work at my various tasks, which include writing manuals, producing graphics, and reading e-mail. When I attend to my business, I am comforted to use a command structure of simple, value-neutral active verbs, such as

"Open," "Close," "Quit," "Save," "Copy," "Cut," "Paste." At the top of almost every application screen I find the familiar "File Edit" menu bar.

The language of UNIX is almost entirely counterintuitive. For instance, in trying to read from my list of mail, I can find no "Read" command. In the UNIX environment, I must say "Show" the message. To see the list of my incoming mail, do I ask the mailer to open the mailbox or list the contents? No, I request that the program "Scan" my mail.

And when the language is absolutely clear and simple, it is often threatening and definitely not value neutral. Commands such as "Abort" (also a DOS command) and "Kill" leave me feeling helpless. "Kill" is so very final that whenever I encounter it as a possible choice, I am afraid that I will break something if I issue it. And "Abort," no matter which side of the political question of choice you're on, is a term fraught with significance, far beyond the simple "end process now even if you're not finished," which is probably meant.

Should We Be Able to Understand Concepts on Demand, or Is It More Rewarding if We Have to Work at It a Little?

Many of the network applications that are becoming available for Macintoshes and DOS were originally created for Athena, often by enterprising students who saw a need and filled it. (These same creative students often become employees of MIT, and if not MIT, other schools, brokerage houses, Fortune 500 companies, banks, insurance companies, hospitals, and, of course, all the big computer hardware and software companies, where they often continue to be creative.) An example of this is the Discuss system, which lets users on Athena participate in a variety of electronic discussions. The chosen metaphor for the system is that of a "meeting." For a variety of reasons, people felt that they needed an electronic forum for carrying on discussions that often began in physical meetings but hadn't come to closure. Discuss lets subscribers continue the discussion in a more or less open forum. It's a worthwhile program to have, and it does many things, including archive transactions of the various discussion groups, so that new participants can follow a thread forward and back until they get the gist of the discussion. My difficulty with Discuss was its Macintosh interface. The metaphor of the meeting as Discuss moved to the Macintosh environment became more difficult to follow. In the alpha and beta versions, it was not clear which commands to choose or even where to find them. Do I "Check" the meetings or "List" them? What's a "New Transaction"? Should I start with the "File" menu or the "Transaction" menu? (See Figure 1.)

Fortunately, by the time MacDiscuss was released in March 1993, the developer had made quite a few changes, many of them based on the suggestions of a team of two writers and a network user-services consultant. In part, I believe the formation of the team and the changes resulted from a fortuitous event that occurred in early winter. At a daylong conference on computing in the year 2000, one of the directors of my department at MIT gave a presentation on porting Athena to the Macintosh. He chose to demonstrate the beta version of MacDiscuss and proceeded to stumble all over the interface looking for the commands he wanted. I took notes. After the presentation, I encouraged him to write up what had happened for the program's developers. He passed the buck back to me. I sent my notes to the developers. The first response I received was defensive, followed almost immediately by the formation of a new team and the beginning of major changes to the interface. The results are not perfect, but at least the menu items seem to be where people expect them to be. And when the project team was honored recently for getting the program out, I received my t-shirt for persistent *curmudgeonliness*.

Other applications have come along from our department developers in response to perceived administrative needs. But, in general, few of these needs have been driven by the user community at large; rather, they have been driven by the development teams themselves. Not that they are bad ideas. In fact, they are generally great ideas that do meet some need, but they are allowed to move quite far along the development path before the potential users or their representatives have a chance to comment on them as usable products, and by then, it's too late to do anything about it. This is changing. Genuine efforts are being made to make the system responsive to the needs of the user

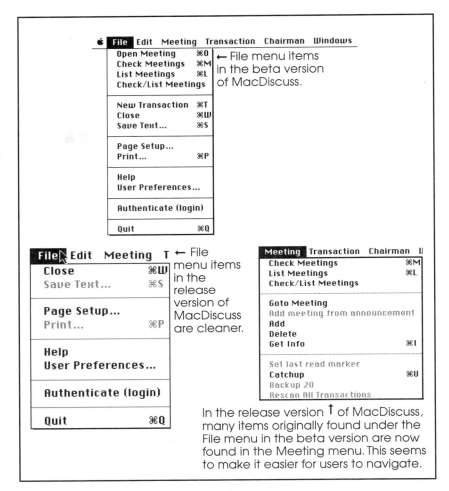

Figure 1. Top: MacDiscuss File menu before usability testing.
Bottom: after usability testing, the MacDiscuss File
menu and Meeting menu. In the release version, many
items were moved from the File menu to the Meeting
menu for easier navigation.

community, but the instinct to just do it and then let the user-services people get involved is still strong.

For instance, Athena developers created an authentication system that is widely recognized and has been widely adopted. When a user logs on to Athena, she enters her username and password, which in Athena is called a "Kerberos Principle." The system validates the entry and grants the user access to the parts of the system for which she has authorization (e.g., she is issued "Kerberos tickets"). Well, this is an interesting and playful use of language that echoes the other classic Greek figures used throughout the Athena environment (e.g., machines with such Greek names as Atlas, Agamemnon, and Menelaus), but what does "Kerberos Principle" mean to most users? One day when I was standing around in the Athena consulting office, I heard this conversation:

"Enter your Kerberos Principle, and then . . . What's your Kerberos Principle?"

"Oh, that's your username and password."

If a Command or Syntax Is Understandable and Easy to Use *Once It Has Been Explained,* Is it Good Enough? Is It Cost Effective to Take the Time to Find Clearer Terms at the Outset?

So why not just call it what everyone else calls it? It certainly would make my writing job easier and the consultant's job easier if we didn't have to stop mid-thought and explain "Kerberos Principle." It is true that, for the developers, Kerberos Principle means an awful lot more than my glib explanation. But the point is that it is important to the developers and to the system people; it isn't important to me when I want to get to my files or e-mail. And, in fact, this is how Kerberos and Kerberos tickets are described in Athena documentation (*Working on Athena. version 2*):

5.1 Your 10-Hour Kerberos Tickets

One of the many important activities that occur behind the scenes when you log in is that Athena *authenticates* you, which means that Athena gives you "Kerberos tickets." These tickets prove to particular programs that you are the user you claim to be. For security reasons, the Kerberos tickets (and the privileges associated with them) are valid for only 10 hours, or until they are destroyed when you log out. (*Don't worry about the details of getting and using the tickets; it happens behind the scenes.*) . . .

This discussion of Kerberos tickets continues for several paragraphs and includes instructions on how to renew tickets. The section from which this passage came, however, is introduced with this paragraph:

> To protect your account, a valid login session on Athena lasts only a certain amount of time (ten hours), after which you must *renew* the session in order to continue working. To renew your account, you just issue the "Renew" command at the athena%prompt (you do not have to log out and log back in).

Aside from the fact that screen messages about time running out for your session and various other messages from the authentication system talk about "expired tickets" and "Kerberos permission denied," the author of the documentation quoted here could have skipped the entire discussion about the Kerberos tickets. (Who was Kerberos? Kerberos, or Cerberus, was a three-headed dog with a mane and tail of snakes. He was the offspring of Typhon and Echidna. Cerberus guarded the entrance to Hades. One of the twelve labors of Hercules was to capture him. Interesting.)

Complex Tasks Are Not the Same as Complex Language, and the More Complex a Task, the More Carefully Chosen the Language That Describes It Should Be

We are in the process of writing a forms-creating system. This system will enable offices and departments at MIT to automate many of the procedures involved in producing and completing forms. It is a simple enough task to create an electronic form similar to a paper form and to let people complete it online. It is not so simple to authenticate the identity of the individual who issues or completes the form and to send a form electronically along a route, collecting all of its proper authorizations.

At MIT, for instance, if I attend a meeting out of town, I file a travel voucher on my return. Right now, a version of this form is available electronically. I get a copy of the electronic form and fill in all the information that will get me a reimbursement check for my travel expenses—and then I print it out, sign it, and give it to our secretary, who makes sure I've done everything properly and either hands it to our boss for her signature or retypes the form and returns it to me for my signature. When everything is ready, she sends the form to the travel office through the campus mail. Eventually, I am reimbursed. The forms project would automate this procedure.

Guess what they have decided to call this system? I, in a moment of indulgence, suggested "Timaeus," but wisely it was rejected because it was too arcane. Instead, the development team chose a more familiar name, "Phaedo." Remember *Phaedo*, the Socratic dialogue on forms? You may have read it as a first-year student. But those of us who actually understand the name represent a small insider group, and there are no clues for those who don't get it. Perhaps they will call it "Phaedo forms." That would help.

Documentation and Training That Focus on Explaining a Complex Interface and Complex Language Do Not Fully Compensate for Designing an Interface That Uses Clear Language and Symbols Wherever Possible

Athena has a real-time message system called Zephyr (another of those Greek allusions; Zephyr, the west wind, was one of the children of Eos, goddess of dawn, by Astreus). You may be familiar with real-time message programs on VMS ("Send") or CMS ("Tell"). This is the same kind of program. The full Zephyr program allows for some fairly sophisticated messaging, including system messages, group messages, and weather reports. But its simplest use is for one-to-one messages. It's easy, if you use it from Athena. At the prompt, you enter *zwrite* and the username of the person to whom you wish to "speak." The program prompts for a message and tells you how to send the message when you're done. If the person you're writing to is logged on, your message appears on his screen.

The Macintosh client, MacZephyr, was just what we'd been waiting for—real-time messaging on the Macintosh and across the net to our colleagues on Athena as well. Great! Except that in the Macintosh interpretation, things somehow got more complex. First of all, this "simple" application required a quick guide and a manual and a 30-minute training session to use it, primarily because the central concept was difficult to understand! To receive messages required that you "subscribe" to a "triplet." To send a message you used the "triplet" in the address header. A triplet (a misnomer in itself) is an address that breaks most e-mail addressing conventions (except uunet conventions). It's backwards! Address information is entered from the most general to the most particular. You begin by telling the program the "class" of communication (e.g., "message") and the "instance" (whether public or private) and, finally, the recipient's e-mail address. Fine, if you happen to be a Russian who is used to addressing from the general to the particular. But what about the rest of us, who address every other written communication from the particular to the general?

Although usability testing had shown these problems in the preproduction releases, they were not addressed in MacZephyr 1.0. Luckily, some major bugs were found, which required an upgrade. In the March 1993 release of MacZephyr, part of the addressing problem was fixed. A menu item allows you to select "Personal" as an option. This displays a "Send" message window with the first two triplet fields complete. You need supply only the username of the person you are addressing. This really does make an enormous difference.

The notion of subscriptions presented another problem because, strictly speaking, you don't subscribe to message lists, but rather, make your machine available to receiving messages from a particular class and instance. One of the difficulties for the developers was finding a comparable process in the electronic lexicon that would make this clear. The choice of subscriptions as the metaphor seemed to confuse people more than help them.

In the first version of MacZephyr, error and program messages from Zephyr were obscure, abundant, and mostly about Kerberos and Kerberos tickets. Many of the original MacZephyr beta-users stopped using the program because it was just too hard to remember the addressing and subscribing procedures, which made it not worth the bother. However, the latest release of MacZephyr seems to have done away with most of the obscure system messages and, on the whole, makes the program a much more pleasant and more stable product to use.

At the time of the beta test, with the permission of the developer and the tech writer working with him, I surveyed the testers.

The survey showed that users had mixed feelings about the product. Macintosh users who were familiar with Zephyr on Athena and were Athena "power" users had no problem with MacZephyr, except for the inability to make it *do* even more things. When asked for wishes for future versions, they generally wanted more features. On the other hand, users whose primary system was the Macintosh were generally using only the "Send" and "Receive" personal messages features. A few were also sending and receiving group messages. Many of these users found the triplet syntax and the subscribing function mystifying, and many confessed to having used the product for a while and then stopped, finding it not all that useful.

An Interface Is the Place at Which Independent Systems Meet and Act on or Communicate with Each Other

I had originally hoped to discuss here how we in the documentation group had begun to work more closely with developers to address some of the issues of language use in interface design in order to avoid transporting Athena jargon along with the porting of Athena applications to lower-end systems. Unfortunately, I must report that it seems to be a losing battle—or, at least for the moment, we are not making a lot of progress. The status quo holds. Developers are still developing, and writers are still filling in the holes with explanations. The bad news is that we must be insistent, vigilant, and noisy to get ourselves invited to provide the language of the interface or to participate in its design. But, even though we may not be as popular as we'd like, we are now being invited to take a much more active role in the development and design process. Why aren't we automatically included? Perhaps the answer lies in the following.

These may be fighting words, but one real part of the problem is that many developers believe they are smarter than writers. In many respects, they are probably correct. They certainly know more than I will ever begin to know about computers. However, I suspect their belief in their superiority stems from other sources as well. In general, our developers are male and under 40, many under 30. In our documentation group, we are mostly female with a *median* age of 40! I am not ready to cede total superiority to them.

I think that, as older women technical writers, we probably know some things that these guys don't.

In creating programs, developers also create their own metaphors, ones which make it easier for them to talk to each other and to think about how a program works. For example, the Kerberos metaphor for the MIT authentication system is wonderful for system developers. It gives them a way to speak to each other about how the system will authorize and keep track of users who have proved their authenticity by giving appropriate passwords and usernames. They speak in terms of issuing or denying tickets to users who request access to services requiring permission. But the ticket metaphor, which appears only in system messages to users, is not a particularly useful metaphor for you, the user, trying to use the program.

On our side, we sometimes need different metaphors, metaphors that are about how we work, not how the system works. This has not always been possible. Before graphical user interfaces, every interaction with the computer was direct. That is, you typed something and pressed "Enter" and the program or system would interpret it directly—sort of. So the meaning of a command *had to be* unique and singularly recognizable by the program. But if you are using a graphical interface, complete with labeled buttons on which to click, what is written on the buttons matters only to you, the user, not to the computer. The buttons are simply graphics that connect to lines of code that the computer understands. Or conversely, the lines of code connect to buttons with labels that you and I understand.

Unfortunately, for some of us, developers and programmers are also end-users, and they like to look straight through the interface to see what's happening inside. When this is coupled with a kind of elitist mentality on the developers' part and an apparent inability to empathize with less erudite computer users, we end up with screens that require manuals to decrypt instead of quick guides to get users started.

Here's a true story: One day our Macintosh network connections were not working. A colleague wanted to read her e-mail. I suggested that she read it on Athena, since she has an Athena workstation in her office. But there was one problem—she had never read e-mail on Athena before and had no idea how to go about it; could I show her how? Instead of showing her how to use the mailer, I asked her to use a little piece I had written several days earlier, when I was thinking about how to explain graphically the problem of language and access. I gave her the piece of nonsense in Figure 2 and advised her to select all the wrong answers and she'd have no problem reading her mail. She did as instructed, and she didn't have any problems.

Is Access a Problem if Users and Developers Have Exceptionally Different Definitions of Electronic Literacy, in Particular, Computer Literacy?

In preparing for this chapter, I have been speaking with my colleagues and friends around the institute. I've been asking them, for instance, what they think computer literacy means in the MIT environment; what they think the actual role of the technical writer is; and what they think technical writers should be doing. The answers have been revealing. The best answer on computer literacy came from an old friend and former colleague. I couldn't have said it better. Interestingly enough, although I sent her the question via e-mail, and she responded via e-mail that she'd think about the question and would be happy to answer it, her answer came in the campus paper post.

Phyllis's Random Thoughts on Computer Literacy

A person who is computer literate *knows*

- how to turn a computer on and off;
- how to keep it clean;
- what not to eat or drink in its presence;
- that, like any machine, a computer is made up of parts that work together;
- how to use it safely;
- the difference between hardware and software;
- what his or her computer can and cannot do;
- what is sensible to ask a computer to do;
- when the computer he or she is using is behaving normally and when erratically, and therefore when to call for help.

Here's a test. Choose the word that best completes the following sentences:

Oh, look. There's the mailman. Hey, Ma, I'll (<u>inc, get</u>) it. Oh, look, there's something for me. Great, here, I'll (<u>open, show</u>) it. I wonder if there's anything else for me. Let me (<u>scan, see</u>) the rest of the mail. Here, Ma, there's something from Grandma. Oh, my goodness, it's a check for a thousand dollars. I'd better (<u>write, compose</u>) a thank-you note right away.

Figure 2. Nonsense exercise.

A person who is computer literate *has a sense of*

- what functions are common to various computers;
- how to adapt to different models of computers;
- how to learn to use various kinds of software;
- what kinds of questions to ask about how a computer works.

A person who is computer literate *does not necessarily need to know*

- the names of the parts of a computer;
- the history of computers;
- how a computer works internally;
- how to write a program;
- how to speak computerese.

Unfortunately, too often what Phyllis calls "things you don't necessarily need to know to be computer literate," and thus be electronically literate, fall precisely within the category of things that technical people think users should know. What is implied by knowing this stuff is initiation into the circle of computer *cognoscenti*. The computer is no longer a tool to be used for making complex tasks more manageable, but a discipline, not unlike other disciplines, with its own history, philosophy, mores even, and, of course, language for discussing ideas too difficult to discuss in everyday language. I asked a friend what he thought technical writers should do. He told me that writers should be able to take the high technical concepts of the developers and translate them into terms that users can understand so that they will be able to understand not only how to use a program or a computer, but also how and why that program or computer does what it does. I think he means that we're supposed to translate the computer guru's jargon into everyday language. What he really wants is for the user to know "when the computer he or she is using is behaving normally and when erratically, and therefore when to call for help."

I think he is wrong. I think that one of the problems with program development at MIT is that when a program moves from project (someone's good idea and initial creation) to product (something available to users and supported by our department), the interface issues (including documentation) should not be driven or decided by technical developers but by professional communicators (designers and writers). At present, almost all of the writing we do is driven by the needs of the technical staff. All of our writing is subjected to intense review by the technical staff for technical accuracy (as it should be) and editorial and stylistic form (as it probably shouldn't be). But very rarely are the writers seriously invited to critique the design of an interface, which I will argue is the primary documentation of an application.

I received two more answers to my survey: one from a person in the development group, the other from an administrator. Can you guess which is which?

Answer 1:

To me, computer literacy in the MIT distributed computing environment means knowing how to find your way around the endless maze of electronic pathways that exist that will connect you with more than you ever wanted to be connected with in the first place!!

Answer 2:

Computer literacy at MIT really has several dimensions, including being able to:

1. use one or more of the many information technologies or tools that already exist in offices, and, in the MIT infrastructure, to support significant daily activities in administration, research, learning, or pedagogy.

2. evaluate the fitness of new technologies and tools, either as they become available in the marketplace, or as they are incorporated in the MIT infrastructure.

3. use information technology to harness the "fire hoses" of data that are popping all around the world, to synthesize information, generate knowledge, and to produce an environment conducive to the development of great wisdom across a broad spectrum of disciplines.

The first definition of computer literacy comes from the administrator. Her answer speaks directly to problems of access by positing an endless maze of electronic pathways that she needs to navigate.

Conclusion: There's a Light at the End of the Tunnel

Computers are everywhere, and computer networks make it possible for us to go anywhere electronically. In order to ensure that everyone has the access he or she wants and needs to computers and the resources they make available, technical writers must become technical communicators and join with developers to make products that are usable. Our role should be to help computer users become more adept—literate—in this electronic milieu. Our goal should be to include rather than exclude. By participating in the process of development and applying our particular expertise to the task of interface design, we are sometimes able to reach these goals.

It isn't easy. We are very rarely sure that anyone is really paying attention to us. And even when there is progress, we can never be sure that we had anything to do with it. But we can be certain that it will not happen unless we, as technical communicators and as end-users, speak up and tell the developers what we want and need. And the ability to do this is part of electronic literacy.

Chapter 3

Electronic Mail in Two Corporate Workplaces

Brenda R. Sims
University of North Texas

This study contrasts the social context, format cues, and linguistic features of electronic mail—asynchronous computer exchanges—taken from a telecommunications company and a computer company. In the less hierarchical and controlled computer company, where electronic mail use is global, the participants used more unconventional punctuation, capitalization, and spelling than those in the more hierarchical, controlled telecommunications company, where electronic mail use is localized. Linguistic features of written and oral discourse occurred in the computer exchanges from both companies.

The speed and ease of delivering electronic mail is changing how professionals communicate. Hewlett-Packard's electronic mail network, for instance, delivers more than 350 million messages every year to its 90,000 employees (Perry, 1992). Companies such as Hewlett-Packard report that electronic mail leads to increased communication—it assists employees in overcoming such problems as telephone tag, time-zone differences, and varying work schedules. Electronic mail ignores time and work schedules and "is not as intrusive as a phone call. It does not interrupt the recipient, and for the sender, takes less time since he or she need not run through the social amenities" (qtd. in Perry, 1992, p. 25). Electronic mail and other computer-based interchanges limit cues about age, gender, race, socioeconomic status, and even appearance (Ferrara, Brunner, & Whittemore, 1991; Perry, 1992; Selfe & Meyer, 1991); as Perry (1992) explains, with electronic mail, "people are judged only by the value of their ideas, so all ideas can get an equal hearing" (p. 28). Indeed, electronic mail has great

41

power and is changing how we communicate in business and industry; yet, how is this growing communication tool affecting how people write and even what they write?

In this chapter, I examine electronic mail in two corporate environments and how these corporate environments have—at least indirectly—affected the ways in which their employees use electronic mail. Throughout this chapter, electronic mail refers to text sent via computers; electronic mail is asynchronous—it occurs in nonreal time. Electronic mail messages can be instantly transmitted but are frequently stored for later reading, unlike interactive computer conversations or online conferences that occur in real time (Ferrara, Brunner, & Whittemore, 1991; Murray, 1991). Specifically, I will present an overview of current research on electronic mail and then discuss my study of electronic mail at two Dallas-area firms, Convex Computer, Inc., and Southwestern Bell Telephone.

Research about Electronic Mail and Other Media

Researchers have looked primarily at two types of computer interchanges, real-time (or synchronous) and nonreal-time (or asynchronous). The research on real-time computer interchanges has focused on interactive chat programs, while the research on nonreal-time discussion has focused on electronic mail—the subject of this chapter. The research on real-time, interactive exchanges provides a valuable backdrop for understanding electronic mail in the corporate workplace. This research has pointed out the absence of gender and status cues in computer interchanges and on the hybrid nature of these interchanges (Selfe & Meyer, 1991; Ferrara, Brunner, & Whittemore, 1991; Sproull & Kiesler, 1991). In studying real-time interchanges, Ferrara, Brunner, and Whittemore (1991) found computer-linked communication to be emerging as a hybrid language that shows characteristics of both oral and written language.

Murray (1985; 1988) has also studied the characteristics of oral and written language in computer interchanges. She discovered that a computer scientist's electronic mail was "more formal than face-to-face conversation and telephone conversation, but less formal than written memos and documents" (1985, p. 224). The electronic mail messages that Murray examined illustrated "discourse features from both oral and written discourse" (p. 224). Because of this duality, electronic mail has the potential for breakdowns in communication resulting from "nonexplicit referencing, unmarked topic shifts, possible brusqueness, and use of quotation marks" (p. 224) and from a lack of the full range of paralinguistic cues (Ferrara, Brunner, & Whittemore, 1991). Since electronic mail writers don't always wait for a reply before sending another message, writers with different problem-solving techniques can continue along different paths for a long time before recognizing the differences (Murray, 1985). Finally, Murray explains that communicating by way of electronic mail is not acquired along with spoken language in childhood, and it—like written discourse—must be learned if it is to be effective (p. 225).

Sproull and Kiesler (1986) studied the effect of electronic mail on social behavior in a well-established electronic mail community of a large office equipment firm. They found that electronic mail reduced social context cues; electronic mail writers focused more on themselves than on the readers (p. 1509). They also discovered that electronic mail messages from "superiors and managers did not look different from messages from subordinates and nonmanagers" and that the writers behaved irresponsibly more often in their electronic mail messages than they did in face-to-face conversations (p. 1509). Their research also suggests that the often uninhibited behavior among electronic mail users "may lead to more new ideas flowing through" electronic mail than through more traditional communication media (p. 1510). Sproull and Kiesler (1991) also found that, with electronic mail, people gain greater accessibility to each other's ideas, regardless of their race, gender, appearance, etc.; therefore, readers focus on the message rather than on the writers.

Also examining electronic mail and social behavior, Schaefermeyer and Sewell (1988) surveyed electronic mail users by way of BITNET (Because It's Time Network). They found that writers used electronic mail to replace other communication media, especially the telephone and face-to-face communication.

Likewise, Stein and Yates (1983) suggest that electronic mail may replace "more formal and longer communications" such as printed memoranda (p. 101). However, from their interviews with electronic mail users at Digital Equipment Corporation (DEC), Stein and Yates believe that electronic mail replaces few face-to-face communications; instead, electronic mail "falls between a telephone call and a memo in both formality and detail of explanation. What results is a message that is less formal and less inhibited in style than a traditional communication but more structured than a phone call" (p. 101).

This research has emphasized that electronic mail and real-time computer interchanges blur the distinctions between oral and written language. It has also pointed out how electronic mail and real-time computer interchanges are replacing the telephone and face-to-face conversations for some users and how electronic mail breaks down social barriers, such as gender, race, or appearance to give people a supposedly more equal voice via electronic mail. Some of these studies have used linguistic analysis to examine the characteristics that real-time computer interchanges share with oral and written communication (Wilkins, 1991; Ferrara, Brunner, & Whittemore, 1991). However, these studies have not used linguistic analysis to examine the characteristics electronic mail texts share with oral and written communication.

Convex Computer, Southwestern Bell Telephone, and Their Electronic Mail Environments

This study attempts to fill that gap by examining electronic mail as a hybrid medium, a medium that borrows characteristics from oral and written discourse. Unlike the previous studies, this study looks at electronic mail texts (asynchronous, or nonreal-time) from two companies, Convex Computer, Inc., in Richardson, Texas, and Southwestern Bell Telephone's regional office in Dallas, Texas, that have different corporate cultures and different rationales for using electronic mail. The employees of these companies are experimenting with ways to use electronic mail; they use pictures to "decorate" their messages, and emoticons, unconventional punctuation, and spelling to express emotions normally expressed only in oral discourse.

The different corporate environments at Convex and Southwestern Bell influence their employees' use of electronic mail and the results of this study. At Convex, the management encourages all employees to use electronic mail, and in fact they use electronic mail themselves, as illustrated by the messages from the company president that appear in this sample. The Convex employees who participated in this study were comfortable using this company's common electronic mail system. At Southwestern Bell, the company management does not encourage using electronic mail. During the interviews, several Southwestern Bell employees reported that many upper-level managers don't use electronic mail. Using electronic mail at Southwestern Bell has been a grassroots movement—in other words, several employees low in the company hierarchy started using electronic mail. Through these employees, more and more employees are using electronic mail, but the use has not come from top down in the company as it has at Convex; as a result, the employees don't use a common electronic mail system. The lack of encouragement to use electronic mail and the absence of a common electronic mail system at Southwestern Bell create primarily localized use; at Convex, where employees are encouraged to use electronic mail, the use is global—electronic mail is their primary medium of communication. This localized use of electronic mail at Southwestern Bell is illustrated in part by the 195 messages that I received during a 5-day period from 18 employees, as compared with the 687 messages from 31 participants during a 24-hour period at Convex.

Thirty-one Convex employees participated in the study (11 males and 20 females). Twenty-one Southwestern Bell employees participated (10 males and 11 females). At both companies, the participants completed a questionnaire about their writing habits while using electronic mail and their views about electronic mail when compared with other traditional communication media. The Convex participants then submitted paper copies of the electronic mail messages that they had sent or received during a twenty-four hour period, while the Southwestern Bell participants submitted copies that they had sent or received during a five-day period. I received 687 electronic mail messages from the Convex participants and 195 messages from the Southwestern Bell participants. At Southwestern Bell, I also interviewed five participants to discuss their electronic mail messages and their impressions of their corporate environment's effect on electronic mail.

Using the questionnaires as background about the participants and the electronic mail systems at Convex and Southwestern Bell, I wanted to investigate the following questions:

- *What social context cues, if any, did the writers use in their messages?* How did the social context cues in the messages from the two groups compare? How did the messages correspond to the corporate environment? Did the writers seem concerned with the needs of the readers and with making a good impression, or did they seem relatively unconcerned? Did the writing seem to be regulated by traditional conventions? How did the messages correspond to the corporate environment?

- *What format cues, if any, could the readers use to differentiate messages from employees at different levels in the corporation?* What cues, if any, did the writers use to indicate the type of message? Did the format cues in messages from the two groups differ? Did they use cues to differentiate a personal message from a business message or an urgent message from one that was not urgent?

- *Did the messages exhibit more characteristics of written or of oral discourse?* How did these characteristics in the messages from the two groups compare? Did the messages demonstrate an intimacy with the reader, as is typical for a speaker, or a detachment from the reader, as is typical of much written communication?

Convex Participants and Their Impressions of Electronic Mail

The Convex participants ranged from 20 to 55 years of age; two-thirds of the participants were female and one-third were male. The majority of the participants had college degrees, with more than half of those having some graduate work. The participants worked in a variety of areas (administration, engineering, human resources, manufacturing, marketing, technical support, and quality control)—the largest group (13 participants) from engineering. Thirty of the participants had been with the company for five or fewer years, and 20 had been using electronic mail for ten or fewer years.

All the Convex participants had computer terminals at their desks. These participants used electronic mail as their primary medium for communicating with other Convex employees. Twenty-two of the participants reported that the ease of use of the electronic mail system was good, while four reported that the ease of use was fair (five participants didn't respond to this question).

All the participants primarily used electronic mail to send work-related messages; 30 of the 31 participants also used electronic mail to send personal messages. When writing electronic mail messages, 26 of the participants sent first drafts of their messages, while 5 revised their first drafts before sending them. Twenty-eight of the participants said that they waited less than one hour before sending an electronic mail message.

Southwestern Bell Participants and Their Impressions of Electronic Mail

The Southwestern Bell participants ranged from 31 to 50 years of age. All but six of the participants held college degrees. The participants worked in proposal development, data management, operator services, marketing, human resources, budgeting, and facilities. The participants had been with the company from three to twenty-three years, and all had been using electronic mail for at least one year.

The participants did not all use the same electronic mail environment. Those participants in proposal development used a Macintosh-based environment, while those in data management and operator services used the UNIX system; therefore, ease of use varied for the participants. During the interviews and informal conversations and as noted on the questionnaires, many participants, especially those using the Macintosh-based environment, reported that the lack of a single electronic mail environment made communicating via electronic mail difficult across the various groups.

The Electronic Mail Messages

Using the questionnaire information as background about the participants and their use of the electronic mail system, I examined 687 electronic mail messages from the Convex participants and 195 messages from the Southwestern Bell participants. I specifically examined the format and social cues and how these cues affected the writing. I then looked at whether the messages exhibited characteristics closer to oral or to written discourse.

The Lack of Social Cues, Format Cues, and Traditional Conventions in the Messages

We determine the social context of a situation through static cues such as the heading of a memorandum and through dynamic cues such as facial expressions and other nonverbal behavior. With electronic mail, many, if not most, of the dynamic cues are naturally lost, and the static cues are weak. As Perry (1992) explains, electronic mail "eliminates cues about age, gender, race, and appearance: people are judged only by the value of their ideas, so all ideas can get an equal hearing" (p. 28). When a communication lacks personal information, readers focus on the message rather than on the writer. On the other hand, according to Sproull and Kiesler (1986), communicators determine the social context of a situation through static cues such as a person's appearance and through dynamic cues such as facial expressions and other nonverbal behavior. When these static and dynamic cues are weak—as in electronic mail messages—the communicator's sense of anonymity may lead to relatively self-centered and unregulated behavior. Sproull and Kiesler (1986) add that writers become relatively unconcerned with making a good impression: "[T]heir behavior becomes more extreme, more impulsive, and less socially differentiated" (p. 1496). The writers then change or omit traditional conventions of capitalization, spelling, and punctuation (Murray, 1988; Ferrara, Brunner, & Whittemore, 1991). Do the social context cues, format cues, and conventions in the Convex messages and the Southwestern Bell messages conform to these conclusions?

The Convex Messages

The Convex messages all have the same format (see Figure 1). This format does not indicate the job title or position of the writer or the reader. Many of the writers use only their login name (such as jjackson for Jim Jackson). The only static social context cue the readers receive is through the subject line, which is hard to see; if the subject and the writer are unfamiliar to the reader, the cue does not give the reader any useful information about the content of the message or about the writer's position and status in the company. So, a message from the president looks like any other message, and a personal message looks like a business one. Figure 2 shows a message from the president of Convex. Notice how the message does not indicate that the writer is the president; the message looks like those written by employees lower in the organizational hierarchy.

As Sproull and Kiesler (1986) point out, when the social context cues are weak—as in electronic mail—the communicators become unconcerned with impressing the readers, and their communication often becomes uncontrolled. The Convex electronic mail messages frequently exhibited uncontrolled behavior through spelling errors, unconventional punctuation, and infrequent use of capital letters; in several messages, writers did not even use any capital letters. The following excerpt from their messages shows some of the misspelled words and the missing capitals. Notice how the writer omits capital letters not only at the beginning of sentences, but also in proper names:

Excerpt 1
it *is* a high res [resolution] machine and i checed [checked] the light levels on the fiber. it was low so i went through and made a recheck of all fiber. after tightening everything, i go [got] better readings on the light level on the fiber. i believe

```
>From ernst@trojan   Tues     Jul  31  15:57:07      1990
Received:         by yagaman     (5.51/4.7)
                  id AA10552;   Tue, 31 Jul 90  15:57:06   CDT
Received:         by trojan      (5.61\4.7)
                  id AA22509;   Tue, 31 Jul 90  15:57:04   –0500
From:     ernst@trojan     (Daniel Ernst)
Message–ID:          <9007312057.AA22509@trojan>
Subject:     test
To:  marvin@trojan
Date:     Tue, 31 Jul 90  15:57:04    CDT
X–Mailer:          Elm (version 2.1 PLO)
```

Figure 1. Typical heading format for Convex messages.

Excerpt 1 *continued*

that things should be ok for her now except for the windows that she runs on convexs. it runs share. if her shares are not up to snuff, there is nothing that can help her run faster on her convexs windows.   markus

The unconventional punctuation appeared primarily in the writer's use of apostrophes and asterisks. As the following excerpts from the messages show, the writers frequently omitted apostrophes in contractions and possessive nouns. They used ellipses as periods or dashes; these ellipses often consisted of more than three periods. (Notice how the writer of excerpt 3, below, doesn't even use a consistent number of periods for the ellipses; the ellipses vary from four to seven periods.) The writers also occasionally used asterisks instead of quotation marks:

Excerpt 2

Ive [I've] just received 3 (three); ones in the tool box in the PE Lab, ones by the Javelin HMUs and since they seem to grow feet and walk off I have one in my bottom filing cabinet. Thought Id [I'd] keep it there until Neptune gets started.

Excerpt 3

can you possibly tell who messed with this last. . . . . the scoop is, oracle shows that it was shipped to hmu on 5/26/90. . . . . however i pulled up the queue 3 weeks ago when it was empty and it was . . . . (this board wasn't on it). . . . . well needless to say we don't have this board and haven't had it

```
>From paluck@starman  Thu Jul 26  18:28:03      1990
Received:          by yagaman         (5.51/4.7)
                   id AA16515;  Thu, 26 Jul 90 18:28:02   CDT
Received:          by starman  (5.51\4.7)
                   id AA15208;  Thu, 26 Jul 90 18:26:40   CDT
Date:     Thu,     26 Jul 90 18:26:40     CDT
From:     paluck@starman    (Bob Paluck)
Message–ID:    <9007262326.AA15208@starman>
To:  cruisers@starman,  schroedr@starman,  wise@starman
Subject: IMPORTANT; PARSEC PONY THREW A SHOE!!!!!!!!!!!!!!
Status: RO
```

You won't believe what happened last night. As Dave and Trish
have been working every night for the last several weeks cutting
200 hours of home movies into the infamous and long awaited movie
"Parsec

Pony Rides Again", the movie itself got cut onto the cutting room
floor. (Yes, all software people know how to do back ups, but Dave is
a world renowned hardware designer!) We lost most all their work
and the nearly have to start over again.

So unfortunately we will need to postpone the party for two weeks
to redo and finish the movie. The party is now set for Auguest
11, 1990 (Saturday night two weeks away).

Sorry for the surprise, but feel even more sorry for Dave and
Trish who have been donating their time to make a great movie
that each of use will keep forever.

In order to be sure everyone that was coming knows about this
change, please send me mail back so I know you know.

. . .happens sometimes, but in the scheme of life we won't let
Murphy get us down on this one?

bob

Figure 2. Message from the Convex president.

Excerpt 3 *continued*

for a long time. . . . . . coold [could] someone have possibly
changed the date and destination. . . . . . . i have sent mail to
freddie to see if he has it out in systems . . . . cause it's not on
this side of the house . . . . . other than that i guess it's a lost
board.

Excerpt 4

Are the communication registers considered to be the type of shared memory that would reside in the cache, or are they *real* registers?

Although many dynamic social context cues are eliminated in electronic mail messages, some of the writers of the messages used unconventional punctuation to convey dynamic social context cues that they normally would have conveyed through facial expressions or voice intonation. For example, in the following two excerpts, the writers use emoticons to show happiness [:-)] and sadness [:-(] and asterisks to emphasize a word:

Excerpt 5

Use at your own risk until tomorrow morning!! We've got hardware problems that affect four disks :- (. /scratch and / texec have *not* been mounted.

Excerpt 6

This could be the highlight of Siggraph :-).

The Southwestern Bell Messages

The format of the Southwestern Bell messages varied according to the environment that the writer used to create or that the reader used to receive the message. Figures 3 and 4 illustrate two typical formats. The message in Figure 3 was written and received on the DEC system. The message does not indicate the job responsibility, title, or even the department of the writer. In my interviews with the Southwestern Bell participants, they explained that some messages at Southwestern Bell can be automatically generated by the DEC system; so a new employee might not know whether a message is generated by the system or by a human.

The format of the message in Figure 4, which was created and received on the Macintosh system, gives the reader more static cues through format than does the message in Figure 3. The writer always uses headings with pictures and captions—her messages are easily identifiable. The readers know when they are getting messages from her even before reading them. Yet, even the messages created on the Macintosh system lack format cues, such as

```
From rx2587  Mon     Mar     2  17:59 CST 1992
Subject:      Forwarded mail. . .
To:  houda!rwl787    (Ramona Whitely)
Date:    Mon, 2 Mar  92 17:59:41   CST
From:     Bob McElroy   <texos!rx2587>
Cc: texos2!dh9950        (David Holmes)
X–Mailer:    ELM     (version  2.2 PLO)


             Ramona,
             I recommend that you either update the forward
             that you have in the /usr/mail/fyi, or you
             change the manner of distribution of fyi's.
```

Figure 3. Message on Southwestern Bell's DEC system.

```
Printed By:  Kerry Moskop                      Page:  1
   From:  Kerry Moskop (3/2/92)    Rebecca Kavanaugh (3/2/92)
     To:  Neil Cobb, Jeff Fields, Monna Haley, Mary Anne Hicks,
          Kerry Moskop, Barbara Payne,
    CC:
   BCC:
Priority:  Normal                    Date sent: 3/ 2/ 92
```

"Go ahead ... send my mail!"

Conf Room B	
3/2/92	4:50 PM

HI Guys!
I need to reserve this room for TI project on
Thursday 3–5 and Friday 3–6. Any problems?
If so, will "A Fistful of Dollars" help?? ha.

You ain't one of them programmer types, are you?

Figure 4. Message on Southwestern Bell's Macintosh system.

the department and job title of the writer. However, this lack of format cues was not as problematic for the Southwestern Bell employees as for those at Convex because the Southwestern Bell employees tended to correspond via electronic mail primarily within their own departments or groups.

The Southwestern Bell messages also exhibited uncontrolled behavior through unconventional spelling, punctuation, and capitalization. In fact, 154 of the 195 messages from Southwestern Bell writers exhibited at least one of these characteristics. The examples below illustrate some of the unconventional spelling, punctuation, and capitalization:

Excerpt 1

marla, okay. i love it when someone tells me not to work on anything. see ya on the video.

Excerpt 2

Would you pls [please] check to see if you have a form on file for [names of three employees]? And, if not pls send them a blank form to complete and return to you.

Excerpt 3

I put a copy of the BDS/LAN file on our server - I need to reference Houston's documents and do a little work on the file. So - don't make any changes until I finish.

Excerpt 4

HI, LADIES!!! HOW ARE THINGS? I'M JUST CHECKING TO SEE IF YOU'RE STILL PLANNING TO KEEP UP YOUR HEALTH WALKS.

In excerpts 1 and 4, notice how the writers use unconventional capitalization. In the first excerpt, the writer doesn't even capitalize the name of the receiver or begin sentences with capital letters. Although present, these characteristics were not as prevalent in the Southwestern Bell messages as they were in the Convex messages. Notice also the unconventional use of dashes in excerpt 3 and of exclamation marks in excerpt 4. The writer of excerpt 4 seems to be using exclamation marks to show emotion or to simulate voice intonation.

Overall, the behavior exhibited in the Southwestern Bell messages was much more controlled than that in the Convex messages. The Southwestern Bell messages did not contain as much unconventional capitalization, punctuation, and spelling as did the Convex messages. I attribute this difference to the corporate culture at Convex, which is untraditional, relaxed, and creative, while that at Southwestern Bell is highly structured, hierarchical, and controlled; therefore, the employees at Southwestern Bell feel more pressure to conform to norms of traditional communication. Also, the uncontrolled behavior exhibited in the Southwestern Bell messages occurs primarily in messages from one employee to another at the same level in the company—not from one employee to another higher in the company hierarchy, a feature indicative of its grassroots uses.

The Blurring of Oral and Written Discourse in Electronic Mail Messages

Now that computer technology has advanced, "the old distinction between written and oral language becomes less viable" (Ferrara, Brunner, & Whittemore, 1991, p. 22). Indeed, in reading the electronic mail messages written by the Convex and Southwestern Bell employees, I saw the lines between oral and written discourse blur through the involvement with or detachment from the reader. According to Ong (1981), oral discourse is empathetic and participatory rather than objectively distanced. Similarly, Chafe (1982) states that "involvement with the audience" is typical for a speaker and that "detachment from the audience" is typical for a writer (p. 45). Chafe also suggests that oral discourse is more fragmented than is written discourse. In oral discourse, the audience does "not need many 'logical' connections . . . because the concrete situation supplies a full context which makes articulation, and thus abstraction, at many points superfluous" (Ong, 1981, p. 40). Yet the writer must "learn to be 'logical,' to put matters together in a sequential, linear pattern so that anyone who comes along . . . can make complete sense of what is being written" (Ong, 1981, p. 40). Written discourse, then, is more integrated or connected than is oral discourse.

To determine the detachment in the Convex and Southwestern Bell messages, I looked for three characteristics (I have included examples from each group; all italics are mine):

> **Passive voice constructions:** "The beach party *is designed* for and intended for Convex folks only." (Convex) "If the Michelangelo Virus *is found*, the PC should *be turned off* until disinfected properly." (SWB)

> **Nominalizations:** "I apologize for the wide *distribution*." (Convex) "I strongly encourage your *participation*." (SWB)

> **Periodic sentences:** "If you know of someone who *does* have an interest in this, but has not been included in the mail, please inform them of the meeting." (Convex) "For example, if you will be using Uniplex as your mailer during the study period, i.e., March 2-6, then each time you receive a mail message, pls [please] remember to forward it to bsu." (SWB)

Passive voice constructions and nominalizations occur more frequently in spoken than in written discourse and may indicate detachment (Gibson, 1969; Chafe, 1982), while periodic sentences are more characteristic of written than of oral discourse (Gibson, 1969). Table 1 shows the percentages of passive voice, nominalizations, and periodic sentences in the messages. The Southwestern Bell messages had a lower percentage than did the Convex messages in all three characteristics. However, both groups of messages overall showed little detachment.

To examine the personal involvement in the messages, I examined four characteristics (each characteristic is followed by one or more examples from each group; all italics are mine):

> **First-person pronouns:** "OK. *I* have some good news (maybe), and some bad news (maybe). . . ." (Convex) "Of course, if you are predisposed to cynicism or paranoia, you are probably saying to yourself . . . How do *I* know this file doesn't actually have some kind of new insidious virus on it?" (SWB)

> **Second-person pronouns:** "I hope *you* and *your* family will enjoy the beach party this Friday." (Convex) "If *you* are one of the following, *you* have an assignment in the event of a fire or fire drill. THANK *YOU* FOR VOLUNTEERING." (SWB)

Table 1. Detachment characteristics in the electronic mail messages from Southwestern Bell and Convex.

	Southwestern Bell in percentages	Convex in percentages
Passive voice	34	42
Nominalizations	24	37
Periodic sentences	4	12

References to the writer's mental process and statements that monitor the flow of information: "I *guess* the purpose of the meeting had to do with sail boat racing." (Convex) "We'll know tomorrow, I *hope*." (SWB)

Informal diction: "I'm sorry, but my .mailre file was *hosed*." "I *screwed up* a quasar entry by entering the wrong *bleeding* serial number." "Can you delete that number for me. . . . I made a *Boo Boo!* :)" (Convex) "*Hi, Gang.*" "*FYI.* I've got a conference call on the NCS IWS deployment plan tomorrow." "*Thankee.*" "If you concur, *'make it so,' (as Captain Picard would say)*." (SWB)

Chafe (1982) explains that "a speaker's involvement with his or her audience is manifested . . . in a speaker's more frequent reference to him- or herself" (p. 46) and that these references are much less frequent in written discourse (Chafe, 1982; Biber, 1986; Ferrara, Brunner, & Whittemore, 1991). This same involvement is also indicated by frequent direct address of the audience or reader as "you" and by frequent second-person pronouns (Gibson, 1969; Biber, 1986; Ferrara, Brunner, & Whittemore, 1991). Another means of determining the degree of personal involvement and orality is through statements that refer to the writer's mental process or that monitor the flow of information—statements such as "I had no idea," I guess," "well," "I mean," "you know" (Chafe, 1982). Finally, informal diction can also indicate a high degree of personal involvement and orality (Lakoff, 1982). Informal or colloquial style in written discourse "is not natural"; it obscures the distinctions between oral and written discourse (p. 254). According to Lakoff, this obscuring occurs in the works of writers of great subtlety and skill; these writers deliberately obscure the distinctions between the two mediums (1982). However, electronic mail frequently takes on an informal, colloquial style even among the neophyte writers in this study. This style might include slang, jargon, colloquial phrases, uncommon abbreviations, humor, or sarcasm (Ferrara, Brunner, & Whittemore, 1991; Murray, 1985, 1991).

Table 2 shows the percentages of these characteristics in the electronic mail messages from Southwestern Bell and Convex. These percentages represent the number of messages that contain at least one occurrence of the characteristic listed in the first column. Many of the messages contained two or more of the occurrences, but my count does not reflect this. These percentages show that both the messages from Southwestern Bell and from Convex show a higher percentage of personal-involvement characteristics than detachment characteristics. The Southwestern Bell messages show a higher percentage of first- and second-person pronouns and of informal diction than do the Convex messages.

Along with the personal-involvement and detachment characteristics, I also looked at the integration in the electronic mail messages. As writers write down one thought, they have time to move ahead to the next thought—time to integrate or connect a succession of thoughts into a coherent whole in a way unavailable to spontaneous oral discourse. In integrating their thoughts, writers use a variety of devices to incorporate additional elements into an idea unit, whereas speakers generally use few if any such devices. The following list gives examples of the characteristics of integration that I examined in the Southwestern Bell and Convex messages (the italics are mine):

> **Present participles:** "you are a senior engineer, and as such ought to be involved in the process of *interviewing* new folks for the group." (Convex) "We'll plan on *leaving* the center no later than 11:30 AM." (SWB)
>
> **Attributive adjectives:** "she is a *better* therapist." "The Convex Beach party is a *unique* event." (Convex) "[Name of customer] is a *tough* customer." (SWB)
>
> **Nominalizations:** "*Extensions* under *development* include *incorporation* of Data and Spreadsheets, Colour, Security. . . ."

Table 2. Personal involvement characteristics in the electronic mail messages from Southwestern Bell and Convex.

	Southwestern Bell in percentages	Convex in percentages
First-person pronouns	79	63
Second-person pronouns	60	43
Informal diction	61	36
References to mental processes/ statements that monitor the flow of information	10	24

(Convex) "I have gotten the *impression* that there is not any question about our *viability* or continued *existence*." (SWB)

Relative clauses and complement clauses: "also no one *who is MY vball* [volleyball] *partner* can go for the above mentioned reason." "it would seem appropriate *to investigate the suitability of ODA for Internet purposes*." (Convex) "THIS IS JUST AN 'FYI' SO THAT YOU WILL KNOW *TO SUPPORT THE MANAGERS AND 'DELIVER THE MAIL'* WHILE I AM AWAY FROM THE OFFICE." (SWB)

Integrated discourse is characterized by a variety of elements such as present participles, attributive adjectives, and clauses introduced by "that," "to," "who," "whom," or "which" (Murray, 1985; Chafe, 1982; Ferrara, Brunner, & Whittemore, 1991). In looking for the frequency of present participles, I omitted progressive constructions such as *she is thinking* and lexicalized words such as *meaning* which behave as adjectives. Like present participles, attributive adjectives characterize integrated discourse, allowing the writer to express an idea as a modifier rather than as an assertion. Integrated discourse also contains a high frequency of relative clauses (clauses that begin with "that," "to," "who," "whom," or "which") and complement clauses (normally introduced by "that" and "to") (Chafe, 1982).

Table 3 summarizes the occurrences of the integration characteristics in the electronic mail messages from Southwestern Bell

Table 3. Integration in the electronic mail messages from Southwestern Bell and Convex.

	Southwestern Bell in percentages	Convex in percentages
Present participles	32	56
Attributive adjectives	12	54
Nominalizations	24	37
Relative and complement clauses	31	42

and from Convex. The Convex messages showed a higher level
of integration than did the Southwestern Bell messages, especially
in the percentage of attributive adjectives and present participles.
These higher percentages indicate that the Convex messages are
closer to written than to oral discourse. This indication is surprising because of the relaxed environment at Convex and the Convex participants' preference of electronic mail over verbal communication. This preference is illustrated by the 687 messages from
31 Convex employees during a 24-hour period as compared with
the 195 messages from the 18 Southwestern Bell employees during a 5-day period.

Conclusion

Written communication via computers poses a special problem for scholars of orality and literacy because it blurs the traditional distinctions between oral and written discourse. As Ong
(1977) explains, the new orality bears striking resemblance to the
old in its participatory mystique, its fostering of a communal sense,
and its concentration on the present moment. But this new orality
"is essentially a more deliberate and self-conscious orality, based
permanently on the use of writing and print" (Ong, 1982, p. 136).
As part of this new orality, electronic mail and other types of computer interchanges take on the characteristics of oral and written

discourse. Like traditional orality, real-time computer interchanges encourage involvement (Ferrara, Brunner, & Whittemore, 1991; Selfe & Meyer, 1991; Wilkins, 1991; Murray, 1985). This study supports this idea of involvement in nonreal-time electronic mail. The electronic mail messages from Convex and Southwestern Bell exhibited more characteristics of personal involvement than of detachment, a characteristic of written discourse.

Like traditional orality, electronic mail also concentrates on the present. Traditional orality is spontaneous and allows for immediate feedback from the audience, while written discourse is nonspontaneous, planned, and organized with no feedback (Lakoff, 1982; Ong, 1981). Electronic mail has some of the spontaneity of oral discourse and frequently allows for quick (if not immediate) feedback. This feedback can occur within minutes of sending a message. However, electronic mail is more deliberate in that the writer has the opportunity to plan and organize the discourse. Yet, in the questionnaires completed by the participants at Convex and Southwestern Bell, most reported that they spent little time planning and revising electronic mail messages and sent messages within seconds of writing. The spontaneity of electronic mail may encourage the misspelled words and unconventional punctuation, diction, and capitalization exhibited in the electronic mail from Convex and Southwestern Bell. The more frequent appearance of these characteristics in the Convex messages may further strengthen the link between spontaneity and informality because the Convex employees use electronic mail as their primary communication medium—frequently replacing oral media such as telephone and face-to-face conversations. However, the messages from one group of Southwestern Bell participants—those in the proposal-development division—contained more unconventional punctuation, diction, and capitalization than did the messages written outside the proposal-development division. These participants also used pictures to personalize their messages. Similar to the Convex participants, the proposal-division participants were beginning to use electronic mail to replace face-to-face and telephone communication. With the unconventional diction, punctuation, and mechanics and the pictures and emoticons, these participants at Southwestern Bell and Convex are developing their own rhetoric for electronic mail—a rhetoric that borrows from traditional oral and written discourse (Ferrara, Brunner, & Whittemore, 1991).

As Ong (1977) writes, the new orality is "more deliberate and self-conscious" than traditional orality. Indeed, the electronic mail in this study was more deliberate and self-conscious than traditional orality through the integration characteristics and the lack of social cues. Although the level of integration in the messages was not extremely high, the messages did show some integration. The Southwestern Bell messages did not show as high a level of integration as did the Convex messages. This integration shows that electronic mail is not completely divorced from the traditions of written discourse—it too is often planned and deliberate. The messages from all participants, except those prepared on the Macintosh system, seem to eliminate the self-conscious nature not part of traditional orality through the absence of format cues. The messages contained few, if any, format cues to indicate the organizational level, area of responsibility, subject matter, etc. A message from the president of the company would look the same as one from any other employee. The lack of traditional format cues (headings, job titles, departments, etc.) was less important for the Southwestern Bell readers because the participants communicated primarily with people they knew and with people within their work groups. Both at Convex and at Southwestern Bell, the only format cue that a reader might use to determine the subject matter of the message or area of responsibility of the writer is the subject line. On the surface, it would seem that this lack of format cues would make the messages less self-conscious—that all users would have a democratic voice. However, this attempt at democracy can seem self-conscious and contrived, for example, when the employees know that the message is from the president, or when the employees know that the president can track down who they are and what they do in the company. The employees may try to treat everyone as an equal in the electronic mail environment. But in reality—as in the case of electronic mail to the president—the employee at a much lower level in the corporate hierarchy becomes self-conscious when trying to write to the president, as if the president is his or her co-worker.

Welch (1993) says that our classroom practices have been deeply conditioned by this new power of the spoken word in its electronic manifestations. Indeed, electronic mail is a powerful tool now available to us and to our students, but it is a medium which follows only part of the rules of traditional written discourse. Instead, it borrows from the rich traditions of orality and literacy and is creating new traditions of its own. We should help our students understand how to use the written traditions of deliberate planning and integration when writing electronic mail. We should also encourage them to use, but control, the spontaneity of electronic mail. This spontaneity is one of the advantages of electronic mail, but it can cause uncontrolled writing. For instance, our students should learn when it is appropriate to use emoticons, pictures, and unconventional diction in electronic mail. Electronic mail may one day replace most paper communication; therefore our students need to understand electronic mail and its rich borrowings from oral and written discourse.

References

Biber, D. (1986). Spoken and written textual dimensions in English. *Language, 62*, 384–414.

Chafe, W.L. (1982). Integration and involvement in speaking, writing, and oral literature. In D. Tannen (Ed.), *Spoken and written language* (pp. 35–53). Advances in Discourse Processes, Series 9. Norwood, NJ: Ablex.

Ferrara, K., Brunner, H., & Whittemore, G. (1991). Interactive written discourse as an emergent register. *Written Communication, 8*(1) 8–34.

Gibson, W. (1969). *Persona: A style study for readers and writers*. New York: Random House.

Halpern, J.W. (1985). An electronic odyssey. In L. Odell & D. Goswami (Eds.), *Writing in nonacademic settings* (pp. 157–201). New York: Guilford.

Lakoff, R.T. (1982). Some of my favorite writers are literate: The mingling of oral and literate strategies in written communication. In D. Tannen (Ed.), *Spoken and written language* (pp. 239–260). Advances in Discourse Processes, Series 9. Norwood, NJ: Ablex.

Murray, D.E. (1985). Composition as conversation: The computer terminal as medium of communication. In L. Odell & D. Goswami (Eds.), *Writing in nonacademic settings* (pp. 203–227). New York: Guilford.

Murray, D.E. (1988). The context of oral and written language: A framework for mode and medium switching. *Language in Society, 17,* 351–373.

Murray, D.E. (1991). The composing process for computer conversation. *Written Communication, 8*(1) 35–55.

Ong, W.J. (1981). Literacy and orality in our times. In G. Tate & E.P.J. Corbett (Eds.), *The writing teacher's sourcebook* (pp. 36–48). New York: Oxford University Press.

Ong, W.J. (1977). *Interfaces of the word: Studies in the evolution of consciousness and culture.* Ithaca, NY: Cornell University Press.

Ong, W.J. (1982). *Orality and literacy: The technologizing of the word.* London: Methuen.

Perry, T.S. (1992, October). E-mail at work. *IEEE Spectrum,* 24–28.

Perry, T.S., & Adam, J.A. (1992, October). E-mail pervasive and persuasive. *IEEE Spectrum,* 22–23.

Schaefermeyer, M.J., & Sewell, E.H., Jr. (1988). Communicating by electronic mail. *American Behavioral Scientist, 32*(2), 112–123.

Selfe, C.L., & Meyer, P.R. (1991). Testing claims from on-line conferences. *Written Communication, 8*(2), 163–192.

Sproull, L., & Kiesler, S. (1986). Reducing social context cues: Electronic mail in organizational communication. *Management Science, 32,* 1492–1512.

Sproull, L., & Kiesler, S. (1991). *Connections: New ways of working in the networked organization.* Cambridge, MA: MIT Press.

Stein, J., & Yates, J . (1983). Electronic mail: How will it change office communication? How can managers use it effectively? In R.W. Beswick & A.B. Williams (Eds.), *Information Systems and Business Communication* (pp. 99–105). Urbana, IL: American Business Communication Association.

Welch, K. (1993). Reconfiguring writing and delivery in secondary orality. In J.F. Reynolds (Ed.), *Rhetorical memory and delivery* (pp. 17–30). Hillsdale, NJ: Erlbaum.

Wilkins, H. (1991). Computer talk: Long-distance conversations by computer. *Written Communication, 8,* 56–78.

Chapter 4

Writing Technologies at White Sands

Powell G. Henderson
White Sands Missile Range, New Mexico

Increased technology in a workplace creates the potential to dra-matically change the basic structure of written communication in that workplace. However, that potential may not always be real-ized. This ethnographic study of a government organization iden-tifies patterns of local use, resistance to standardization, and the persistence of paper forms that complicate writing with electronic tools in a traditional bureaucracy.

This chapter summarizes the results of an ethnographic study of written communication in a moderately sized government or-ganization during a period of approximately twenty-seven months, from May 1991 through August 1993. My research ad-dressed how the influx of technology is affecting written commu-nication there.

Many studies of writing in the workplace have concentrated on relatively homogeneous groups of writers. Paradis, Dobrin, and Miller (1985), for example, studied the writing done by 33 engineers and scientists at an R&D organization. Winsor (1990) conducted case studies of two engineers. Faigley and Miller (1982) surveyed 200 workers, all college graduates, from a broad range of occupations. Flatley (1982) surveyed 89 managers in the San Diego area. Couture et al. (1985) surveyed employees in 50 occu-pations, but limited their study to "competent writers" (p. 405). As an employee of a large government installation and a gradu-ate student of technical and professional communication at New

I thank Paul Meyer and Steve Bernhardt of New Mexico State University for their help with this project and this chapter.

65

Mexico State University, it seemed to me that much of this research did not adequately address the kinds of writing I saw going on around me.

It is natural for a writing researcher to focus on significant documents. After all, if one is to study writing, what better place to start than to study manuals, reports, or newsletters? While I do not question the value of this research, it is important to know whether these documents are really representative of workplace writing, or whether they just illustrate writing that is highly visible. By addressing primarily the most significant documents, or the writing done by only a few people (technical writers, engineers, managers), I felt most workplace composition studies had failed to adequately address the day-to-day writing done by most of the employees in my organization. It seemed analogous to a researcher studying a family's diet by observing only mealtimes and ignoring the potato chips, peanuts, candy bars, and apples snacked on throughout the day.

The organization I worked in and studied was the White Sands Missile Range's Directorate of Information Management. White Sands Missile Range is a Department of the Army installation that provides perhaps the premier overland missile testing capabilities in the entire world, although the range's testing is no longer limited to missiles. The range is a massive chunk of real estate (about the size of Delaware and Rhode Island put together) in the desert of southern New Mexico. Although commanded by an army general, the White Sands workforce, including contractors, is overwhelmingly civilian. The range is also home to contingents from the U.S. Air Force and the U.S. Navy.

The Directorate of Information Management, where I work, is a support organization to White Sands, providing information services for everything from photographic support of missile firings, to mail and distribution for the entire range, to planning for the range's computer networks. The organization also operates a video-teleconference facility and a cable television station offering limited programming. Parts of the organization have made army documentaries and training films for years. We provide data-processing support to White Sands, with its IBM mainframe and networked UNIX minicomputers. We also provide software and hardware troubleshooting and training for the several thousand personal computers on the range.

In our organization, no one has the title of technical writer. What we do have is an organization of more than 300 electronic technicians, budget analysts, photographers, secretaries, management analysts, engineers, engineering technicians, computer programmers, and a smattering of military personnel. All are involved daily with a wide variety of information services.

The Nature of the Research

What I attempted to do was quite simple. I wanted to observe and document the written communication that went on around me and to identify patterns and trends in the ways in which increased technology in the workplace was changing, or not changing, written communication. The study was undertaken on a part-time basis in my own organization and was done with the support of the organization. I estimate that I averaged two to three hours per week of work time devoted exclusively to the research.

I chose a qualitative approach, with data derived from multiple sources, as the research course that would best permit me to identify patterns in written communication. Since I was studying written communication, it seemed logical to start with the documents themselves, and I set about gathering as many as I could. I collected thousands of documents and subjected several hundred to intensive analysis. My definition of written communication was quite broad and included handwritten documents, forms, memos, and e-mail.

As a longtime employee of the organization, I was by definition a participant. My own position is that of a computer programmer/system analyst. For most of the study period, I was a team leader of a small team in the areas of personal computer software development and mainframe database administration. I had worked in the same building since 1975, except for a three-year assignment in Germany. During several months of the study, I was able to observe the workplace from the perspective of a supervisor.

As a part-time graduate student studying writing in the workplace, I also attempted to look at written communication at White Sands as a disinterested observer. I took copious notes throughout the study and spent considerable time sorting my observations.

I conducted more than twenty formal, sit-down interviews and hundreds of shorter, more informal interviews with personnel throughout the organization. In the spring of 1993, I also distributed a five-page questionnaire to all employees of the organization. (The response rate was greater than 40 percent.)

Major Patterns in the Writing at White Sands

Several patterns or generalizations seemed to be true for understanding communication within the directorate and would potentially have far-reaching ramifications for understanding writing in the workplace. The patterns I note here should, of course, be considered in the light of the limitation of my research. Considering the number of offices and employees in the organization, and the number of documents created, my research touched on only the smallest fraction of the organization's written communication. Nonetheless, the patterns I discovered should be of interest to those who teach and study writing in the workplace. This work accounts for the experiences of working professionals who do not define their professions as "technical communicators" but who nevertheless do a great deal of writing at work. This study should illustrate the need for further research into their experiences. The most significant of my findings form the basis of this discussion:

- Most writing created within the organization is event-driven. In other words, some event, either in the past or in the future, causes the document to be created. Such events can also be part of larger institutionalized processes.

- Most written communication in the organization is part of a process that aims to get something done. Moreover, most written communication is a by-product of a process, rather than an end product.

- A considerable amount of written communication in the organization involves preprinted forms.

- Some documents suffer from a worth/benefit imbalance.

- New technology tends to augment, not replace, old technology.

- While written communication is important within the organization, and a great deal is produced, most written communication requires only the simplest of technology to create.

- Benefits to document creation caused by increased technology must be balanced against the cost in equipment and human resources required by the technology itself.

- Technological improvements, like any tool, are of greater value in some offices than in others.

- Improvements resulting from the introduction of technology in the workplace tend to be incremental and slow. When something goes wrong with the technology, however, the impact is likely to be severe and rapid.

Most Writing in the Directorate Is Event-Driven

One thing that was immediately apparent from an examination of documents at White Sands was that most written communication there is event-driven. Some event happens, or is about to happen, that serves as a catalyst for the writing. Typical events that initiated writing in the study were

- notification that an inspection team was scheduled to arrive;

- an employee requested training;

- an accident happened on the job;

- new key control officers were appointed for a building;

- new software was installed on a multiuser computer system;

- an employee retired; and

- a computer virus was found in another installation, and employees were reminded of the availability of virus-checking software.

Many events are unpredictable and add to the tension and excitement of the workplace. People described these by using such phrases as "stamping out brush fires." They may be initiated by a personal visit from a manager or customer, a scribbled "Your Action" on a memo, a phone call or a message on a voice-mail system, or an e-mail message. Not all events require written communication, of course, but many do. A corollary is that very little writing is created spontaneously, with the possible exception of doodles.

Understanding that documents are spawned by events is important. Receiving a document can in itself be an event that causes the creation of other documents, so that a single event can cause a chain reaction of activity. Few employees in the organization can accurately predict on Monday morning what their coming week will be like. The next phone call or office distribution may contain a catalyst for many hours of effort.

Not even the simplest documents exist in isolation. Even the most basic written communication is, as Faigley (1985) has pointed out, "inextricably tied up in chains of communication" (p. 241). So, much of the corporate lore seems to be tied up in what a co-worker of some years ago called "the great oral tradition." "Here is what you do when someone is injured at work. . . ." "These are the steps you must go through in order to turn in equipment as excess. . . ." "You want a CD-ROM reader? Fine, here is what you must do. . . ."

When events are cyclical and/or repetitive, they are still events. The Biweekly Status Report, for example, is a report to the directorate commander which is a roll-up of information submitted from every office in the organization. Because it is a biweekly report, it can be plotted for months in advance. As another example, a supervisor with twelve employees knows that during the course of the year he or she must write twelve annual appraisals. In many cases, these events have been around for decades and have become institutionalized, perhaps documented somewhere—in SOPs (Standard Operating Procedures) or regulations. Within the directorate, for example, processes may be governed by:

- organizational units within the directorate;
- the directorate itself;

- White Sands Missile Range offices;

- TECOM (the Test and Evaluation Command, the parent organization of White Sands);

- AMC (the Army Materiel Command, the parent command of TECOM and grandparent command of White Sands);

- DA (the Department of the Army);

- DoD (the Department of Defense);

- OPM (the Office of Personnel Management); and

- other government agencies (the Department of Labor, for example, has forms and procedures to be used when there is a serious on-the-job injury).

Most Writing in the Directorate Is a By-Product of a Process

We can define a process as a grouping in sequence of all the tasks directed at accomplishing one particular outcome. Examples are the steps in producing a product, hiring or training a new employee, or filling an order. In this light, we begin to see that every activity is part of a process, and there are thousands upon thousands of processes in every organization (Scholtes et al., 1988).

Applying this process-oriented thinking to written communication, nearly every piece of writing is a part of some larger process, whether the communication is recorded on paper or in an electronic message on a computer. It might even be a plastic room number attached to a door. The process may be as simple as taking a phone message for a co-worker or as important as justifying the work existence of an employee, office, or organization. Every process has, or logically should have, its own scorecard detailing what is important to that process. There should be some means of determining, at the completion of the process, the degree of success of each particular step in a process. Sometimes the speed of the process is important, but, at other times, complete and total accuracy of data may be essential to the success of a process.

Some documents created within the directorate are end products of a process. The creation of a manual or an SOP or a class diploma has as the final result a paper document. The worth of the effort for the process should be judged by the quality of the document. An award certificate with coffee stains does not reflect a successful effort. One "certificate of appreciation" presented to one of my co-workers, a nicely printed document, had the state printed as "New Mixico."

The output of other processes, however, may not be a document at all. The output of a request for an account on one of the directorate's computers, for example, is the assignment of the account. The output of a training request is the training itself. The process may generate a trail of paper along the way, but these documents are not products but by-products. Their worth should be judged by how well they further the processes they serve.

An analogy with sports might make the point clearer. In downhill skiing, contestants are scored on their speed through the course. As long as the contestant stays within the course boundaries and perhaps obeys a few other rules, it is the final time that counts. Form counts for nothing in scoring such a race. Presumably, a skier could ski part of the course backwards. In platform diving, on the other hand, the worth of a dive is not based on how quickly the diver enters the water, but rather on the form exhibited between the platform and the water.

There seems to be a real danger in confusing products with by-products—with judging a downhill skier on form. Effort aimed at improving what are essentially by-products may be wasted, if not detrimental to the process. If a document must be returned to its originator for trivial cosmetic reasons, or if it waits in an "in" box for approval by an official who is on vacation, the by-product may be served, but the process is not. All this is not to say that by-products are unimportant, only that their worth must be balanced against the total process.

A Considerable Amount of Communication Involves Preprinted Forms

Preprinted forms, both official and unofficial, are central to most of the processes I studied. They come in all sizes and colors. Some include carbon paper, some are carbonless, while still others are single-part forms of only a few square inches. With few exceptions, forms are mostly by-products of processes. I would like to discuss forms at some length here because they are so integral to the processes and writing I studied. Together with regulations and custom, they constitute "the system" that must be lived with at White Sands. Whether or not this system is efficient, it is the way things are, and it is not easily changed. One document collected in my study, a yellowing, typed summary of codes used in the army's supply system that was unearthed during an office move, was written in 1961. The information was still, by and large, applicable more than thirty years later.

While there are a few forms that are end products (such as forms that are designed to be placed on walls, or security stickers stuck on telephones, or the open/closed sign that is attached to a safe), most forms are designed to improve a process. The White Sands forms warehouse, which is administered by the Directorate of Information Management, stores more than a thousand individual form types (these are only the official ones). Sometimes it seems that there is, indeed, a form for every purpose. There is even a form for establishing an official form.

Forms often carry efficiency to an extreme degree. One of the best examples of this is DD Form 1556: Request, Authorization, Agreement, Certification of Training and Reimbursement. As the title indicates, this form is used throughout the process of getting a single individual through a single training class. It is the form that is used to request training. It is used to approve or disapprove the training. It is used to certify that funds are available for the course. There are spaces where the school indicates whether or not the applicant was accepted for the training. A section is provided to record that the fees were paid. In case of nongovernment training of more than eighty classroom hours, there is a place for the student to certify that he or she will remain in the government for a certain period after the completion of the training. Finally, the form is used to record the student's evaluation of the course as well as comments for the student's supervisor on the usefulness of the training.

To achieve all this, DD Form 1556 is a 10-part carbon form. Together with a front page of instructions, the entire package contains 11 sheets of paper plus 8 sheets of carbon paper. Eight of the form pages also use the reverse side of the page.

This form is a mechanical marvel. Through the use of short and long carbons, blacked-out on some pages, and clear insets on some of the carbon paper, each page within the form allows it to be used for many different purposes. Yet, the student's name is reproduced on each page and needs to be typed only once. The key word here is *typed,* for the DD Form 1556 is a model of efficiency only within the old mechanical office paradigm. Within an office with clerical personnel, typewriters, a mail-distribution system, and file folders, the form is, in its own way, extremely efficient. As long as there is someone available to type the form, reverse carbons, and decollate and distribute the parts of the form to the proper offices, the system served by this form has the potential for operating quite smoothly.

In a sense, then, forms are not just a product of the existing paradigm, they *are* the paradigm itself. As long as these paper forms exist, the old paradigm will exist. Revising forms merely polishes the process. Even when such forms are automated, they still operate within the paradigm. Unless a system were devised that could totally eliminate the forms, the basic process would remain intact. In any case, there seems to be little an individual, an organization, or an entire installation can do about a standard form. As long as the DD Form 1556 continues to be the only approved means of requesting training, for example, technology can do only so much. As soon as the form is created, it ossifies the process, capturing a business process as it existed at a given point in time. Once printed in massive quantities and distributed to many offices, the form tends to be the master, and not the slave, of the process.

The implication for written communication here is that there may sometimes be more effort put in to improving by-products than to improving the process. An employee who corrects spelling errors in a form notifying employees that it is time to pay their coffee dues may be improving the by-product of the process, but may not be improving the process. An employee who provides a flawless, written report on, say, the need for additional telephones in an office may see the report as an end product, and, indeed, to that employee, the report is an end product. Yet, in the context of the larger process, the report is a by-product. An inappropriate treatment of all writing as an end product may be misguided and ultimately disruptive to the work processes within the organization.

Document Balance—Worth versus Effort

Those processes described above sometimes involve conditions that are not always easy for a writer to work under. Sometimes documents do not receive the effort they should and are served up half-raw, so to speak. Other documents, on reflection, seem clearly overcooked.

An important feature of our workplace is that work must often be done at a feverish pace. It was not unusual for workers there to be asked to meet absurdly short deadlines. Our group was once told shortly after 9 a.m. that information was needed for a briefing early that afternoon; we had to provide a list of all computer systems we supported, along with a short description of each, by 11 a.m. The list provided was woefully inadequate. Given an entire day, we would have produced a much more complete and valuable list. With a week, it would have been even more complete. But this deadline was nonnegotiable, and "I can't provide that information on such short notice" was not an acceptable response. Those who requested the information knew it was incomplete and certainly did not complain about the format or content of the information we provided. However, had writing specialists examined the slips of paper left behind, they might have assumed that the organization was staffed by workers in desperate need of training in grammar, spelling, and handwriting. The information collected, collated, edited, and transferred to slick transparencies and handouts reflected the two-hour lead time we were given before the briefing.

This raises an important question for further research. How common is this lack of opportunity for editing in technical writing environments? University training, which assumes leisurely revision and careful editing, may mislead students who eventually face such conditions.

If some documents are denied the attention they need, others receive too much. Time and again I saw employees, especially managers, look at a painfully wrought document, scan the first few pages, and hand the document back to its author with a nod. Few documents were savored and digested to the extent the creators felt they deserved. Part of this has to do with time. Just as there is often not enough time to prepare a document, there is just as often not enough time to study it once it is completed. Therefore, many workers have learned that it is preferable to err on the side of brevity rather than on completeness.

Some documents are created in response to a set of requirements, and those requirements can change, often as a result of further clarification of the problem. Since some requests for documentation eventually seem to go away, writers sometimes delay projects until the last moment, in a variation of the "just-in-time" inventory system developed in Japan. One interviewee carried this to an extreme: To avoid giving a manager opportunity to make his usual request for wholesale changes in her work, she kept delaying submission until just before the absolute deadline. In the end, her manager had no choice but to approve the document as submitted.

People who think of all documents as products, and not as by-products, of a process are often difficult to please. Concerned with a document's completeness of information and neatness, they are often at odds with those who are more concerned with speeding up the process. One of the glories of e-mail in our organization is that there are no regulations governing the form of an e-mail message, so that it is possible to concentrate on the message. However, my study showed that many e-mail messages still follow a strict memorandum format. Perhaps the creators feel more comfortable with formal memoranda or expect the documents to be printed out. In such cases the e-mail network functions merely as a faster courier service, thus preserving one writing context inside a much different one.

New Technology Tends to Augment, Not Replace, Old Technology

The same cart that wheels a new personal computer into an office does not wheel out the typewriter. There is not a decreased need for knowledge, skills, and equipment because of the increased technology in the workplace. Instead, additional skills are required. Personal computers do not replace typewriters; they augment them.

Typewriters will probably remain in the White Sands offices until the last preprinted form is replaced. Most memoranda seem to be created by using word-processing programs, but forms, especially carbon forms, must be filled out with a typewriter or by hand. Even after the most common forms are stored on CD-ROM, offices will still need typewriters to fill out the more obscure forms.

On the other hand, there are quantitative changes in equipment use. Typewriters may still be required, but they are not used as much. Because employees are doing much more of their own document creation, secretaries do much less typing, but they still must type. Increasingly, however, employees at all levels are called upon to work in more and more complex environments. To send and receive electronic mail, for example, employees of White Sands normally must use the UNIX network. Secretaries must be familiar with at least one of several word-processing programs on the network as well as with a variety of word-processing programs on office PCs. They must be able to use fax machines. Many must dial in to remote databases and use spreadsheets.

As a result of this variety, offices are called upon to juggle an increasing number of "things." New things (hardware, software, processes) appear periodically, but fewer go away. As a result, nearly everyone in the organization, regardless of position, seems to be learning something, and the backlog of needed knowledge is forever increasing.

Most Written Communication Created in the Organization Demands Only Simple Technology

By my broad definition of written communication, the Directorate of Information Management does an enormous amount of writing. Yet, most of the documents produced are similar to those created five, ten, or twenty years ago. The processes used to create the documents may have changed, but the products have not. A memorandum may be created on a computer with a word-processing program rather than on a typewriter, but the end result is still a memorandum. Forms may be filled out using a pen, a typewriter, or a dot matrix or impact printer, but the product is still a preprinted form. Even if the form is created using a software package, such as PerFORM, which creates the form itself, the product is still much the same.

Note that I said that a communication may require only simple technology. Nevertheless, its writer may have used technology that is quite complex and expensive. Yet, the documents themselves reflect little of the technology used to create them. Was a memorandum typed with a typewriter, printed on an impact printer, or printed by a laser printer? If it was created on a personal computer, what word-processing software was used? Was the personal computer a DOS system, or a Windows™ system, or was it perhaps done on a Macintosh? Compared with the technology of a few years ago, much of the hardware and software coming into offices today is like a Ferrari compared to a riding lawn mower, but it is a Ferrari stuck in traffic.

Considerable Effort Is Associated with Technology

Many directorate working hours are expended in what I call "technological pencil sharpening"—time that is indirectly associated with written communication, but that is not associated with the creation of a specific document. Installing hardware and software, learning a word-processing program, configuring a printer, and troubleshooting of one kind or another all fall in this category. Formal training in, say, WordPerfect should be considered here, as would helping a co-worker transfer files.

Because the directorate is a support organization, many of the employees I studied are involved with customer support, handling problems with telephones, terminals, networks, personal computer hardware and software, an IBM mainframe, and even the range's many water wells. Many of the problems do not involve written communication, but many do. The directorate's personnel are the first line of support for customer problems with word-processing software.

Some time ago, in the face of a growing diversity of word-processing software, the directorate was the dominant force in advocating a standard word-processing package for White Sands. Our group argued that we could not adequately support every program, either for technical support or training, and that a standard word-processing format would eliminate many file conversion problems. Thus, in the late 1980s, a common word-processing package was designated for the entire installation.

Designating a standard word-processing package was one thing, but putting it into use was quite another. Some users did not have the package, and, even when we acquired a large number of copies, there were not nearly enough to go around. Within my own section, our copies of the package for personal computers arrived several years after it was named as the standard. Many personal computer users continued to use whatever word-processing software they had always used. Network users faced a different problem. The network was made up of disparate, networked minicomputers, from different manufacturers, with a different word-processing solution on each type of computer. A further problem was that, as different nodes were upgraded, the new machines often contained different word-processing software. Even when a UNIX version of the standard word-processing package was put on the network, the package still did not gain much acceptance (at least during the period of my study), even among users familiar with the personal computer version.

Such diversity of word-processing solutions is expensive in several ways. Learning a new word-processing program is time-consuming, as is converting a document from one format to another. Even those who stay with one word-processing program are not immune to change, as new environments (the Windows™ and UNIX versions, for example) and new releases tend to keep even experienced users from wandering too far from their manuals.

My questionnaire suggested there may be a silent backlash against changing word-processing software. Despite having had a standard word-processing package for several years, and despite its being available in both MS-DOS and UNIX environments, less than a third (30.3 percent) of respondents named the standard word-processing package as the program they used most at work. When asked which program they would prefer to use, the number improved somewhat, to 37.7 percent. But, in what I felt was a telling response, when asked how satisfied they were with their current word-processing package, 58.8 percent said they were "totally satisfied."

The Worth of Technology as a Writing Tool

One pattern which came from my own observation, and which was confirmed by the interviews, both formal and informal, is perhaps the most significant in the study. It is quite simple and makes a certain amount of sense, yet it has far-reaching implications. The generalization is this:

> If technology functions as a tool for an office, that is, if it helps the employees do their jobs better or faster or helps them to improve the final product, then it stands a good chance of succeeding if introduced into the workplace.
>
> If, on the other hand, new technology does not function as a common tool, that is, it does not help them to do their jobs better, then it may have a negative effect on office efficiency.

Restated to focus on written communication, the observation is that, if an office has historically created a specific type of document, improving the technology to increase efficiency with that type of document may pay dividends. But if an office has never created a specific type of document, giving that office the capability to create that document does not mean anyone will do so. Give a carpenter a power saw to augment a handsaw, and he or she will make great use of it. Give a carpenter a soldering iron, and it will probably not be used very much. Give a computer with a spreadsheet package to an office that keeps manual spreadsheets, and the gains in productivity may be spectacular. The same package given to a writing group may lay dormant.

Support for this finding comes from several sources. First, there are the documents themselves. With my classification of documents, there are whole categories of writing that, by their very nature, do not seem to be affected by increased technology. Handwritten documents, for example, seem to thrive in spite of technology. Simple memoranda require only the simplest word processing and may still be created on a typewriter. Forms are also designed for use, for the most part, with a typewriter or a pen.

In the interviews, I attempted to determine the extent to which new documents were being created. Despite having the technology to function as miniature publishing houses (full-featured word-processing packages, laser printers, and desktop publishing packages), most offices do not seem to be creating new documents, although they may be using new technology to create documents they have always created. Documents of some complexity and length, such as user guides and manuals, are created by offices that, in the words of one interviewee, "have done it for twenty years."

Probably, there were documents not collected for my research that would prove exceptions to this rule. My research did, in fact, reveal a few places where people were creating some new documents. However, the tendency seemed to be to stay with traditional forms in any specific office.

Some documents at White Sands (computer-system documentation, for example, or memoranda, or entries on preprinted forms) are governed by strict formatting guidelines. Other documents are not, and these are the ones where writers stand to benefit most from the enhanced technology. This second group includes manuals, studies, proposals, organization charts, fliers for office picnics, and coffee rosters.

Improvements Come Slowly, but Problems Come Rapidly

In general, improvements in written communication in the directorate have tended to come slowly, like dawn. Using word processing, or MS-DOS, or Windows™ takes a certain amount of knowledge. Whether its source is from reading manuals, formal classes, coaching by a co-worker, or trial and error, a certain amount of time is involved in learning new techniques.

During the study period, White Sands started converting to ETS, the Electronic Timekeeping System, a mainframe system that permits an employee's timecards to be entered online. It also permits supervisors to certify these timecards online. While the ETS is generally felt to be an improvement over the paper timecards filled out by hand and signed by a supervisor, the implementation took many months. Timekeepers, a handful at a time, had to be trained on the system, and some offices did not have the proper equipment to allow them to access the system. Such time-intensive improvements are costly and must promise widespread benefits before they can be justified in financial terms.

On the other hand, when things go wrong with advanced technology, they are likely to do so immediately and, apparently, without warning. The copier breaks on the forty-seventh of fifty copies. MS-DOS issues the familiar "Abort, Retry, Fail?" message, and a day's work is lost. A hard drive goes down on a personal computer, putting a year's work at risk. A backhoe slices an electrical cable, cutting power to several buildings. A key employee leaves for another job, taking with her the entire office repository of WordStar lore. Strange page breaks start appearing in documents. Such failures are also costly and may require extensive knowledge to troubleshoot.

There are exceptions, of course, like changing printer ribbons, where improvements are instantaneous while quality degrades over time. In general, however, the greater the technology in an office, the more costly and painful is the process of learning to use the technology, the more likely there are to be problems, and the more specialized the troubleshooting expertise needed. Many directorate employees are familiar with MS-DOS, but fewer are familiar with Microsoft Windows™, and fewer still are familiar with the escape sequences needed to manipulate fonts on a laser printer. Nearly everyone can use an electric typewriter, many can use a word-processing program on a personal computer, but not many can use a scanner.

What Can Writing Students and Their Teachers Learn from the White Sands Example?

The following observations from my study seem particularly important to those who consider the sort of preparation universities might offer people who will eventually work in places like White Sands. They do not all represent easy solutions, but rather reflect issues such preparation should address.

Institutional Constraints Differ from Those of the Classroom

There are many obvious differences between a classroom setting and a business setting, but perhaps the most significant is the attitude toward innovation and change.

In the organizational setting I studied, there is an accepted, or normal, way of doing something, and deviating from this norm is often problematic and outside the scope of authority of any single individual. There is a way to requisition supplies, a way to apply for another job, and a way to request a new telephone line. These "ways," or processes, typically involve many different offices, each with its own area of responsibility and expertise. It is one thing to strive for change, but it is another to actually coordinate such a change for the many offices (including the several layers of corporate headquarters above the organization, such as the Department of the Army or the Department of Defense).

A classroom, on the other hand, is an entity that operates with a great deal of autonomy. Innovation and experimentation are quite properly encouraged, as long as the cause of technical communication is served. Changes do not have to be, to draw a parallel with the workplace, approved by the Board of Regents or the university's president. For those who will enter the workplace as technical communicators, there is probably no better way to encounter this difference than to experience the workplace itself. Co-op programs and internships provide training that is impossible to duplicate in a classroom.

Nevertheless, technical communications faculty could develop assignments which attempt to duplicate some of the conditions students may face on the job. Such an approach might, in a small way, emphasize that most documents exist within a historical context.

These conditions might include

- too little time to adequately prepare;
- equipment that is outdated, unfamiliar, or does not work;
- key personnel/information that is unavailable;

- changing requirements as documents are in process;
- working in small teams.

Technical Communicators and Computer Training

All methods used in this study indicate that there are serious problems with training in the use of word-processing software, e-mail, and personal computers within White Sands. There are just too many products, too many operating systems on too many types of computers, too many people using the products, and too few formal training classes to address even the most basic training needs. What training there is, be it formal classroom training, using tutorials associated with a particular application, reading a manual, or coaching from a co-worker, concentrates on task-oriented procedures: "This is how you set the margins. . . ." Students who will work in environments like this one may need to come equipped with a wide exposure to a variety of systems and an enthusiasm for learning new techniques as they are introduced.

What no training adequately addresses is troubleshooting: "See, it says right here in the book that when I click here . . . but this is what I get . . . looks OK on the screen, but when I try to print it . . . ." Based on my observations, employees are frequently called upon to resolve problems that are only remotely associated with their training and inclination. There is an office joke that the person who has a manual is a recognized expert on the product.

A person with word-processing skills may be called upon to assist when there is any sort of problem in the process of creating, printing, or distributing documents. It may be a problem with the word-processing program itself, but it may just as likely be incorrect settings of DIP switches on the printer or problems with a modem. Technical communication students may not feel that a knowledge of the RS-232 standards for asynchronous cable communication is a valuable weapon in document creation, but in our organization it frequently is.

Most people do not use technology in the way they are "supposed" to. Sometimes this is out of ignorance (years ago, I helped a person who entered figures into a spreadsheet and then added them up on an adding machine), but more than likely it is because the technology fails to help them do the work they do, in the way they would like to do it. Software packages are loaded, fiddled with for a while, and ignored, eventually to become "shelfware." Workers ignore computer-based calendars and make notes of future meetings on desk calendars or pocket planners. Important information is still conveyed orally rather than by e-mail. User guides and manuals are ignored. Printers make weak but fairly effective space heaters on chilly mornings.

New technical communicators should be helped to see that the workplace is not a trade show. An office should not be judged by the technology it has, but on how well the office does what it exists to do. Since the time when computers were showcased in glass-walled rooms, the tendency has been to perceive computing equipment as entries in a glitz race. Classes in technical communication should be designed to prepare students to function in a setting which encompasses not only technology's enticing future, but also its humdrum but functional and familiar past. There may be a small market for technological soothsayers and prophets in some organizations, but what is more likely expected of new employees is that they be able to make immediate contributions to solving today's problems, using the tools that are available now.

Dealing with Change at White Sands

One of the issues I wanted to explore in my study was Zuboff's (1988) description of the "magnetism of the past" (p. xv). I wanted to determine how real this phenomenon was in my own organization. What I found was that the magnetism not only exists but exerts its influence over every aspect of the offices and workers I studied. It is "the way things are done" as well as "the way things have always been done." The ways of the past are entrenched and may be driven out only with difficulty.

This magnetism does not manifest itself so much in an infatuation with the past, or in the lack of knowledge of the workforce, or in a belief by the workforce that the current ways are the best, or in a fear of change by the workforce. Instead, the magnetism exists in the forms, regulations, and traditions of a hierarchy stretching from the offices of the Directorate of Information Management to the Department of Defense and beyond. It exists in standard mainframe computer systems that, in some cases, have been around for decades. It exists in hardware and software that, while still useful, are several versions behind the current version.

Change is expensive. Whether expressed in real dollars, lost productivity, direct or indirect training costs, or by any other means, getting from here to there will be costly. Regardless of how slick and efficient the perceived target might seem to be, resources will be consumed. Pointing out budgetary limitations effectively smothers many new projects. The easiest and least expensive part may be purchasing the actual hardware and software. Changing processes is what is difficult and expensive, and unless the underlying process is changed, improvements may be illusory. Therefore, technical communication education should strive to prepare students for a world in which they will be only one spoke on a wheel, on a wagon which has many wheels. They will play an important part in the organization, but it may initially be only a small part. To a much greater extent than they have experienced in school, new technical communicators may be subject to constraints over which they have no control. Many documents they will be creating will not look much different, or in fact be much different, than those created by their co-workers in the organization for dozens of years.

There is another force at work, a force that is often quite strong. This is the force that looks to the future, that embraces technology and sees its possibilities. It is an anxious and impatient force that is fueled by market forces touting the latest technological advances. People who are touched by this force are aware that the bulk of the range's forms could be stored on a few CD-ROM disks and printed on demand. They are aware that the potential exists for automating entire processes. They are aware of how effortlessly and quickly text, charts, drawings, and photographs from many offices could be brought together seamlessly into a single document.

However, even those who fall under the spell of technological possibility are soon faced with fiscal reality. Need is not an acceptable currency for acquisition, and technological potential is even less so. The monetary pie of any organization is not infinite;

indeed, during my study period, financial resources at White Sands shrank noticeably. In many areas, it is a rather simple matter to design a better or more efficient system, but it is not so easy to implement that system, given that today's pockets are not as deep as yesterday's and may be even shallower tomorrow. I now have a better appreciation of how both forces operate in the workplace I studied. Everyone I interviewed, from rank-and-filer to manager, made a convincing case for the validity of his or her particular point of view. There are, as far as I can tell, no simple solutions to even the simplest problem.

University instruction tends to celebrate potential and to be oriented toward the future. The world I studied, as it is being drawn (or pushed) toward the same future, must also turn to face, Janus-like, the past. The processes and paradigms of yesterday are firmly entrenched and must be accommodated.

At the conclusion of this study, I found that my attitude had changed toward technology in the workplace. I am certainly not antitechnology, but I have tempered any zeal I might have had about the short-term impact of technology in the workplace. During the study, I arrived at certain insights regarding technology and writing that should be understood by those who will enter the workplace as well as by those who will prepare them. On the basis of my observations of this specific workplace, some areas (presentation graphics, for example) have made excellent use of technological advances, while other areas are likely to reap only superficial benefits for years, if not decades, to come.

References

Couture, B., et al. (1985). Building a professional writing program through a university-industry collaboration. In L. Odell & D. Goswami (Eds.), *Writing in nonacademic settings* (pp. 391–426). New York: Guilford.

Crosby, P.B. (1980). *Quality is free: The art of making quality certain.* New York: Mentor-NAL.

Faigley, L. (1985). Nonacademic writing: The social perspective. In L. Odell & D. Goswami (Eds.), *Writing in nonacademic settings* (pp. 231–248). New York: Guilford.

Faigley, L., & Miller, T.P. (1982). What we learn from writing on the job. *College English, 44,* 557–569.

Flatley, M.E. (1982). A comparative analysis of the written communication of managers at various organizational levels in the private sector. *The Journal of Business Communication, 19*(3), 35–49.

Henderson, P.G. (1993). Product, process and paradigm: The way we write at work. Unpublished M.A. thesis, New Mexico State University, Las Cruces, NM.

Paradis, J., Dobrin, D., & Miller, R. (1985). Writing at Exxon ITD: Notes on the writing environment of an R&D organization. In L. Odell & D. Goswami (Eds.), *Writing in nonacademic settings* (pp. 281–307). New York: Guilford.

Scholtes, P.R., et al. (1988). *The team handbook: How to use teams to improve quality.* Madison, WI: Joiner Associates.

Winsor, D.A. (1990). How companies affect the writing of young engineers: Two case studies. *IEEE Transactions of Professional Communication, 33,* 124–129.

Zuboff, S. (1988). *In the age of the smart machine: The future of work and power.* New York: Basic Books.

Part Two

Electronic Challenges to Traditional Notions of Writers and Writing

Chapter 5

Writing and Database Technology: Extending the Definition of Writing in the Workplace

Barbara Mirel
De Paul University

People at work often exchange and interpret tables of information in order to make critical organizational decisions. This study describes workplace readers' responses to standard database output and shows how developing effective data reports is a rhetorical art— perhaps primarily a writing task—not simply a technical process of interacting with the search, retrieval, and formatting functions of a database application. The author discusses key rhetorical and technological skills needed to transform database output into usable information for specific organizational contexts.

A major change is transforming the American workplace. Thanks to distributed computing, nontechnical employees in every department can manage their own data and compose data reports for important business purposes. These reports, which answer business problems or concerns, present information retrieved from electronic databases. Service supervisors, for example, often need to decide about salary increases for technicians. Most helpful to these supervisors are reports on technicians' yearly productivity, with supervisors figuring productivity from electronic data on technicians' number of service calls, their average response times, the time spent per call, and the revenue brought in. Typically, supervisors will organize such data into tables, most likely listing the names of technicians in the rows and the measures of productivity across the columns. In this essay, the term *data report* refers only to printed reports that are composed of tables of numbers, words, or both. I focus on tabular reports because they are the most common, though not by any means the only, form or medium for data reporting.

Reports consisting of data tables are vital to virtually every function in a business: marketing uses them for data on customer demographics and purchasing patterns; budgeting displays tables of revenue and expenses; production reports scheduling and maintains inventory through tables; and sales uses this form to present precise data on past, present, and prospective customers. Sometimes these report writers create tabular displays of data for their own needs (making themselves their own readers); at other times, reports may be intended for other readers. In either case, the fundamental purpose of a data report remains the same: to answer a business concern with relevant data organized to support a reader's interpretive needs and strategies for turning that data into information and knowledge.

The organizational value of data reports for recordkeeping and problem solving cannot be stressed enough. Yet reports have value only if report writers are able to generate a form and content that directly address a pressing business problem. Unfortunately, at present, many businesspersons lack this proficiency. Surveys show that managers are extremely frustrated at having to spend, on average, 500–750 hours per year (one-third to half of their year's work) searching for the information they want (Delphi Consulting Group, 1989–93). Often, this searching involves restructuring data reports that other people have written so that the tables truly answer their business questions. Despite such frustrations, little attention is given in either business or in technical and professional writing classes to building people's skills in writing effective data reports.

In developing and drafting data reports, writers transform raw data (discrete "facts") into meaningful information for a given context, audience, and organizational purpose, and they communicate it in a way that fosters the production of knowledge. This transformation is a rhetorical activity. Yet data reporting as a rhetorical action is rarely taught in technical and professional writing classes. Instead, if people at work formally learn about data reporting at all, it is in computer training courses, which teach users how to execute data retrieval and reporting functions. This training stresses technological over rhetorical skills and knowledge, mistakenly assuming that knowing how to operate a technology is commensurate with knowing how to use it to its full advantage to achieve a purposeful exchange of information.

Data reporting demands a dynamic interplay between a writer's rhetorical and technological skills. As such, it has a legitimate place in technical and professional writing classes. As part of the curriculum of technical and professional writing classes, data reporting will help students develop communication skills that are fast becoming indispensable for exchanging information in business settings. These skills involve, first, using information technologies as media of invention (in addition to actual drafting), with database applications being the source for gathering, filtering, and selecting information and arranging it into meaningful patterns for a given purpose and context. Second, these skills involve being able to present tabular data as the sole content of a communication, part of the emerging trend shaped by electronic writing to communicate networks of relationships rather than linear prose (Bolter, 1991).

In this essay, I explore the unique skills and knowledge that data-report writers need to learn in order to produce effective data reports. Analyzing the dynamic relationship between rhetorical and technological skills and strategies, I argue that if data reports are to serve readers' needs for recordkeeping and problem solving, then writers' technological skills must serve their rhetorical aims and strategies.

To analyze the interactive rhetorical and technological competencies involved in data-report writing, I first present a framework for understanding the communicative dimensions of data reporting. Then, I present results of a study in which I interviewed twenty-five nontechnical project administrators in a research laboratory, scientific and business specialists who regularly use financial data reports for their project accounting tasks. I link the qualities that these respondents look for in reports to the interactive rhetorical and technological skills and strategies that writers should employ to develop a report with such qualities. I conclude by proposing general approaches for teaching data reporting in professional and technical writing courses in order to prepare students for this increasingly common form of communication at work.

Data Reporting as Communication

In data reporting, computers enhance communication and knowledge. But too often data reporting is treated as objective fact giving. Historically, data tables have been associated with scientific rationality—impartial facts, free from the suspect subjectivity associated with rhetoric and communication. But this asocial view of tabular data ignores the inescapable rhetorical intentions and practical consequences of retrieving and reporting data. Many recent researchers, therefore, reject an objectivist view of such communications, arguing that facts are not simply transferred from senders to receivers. Rather, in written information, knowledge is constructed through relationships between readers and writers and the experiences each brings to the interaction (Winograd & Flores, 1986; Doheny-Farina, 1992; Norman, 1986; Cypher, 1986; Lave, 1988; Waern, 1988). This relationship-based view of constructing knowledge casts a new light on the writing of data reports.

Many composition specialists examine computer literacy and electronically produced information through this constructivist lens. Unfortunately, they generally omit databases and nonlinear tabular communications from the technologies they examine, technologies such as word processing, desktop publishing, electronic conferencing, and e-mail (Handa, 1990; Holdstein & Selfe, 1990; Hawisher & LeBlanc, 1992). Some research in rhetoric, visual design, and human factors, however, does focus on database-related communications. This research reveals that (1) key rhetorical strategies inform data searches, retrievals, and reporting; (2) rhetorical and technological skills mutually support and shape each other; and (3) designs for functionally effective tables must facilitate readers' strategies for answering business questions. I will discuss each of these issues in turn.

Key Rhetorical Strategies Inform the Searching for, Retrieval of, and Reporting of Electronic Data

Sullivan (1986) concludes that rhetorical invention is the defining feature of electronic data searches. In a study of bibliographic databases, she finds that searchers must have the following skills, all of which involve invention processes:

- knowing the meaning of the "invisible" data that are stored in the system (discovery);

- focusing on what is at issue in a communication situation (stasis); and

- determining the most effective topical orientation of a particular purpose (*topoi*).

Rhetorical invention also comes into play in reporting data. Boehm-Davis et al. (1989) find that the most important factor in designing effectual data reports—even more important than the format of a table—is for writers to select and present only the information integral to their communication situation. In regard to formatting, these researchers find that writers do not experiment with enough formats. Consequently, they rarely produce the best format for their exact purposes. Rhetoricians similarly advise writers to avoid predefined, static templates for data tables and instead dynamically fit their intentions to the rhetorical patterns that they choose (Comprone, 1993).

As an overview of four qualities necessary for effective data reports, Zmud (1978) identifies characteristics that are all implicitly rhetorical, as noted in the parentheses:

- quality of information (selecting appropriate and relevant data);

- accuracy and sufficiency of information (selecting the right scope and detail);

- quality of format (sequencing, ordering, and chunking information effectively); and

- quality of meaning (evoking emphasis, patterns, and relations through logic and layout).

Skills in Rhetoric and Database Technologies Support and Shape Each Other

A number of studies show an inextricable link between rhetorical and technological strategies in data searching and retrieval. Researchers find that unless people know (or in rhetorical terms, invent) (a) the meaning of electronic data, (b) the significance of data relationships, and (c) the right level of detail for a question, they will have difficulty understanding the basic program logic of search principles and data structures (Linde & Bergstrom, 1988; Chen & Dhar, 1990). Correspondingly, searchers' rhetorical strategies are incomplete without a concomitant technical knowledge, since electronic databases dictate the paths that people must follow in defining and searching for data (Sullivan, 1986).

Designs for Functionally Effective Tables Must Facilitate Readers' Strategies

Developing effective tabular displays of data should lead writers to research on visual rhetoric by Tufte (1990), Bertin (1983), Cleveland (1985), Wright (1984), Holmes (1984), Dragga and Gong (1989), Kostelnick (1989), and Barton and Barton (1993). Bertin especially emphasizes the need to design tables to answer actual questions that readers will ask. He identifies three distinct levels of questions and answers. In the "elementary" level, readers' questions are answered by finding a single element in a table; in the "intermediate" level, by relating two or more elements; and in the "overall" level, by seeing the overall trends suggested by the data reduced to and represented by a single element. Bertin argues that the goal for designers is to choose a tabular image that answers the majority of questions the information is capable of generating.

Tufte also stresses functionality in designing tables, arguing that simplicity as an aesthetic preference is not the best strategy for displaying information. Dense rather than simple tabular displays are often necessary to give readers a big- *and* small-picture view of information, making many choices and comparisons possible. According to Tufte, designers should realize that the effectiveness of a table does not depend on how much information it includes, but on how information is layered and ordered to facilitate readers' interpretations.

As this survey of current research suggests, developing effective data reports requires writers, on the one hand, to be adept at rhetorical strategies for invention, arrangement, and delivery, and, on the other hand, to understand the logic and capabilities that a program offers for defining, searching for, and retrieving data and for organizing it into printed reports. Recent research examines only separate aspects of data reporting, such as the rhetoric of tabular data displays, the rhetorical underpinnings of data searches, and technical skills related to retrieving and reporting information. I aim to unite these aspects into an integrated view of the competencies involved in composing tabular texts that communicate critical information for readers' work. This integrated view aims to capture what it means for writers to develop data tables that are situated, purposeful business communications and what preparation would help them in technical and professional writing classes.

Methodology

To study the rhetorical and technological skills involved in data reporting, I analyzed readers' reported responses to the actual data reports that they receive and use at work. From these responses, I inferred some of the knowledge and skills that writers should have to develop effective data reports.

Respondents

I interviewed twenty-five project administrators in a national research laboratory who regularly read and, at times, customize data reports to conduct their cost-accounting responsibilities. All participants are regular report readers who are competent in and receptive to computing. They belong to fifteen different divisions, with each division having projects with somewhat different accounting needs and structures. Twelve respondents are scientific specialists who actively conduct research in addition to managing projects. The other thirteen are full-time administrators whose area of expertise is business and accounting.

The Report and Its Uses in Context

I gathered information on readers' responses to a report that they receive each month. This report is generated from a mainframe financial system by Information System (IS) specialists. Respondents use this report, the Detailed Charge Report, for tracking costs, managing accounts, and assessing budget over- and underruns. This report itemizes all charges to each project account for the month and the year to date. The Detailed Charge Report, a complex table, presents nine types of charge information for each listed purchase or service (see Appendix A). As Appendix A shows, the report gives readers very few cues for interpreting different codes or distinguishing the meanings of such terms as "commitments" and "encumbrances."

Respondents are able to create and order customized versions of this report by using a PC look-alike program that interfaces with the mainframe financial system. This interface program gives laboratory users an opportunity to tailor their report to their needs by selecting only the data that they want and by organizing it to suit their interpretive strategies.

Interview Questions and Analysis of Responses

My semi-structured interviews usually lasted an hour. I asked respondents (1) to identify their purposes for reading the Detailed Charge Report; (2) to describe their strategies for accessing and analyzing the cost data in the report; (3) to evaluate the content and form of the report in relation to their needs and purposes; and (4) to discuss ways in which they derive the information that they want when the report fails to meet their needs. Five of the twenty-five respondents voluntarily walked me through their processes for accessing relevant data from the report, for turning it into a usable form, for interpreting it, and for making decisions.

To analyze responses, I examined participants' combined responses for patterns in their strategies and purposes for analyzing the report, for their satisfactions and dissatisfactions with the report, and for their methods of overcoming problems with it. To explain differences among responses, I looked at the structure of individuals' projects and project accounts and their expertise in accounting and computing.

My analyses show that respondents uniformly are dissatisfied with the Detailed Charge Report for six main reasons that I will discuss in the next section. Yet only a third of the respondents seek to overcome their dissatisfactions by using technological knowledge and skills to customize the report with the interface program. Finally, all of the respondents use the report for the same general purposes, but they access and analyze data differently on the basis of the specific structures and demands of their projects.

Results: Readers' Responses to Data Reports

Each month, respondents use the Detailed Charge Report to answer four central cost-accounting questions: (1) Are all the charges legitimate? (2) Where do high or unusual charges come from? (3) What are the differences between actual and budgeted costs? And (4) which accounts are likely to run over budget (and how should resources be allocated to avoid that overrun)?

As the report now stands, respondents have a hard time answering these questions. Without exception, they are dissatisfied with the report, with at least 20 percent of them criticizing it for the following reasons:

- *Information overload:* the report has too much data.

- *Overly narrow content:* it does not give a big enough picture of cumulative months.

- *Random data:* it does not group or emphasize data for easy interpretation.

- *Unprocessed data:* it does not calculate key relationships such as variances between actual and budgeted costs.

- *Unintelligible data:* it labels rows or columns with terms that have unclear meanings (such as "commitments").

- *Unpresentable data:* it has low legibility and layouts with little difference between figure and ground.

To overcome their dissatisfactions, three respondents rearrange the Detailed Charge Report by using the interface program. All of the administrators in my study are experienced with this program (using it to order routine and ad hoc reports), but only three of them understand how to take advantage of its capabilities. They know how to use its functions to select only certain accounts or categories of costs and to rearrange the row headings of the table so that the data are layered to suit their cost-accounting strategies.

Five other project administrators also customize the report but use their PC databases to do so instead of the interface program. Each month, these administrators rekey the data from the Detailed Charge Report into their private programs and generate reports tailored to the accounting demands of their projects. Recalling Tufte's insights about tables often needing to be dense but well layered, these PC-customized reports may have more information than the Detailed Charge Report, but they are more functional because information is arranged specifically for readers' cost-accounting logic (see Appendix B).

The six respondents who rearrange the Detailed Charge Report (either with their own PCs or with the interface program) have become report *writers* as well as readers. Unfortunately, the other respondents believe that they lack the necessary technical know-how to customize the report. These individuals have domain and task expertise and, concomitantly, a keen sense of their rhetorical needs for reported data. But they lack a complementary expertise in the technology, without which they cannot transform the information they receive into the information they desire.

Discussion: Strategies for Effective Data Reporting

As Comprone (1993) argues, if deliberate rhetorical intentions are not represented in reports, the reports will "cover a topic" without fulfilling their purpose of helping readers to answer their questions with a minimal amount of effort. The Detailed Charge Report, as a generic report produced by the IS department, manifests few rhetorical intentions. Yet it has rhetorical consequences—unfortunately, many negative ones. Readers are dissatisfied and resent being burdened with unnecessary extra work.

In this national laboratory, as is common in many organizations, the centralized mainframe system for reporting is in the process of being replaced by a decentralized computing environment, thereby passing responsibility for reporting from the IS specialists to individual employees in each department. Once respondents and others like them work in the new client/server environment, they will have an even greater need to manipulate the technology to retrieve data and design tabular reports for their rhetorical purposes. For many respondents, this technological medium is a stumbling block. According to their comments in interviews, what they lack is the knowledge to help them adapt various generic software functions (all of which they learned in inhouse training courses) to their individual cases of tailoring reports to their instrumental goals and analytic strategies. They need to know how to translate their rhetorical aims into a technologically produced document.

To develop effective data reports, writers must learn the database capabilities that enable them to achieve their rhetorical aims for invention, arrangement, and delivery. For each of these aims, Figure 1 summarizes associated rhetorical and technological strategies. In the following subsections, I discuss these aims and strategies in more detail, providing supporting examples from my study and from other common instances of data reporting.[1]

Aims	Rhetorical Strategies	Technological Strategies
Invention	Discover and select meaningful data with an appropriate scope and level of detail.	Understand program definitions of data, relations among data, and ways to write searches to get desired data.
Arrangement	Structure data into tables that support readers' interpretive strategies.	Use program formatting and calculating capabilities to provide tables with clear entry points, relevant data, and related data close to each other.
Delivery	Visually lay out and layer information so that printed reports give readers ready access, appropriate emphasis, and perceptible groupings.	Customize layouts and coordinate them with printer controls and configurations and, if necessary, with other software.

Figure 1. An overview of the aims and strategies of data reporting.

Aims of Invention	Rhetorical Strategies	Technological Strategies
Discover appropriate data.	Analyze readers' questions.	Understand the meaning and structure of data stored in a given program.
Select and retrieve appropriate data.	Define all the information that will answer readers' questions.	Create appropriate search statements. Know the logic of data structures and the data that can and can't be joined. Search repeatedly and incrementally and calculate data if necessary. Display search results and evaluate their accuracy and relevance.

Figure 2. Strategies for invention.

The Aims and Processes of Invention in Data Reporting

As with all composing, the success of data reporting depends on fundamental invention processes, namely writers becoming familiar with a subject, identifying issues and questions that concern readers, understanding the topical orientations that address these concerns, and selecting content accordingly. Figure 2 presents rhetorical and technological strategies related to invention.

In my study, respondents' dissatisfactions with the Detailed Charge Report can be traced to many invention issues. The report does not select and display key data relevant to readers' needs. For instance, it gives a fine-grained level of detail on exact monthly and year-to-date costs that are important for readers' recordkeeping and cost-tracking purposes. But it does not include higher-level figures on variances between budgeted and actual costs or on budget overruns, crucial for evaluating spending and deciding on future budgeting. Without these reported higher-level figures, readers have to compute them themselves.

Many respondents want other content as well, such as more verbal description about purchases and services and clearer distinctions between a charge classified as a commitment and one classified as an encumbrance. To avoid causing readers such problems, data-report writers should understand readers' actual questions, explore the full range of knowledge needed to answer them, and select data accordingly.

To implement these rhetorical choices, report writers need many technical competencies in database applications. Yet databases are one of the most complicated technologies for lay users to manipulate for their specific purposes (Date, 1992). One technological competence required for report writers is knowing the meaning and structure of the data stored in their system. For example, if for budgeting purposes writers want to develop a report on profits for the current year, they need to know which data in their program represent profits. Are profits stored as one precalculated figure, or must writers retrieve and relate many data, such as revenues, costs, overhead, and so on? Writers need to learn how the everyday terms and meanings they use for their business concerns correspond to the names, measures, and relationships among data in the system.

In the same vein, writers need to understand if the connections among data that make sense, practically, for solving a business problem are technically feasible. If, for instance, a company is losing money on a product because certain customers continue to buy it without paying for earlier purchases, then a sales representative needs to know who these customers are. What seems practically simple—a report listing all sales of an item, the sales for which payments are delinquent, and the names of delinquent customers—is actually technically complicated and, in some instances, technically infeasible. It is only feasible if the data are set up in a special way to allow writers to retrieve data from different databases. In conceptualizing and setting up databases, nontechnical report writers often need expert help.

Once databases are created, report writers have to know how to frame their searches for information in statements that a program will accept and process. Writing search statements involves abiding by the syntax of a program and, at times, becoming creative with its search logic. For example, creativity comes into play if a small-business owner wants a report on all of the customers with whom she did not do business that year. She cannot simply search for and retrieve this information from the program because it isn't stored in any one field. Rather, she has to "play" with the data she has to get the information she wants. For instance, she may search her order database, list all the customers who placed orders in the past year, and select from her customer database those people who are *not* on the order-placing list.

Finally, report writers' technological strategies include assessing whether the data they retrieve are in fact the right data for their purposes. As research on human factors reveals, database users rarely check the answers yielded by a search, "failing to search for other levels of data which could supplement or contradict that already found" (Katzeff, 1988; Waern, 1988, p. 181).

The Aims and Processes of Arrangement in Data Reporting

One of the greatest challenges for report writers is to choose an appropriate organizing logic for tables that are multifunctional.

As Bertin (1983) argues, designers must creatively organize tables to "answer any question, whatever its type and level . . . in a single instant of perception" (p. 99). Data-report writers have to experiment with single and combined organizing logics for tabular data displays and multiple drafts. They need to know, as in a case from my consulting experiences, that data reports for marketing purposes may take as many as five drafts of a table before a report convincingly shows a supervisor that, against common sense, it is best to target a very small group of low-volume customers because they generate the highest revenue. Relevant rhetorical and technological strategies for arrangement are presented in Figure 3.

Rhetorical purpose should determine whether the best display is a table or some other graphic form. In my interviews, respondents agree that tables are most appropriate for their accounting needs. But they criticize the arrangement of the tables in the Detailed Charge Report. The preset order of columns results in separating data that these readers want to compare. For example, monthly charges and fiscal year costs with everything figured in (commitments and encumbrances) are many columns apart. Yet this comparison is critical for managing costs. Just as important, row headings do not accommodate the "cut into the data" that some respondents want to take because of the unique structures of their projects. One administrator, for instance, is frustrated with the report for grouping data by accounts (listing each account and the charges it has accrued) instead of by items (listing each item and the various accounts that have ordered it).

Readers can redesign the row groupings to get this desired arrangement if they use the *sort* function of the interface program. But, as noted earlier, few respondents understand the uses of this technical capability. When developing reports in an electronic medium, writers' rhetorical intentions for arrangement are inseparable from their technical skills in implementing them. Database interactions for formatting are often conceptually complex, especially if writers want to experiment with a number of options before choosing the best one for ordering, sequencing, and grouping information. Regrouping data or viewing multiple options at once may require writers to use and combine commands in novel

Aims of Invention	Rhetorical Strategies	Technological Strategies
Structure data to accommodate readers' needs.	For reference purposes, order and layer data so that even dense displays have an apparent organizing logic.	Adapt formatting capabilities for multiple rows and columns of varying sizes.
	For problem-solving purposes, classify readers' questions by Bertin's level and order and reduce data to answer as many questions as possible.	Use calculating functions to define and display the data relevant to readers' needs (e.g., variances).
		Display format results to evaluate if they meet readers' needs.

Figure 3. Strategies for arrangement.

Aims	Rhetorical Strategies	Technological Strategies
Visually present tables with appropriate emphasis, access points, and interpretive cueing.	For reference purposes, create legible visual forms and perceptually highlight key groupings.	Understand and use program capabilities for page layouts, including writing small programs or macros for customized features.
	For problem solving, use white space, typography, headings, location, and positioning to draw attention to key relationships and to give easy access to elements.	Adapt printer controls to desired page designs.
		Display layout results to evaluate if, once printed, they meet readers' needs.

Figure 4. Strategies for delivery.

ways. Just as tricky are such customized formatting efforts as inserting verbal descriptions or altering some, but not all, parts of a table.

The Aims and Processes of Delivery in Data Reporting

Delivering information in effective visual designs involves giving readers easy access to the data and data relationships relevant to their concerns. Figure 4 summarizes rhetorical and technological strategies relevant for delivery.

Reports used for reference usually display large amounts of data in a small amount of tabular space. Legibility is paramount. Factors contributing to legibility include the size and width of columns, space between rows, and typography. These factors also help to reduce the homogeneity of a table and to heighten readers' perceptions of groupings.

Reports used for problem solving need designs that draw readers' attention to key information and that help them to distinguish important types and groupings of information. Table displays should create for readers paths through the table so that readers perceive particular groupings of data as individual "locales" that they may access at random and read as self-contained information. Type size, style, and variation are vital for emphasizing specific elements and relationships; positioning and locating data support people's conventional strategies for reading left to right and top to bottom. One of the most powerful ways for report writers to highlight differences among data and data relationships is to use vertical and horizontal white space and headings advantageously.

In the Detailed Charge Report, respondents report difficulty in finding the data elements that they need, partly because the report lacks sufficient typographic variation, white space, and perceptible headings. These delivery shortcomings also make it hard for readers to find their places in the table again if they look away for a moment. Better rhetorical strategies for graphic design would help. But, as with arrangement strategies, delivery choices require corresponding technical skills. Improvements in database, spreadsheet, and word-processing programs now make it easy for writers to move, resize, add, and delete rows and columns. Yet for some desired page designs, writers still need to write small programs or macros, for example, for numbering every other line (a function that seems simple but actually requires a program to go through many conditional steps). Writers also have to set printer controls appropriately and, in some cases, link data to more powerful layout systems, such as desktop publishing or high-powered word-processing programs. Using other programs is often the best way for writers to experimentally compose and view a variety of graphic presentations and select the best ones for their purposes.

Implications for Teaching and Further Research

In sum, for invention, arrangement, and delivery, writers of data reports must dynamically relate rhetorical and technological strategies to produce accessible and purposeful tables of information. The effectiveness of data reports, as judged by readers in an actual communication context, hinges on writers having chosen and implemented conceptual and visible displays that answer readers' concerns and questions.

Undergraduate students, as prospective report writers in future careers, would benefit greatly from a rhetorical orientation to data tables and reporting, an orientation that technical and professional writing courses are uniquely capable of providing. The design of a detailed curriculum for teaching data reporting in technical and professional writing courses is outside the scope of this study. Yet, as illustrated in Figures 1 through 4, this study does provide a foundation for defining issues that curriculum designers should address.

Curricula may focus on various workplace situations in which tabular data are typically communicated, having students analyze diverse audiences for these reports and the different levels of questions that readers are likely to pose to the data. This focus will extend students' rhetorical skills beyond linear prose paragraphs to graphic forms. Such forms will challenge students to write with a purpose in a design that offers readers multiple entry points and interpretative paths. Students also will experiment with various structures and layouts for tabular data displays and evaluate choices against communication purposes. These forms of communication are common practice in organizational life, yet they are rarely addressed in technical and professional writing classes.

Assignments may start somewhat simply, with students designing standard communications for hypothetical contexts that are limited in scope and purpose. Assignments should become progressively more rhetorically and technologically complex. To link rhetoric and technology, however, students need to learn concepts and operations of database applications relevant to their rhetorical aims and intentions. Teachers of technical and professional writing courses may be daunted by the prospect of simultaneously teaching the necessary rhetorical *and* technological skills and knowledge, especially if they have little database expertise. Since data reporting requires interdisciplinary competencies—competencies in rhetoric and in database systems—collaborative teaching between writing and computer science or information systems teachers would be advantageous.

As attested to by the respondents in my interviews, the technology may become a major obstacle for students attempting to develop data reports. By working together, writing and computing teachers may create pedagogically sound approaches for moving students through report-writing situations that require increasingly complex rhetorical and technological skills and strategies. Collaborations may range from actual team teaching to situations in which writing teachers prepare data-reporting cases and computing teachers design data sets and easy-to-use formatting and printing functions that may facilitate students' computing interactions for these cases.

To better understand the rhetorical and technological competencies involved in data reporting, researchers need to investigate the ways in which various features and functions of database applications enhance or constrain rhetorical choices, including the effects of advances in program capabilities and interfaces on reporting. In addition, more studies should focus on report writers and actual readers in natural work settings, closely assessing the qualities that characterize effectiveness for different types of data reports and the processes involved in producing them. As mentioned earlier, studies of actual readers and writers need to extend long enough for researchers to iteratively test writers' choices and revisions against readers' actual uses of a document. Finally, composition specialists need to extend their research beyond computer-based writing and computer-mediated communication. They need to include the effects of electronic data retrieval and nonlinear reporting on the production of knowledge in actual workplace situations. Findings from such studies will enrich the ways in which teachers prepare students to succeed in communicating in computerized workplaces.

Note

1. Because this analysis of invention, arrangement, and delivery is based on insights from my study, it relates to complex data tables for recordkeeping and problem-solving purposes in real work settings.

References

Barton, B.F., & Barton, M.S. (1993). Ideology and the map: Toward a postmodern visual design practice. In N.R. Blyler & C. Thralls (Eds.), *Professional communication: The social perspective* (pp. 49–78). Newbury Park, CA: Sage.

Bertin, J. (1983). *The semiology of graphics*. Madison: University of Wisconsin Press.

Boehm-Davis, D., Holt, R., Koll, M., Yastrop, G., & Peters, R. (1989). Effects of different database formats in information retrieval. *Human Factors, 31,* 570–592.

Bolter, J.D. (1991). *Writing space: The computer, hypertext, and the history of writing*. Hillsdale, NJ: Erlbaum.

Chen, H., & Dhar, V. (1990). User misconceptions of information retrieval systems. *International Journal of Man-Machine Studies, 32,* 673–692.

Cleveland, W.S. (1985). *The elements of graphing data*. Monterey, CA: Wadsworth.

Comprone, J. (1993). Generic constraints and expressive motives: Rhetorical perspectives on textual dialogues. In N.R. Blyler & C. Thralls (Eds.), *Professional communication: The social perspective* (pp. 92–108). Newbury Park, CA: Sage.

Cypher, A. (1986). The structure of users' activities. In D. Norman & S. Draper (Eds.), *User-centered systems design* (pp. 243–263). Hillsdale, NJ: Erlbaum.

Date, C.J. (1992). *Related database writings, 1989–1991*. Reading, MA: Addison-Wesley.

Delphi Consulting Group. (1989–1993). *Information management: The next generation*. 10th ed. Washington, D.C.: Delphi Consulting Group.

Doheny-Farina, S. (1992). *Rhetoric, innovation, technology*. Cambridge, MA: MIT Press.

Dragga, S., & Gong, G. (1989). *Editing: The design of rhetoric*. Amityville, NY: Baywood.

Handa, C. (Ed.). (1990). *Computers and community: Teaching composition in the twenty-first century.* Portsmouth, NH: Boynton/Cook-Heinemann.

Hawisher, G.E., & LeBlanc, P. (Eds.). (1992). *Re-imagining computers and composition: Teaching and research in the Virtual Age.* Portsmouth, NH: Boynton/Cook-Heinemann.

Holdstein, D., & Selfe, C.L. (Eds.). (1990). *Computers and writing: Theory, research, and practice.* New York: Modern Language Association of America.

Holmes, N. (1984). *Designer's guide to creating charts and diagrams.* New York: Watson-Guptell.

Katzeff, C. (1988). The effect of different conceptual models upon reasoning in a database query writing task. *International Journal of Man-Machine Studies, 29,* 37–62.

Kostelnick, C. (1989). Visual rhetoric: A reader-oriented approach to graphics and design. *Technical Writing Teacher, 16,* 7–88.

Lave, J. (1988). *Cognition in practice.* New York: Cambridge University Press.

Linde, L., & Bergstrom, M. (1988). Impact of prior knowledge of informational content and organization on learning search principles in a database. *Contemporary Educational Psychology,* 90–101.

Linde, L., & Waern, Y. (1985). On searching an incomplete database. *International Journal of Man-Machine Studies, 22,* 563–579.

Norman, D. (1986). Cognitive engineering. In D. Norman & S. Draper (Eds.), *User-centered system design* (pp. 31–61). Hillsdale, NJ: Erlbaum.

Sullivan, P. (1986). Rhetoric and the search for externally stored knowledge. Unpublished doctoral dissertation, Carnegie Mellon University, Pittsburgh, PA.

Tufte, E. (1990). *Envisioning information.* Cheshire, CT: Graphics Press.

Waern, Y. (1988). *Cognitive aspects of computer-supported tasks.* New York: Wiley.

Winograd, T., & Flores, F. (1986). *Understanding computers and cognition: A new foundation for design.* Norwood, NJ: Ablex.

Wright, P. (1984). A user-oriented approach to the design of tables and flowcharts. In D. Jonassen (Ed.), *The technology of text* (pp. 317–340). Volume 1. Englewood Cliffs, NJ: Educational Technology.

Zmud, R.W. (1978). Concepts, theories, and techniques: An empirical investigation of the dimensionality of the concept of information. *Decision Sciences, 9,* 187–195.

Appendix A: Sample page of detailed charge report

Element	Reference #	Identification	Status	Cost this month	Cost this FY	Commitment	Emcumbrance	FY costs + Com. & Encu.
Axx Graphics								
	xxx xxxx xxxx	projectionist		395.00	395.00			395.00
	xxx xxxx xxxx	binding		235.15	235.15			235.15
Ayy Shop Work								
	xxx xxxx xxxx	electrical	3	156.00	335.00			335.00
	xxx xxxx xxxx	install	3	167.35	167.35			167.35

Appendix B: Sample report customized with a PC database

Acct	Oct.	Nov.	Dec.	Jan.	Feb.	Mar.	Apr.	May	June	July	Aug.	Sept.	FY total	Budget	Variance
name															
name															
PD absence															
Total															
name															
name															
Effort															
Total															
travel															
shop															
purchases															
M&S															
Total															
cmptg															
waste															
mgmt.															
GLS															
Totals															
TOT.															
BDGT.															
VAR.															

Starting Point for Analysis

Chapter 6

After Automation: Hypertext and Corporate Structures

Johndan Johnson-Eilola
Purdue University

Stuart A. Selber
Clarkson University

Early claims for hypertext reveal some of the medium's social and intellectual revolutionary potential, but specific hypertexts often merely support and deepen status quo, relatively hierarchical social and textual relationships. Because these texts are seen as ways of automating existing patterns of work and control, they often act only to contract *vital processes of communication. By thinking of hypertext as having the potential to* expand *communication processes, we might encourage a broad-based, positive shift involving not only new emphasis on the roles of the reader and writer, but reconsideration of the social situation and technology itself.*

If a skilled typist could consistently turn out sixty words per minute, why waste her time on filing or answering the telephone? A skilled typist was likely to be kept in her job for as long as her employer could keep her there. . . .

It should be emphasized that there was nothing inherent to the typewriter which compelled such an organization of clerical work. The typewriter, in fact, can be quite useful for people who operate it sporadically. . . . The organization of work is largely determined by the efforts of businessmen and scientific office managers to organize their clerical labor as profitably as possible, and not to make the "inefficient" error of having a typist do work that a lower-paid file clerk could just as easily do.

—Margerie W. Davies (1988, p. 34)

In this chapter, we offer a general framework for complicating the relations between various types of hypertext, corporate structures, and technical communication. We argue that commercial hypertexts, as they are currently constructed by technical writers, frequently tend toward automating and conserving traditional, hierarchical corporate structures and contracting the scope and importance of communication.[1] Although such forms of automation often constitute valuable improvements over old ways of work, an overreliance on the automation of communication activities often disempowers both users and technical communicators. The majority of our discussion centers on readers, rather than writers, of hypertexts in technical communication settings. We are convinced that the low value placed on the act of *reading* and *using* technical documents in the "automating" view of hypertext bears much of the burden for the parallel low status of the writers of such automatic texts. (Similarly, see Dautermann's claim in this volume that users who underutilize computers "may devalue writing in general.")

We begin with a brief sketch of the current state of hypertext in business and industry. Comparing historical conceptions of hypertext to the medium's most popular current uses, we argue that some important and powerful aspects of hypertext have been left largely undeveloped or restricted to specialized sites and users. A large degree of this uneven development is due not to the isolated technology itself, but rather, to emphases on efficiency and short- over long-term profit and productivity in some versions of corporate and industrial cultures (see Wieringa et al., this volume). Such dynamics are not in themselves repressive or disempowering, but often become so dominant that they override other concerns and spaces of action. In the final sections of this essay, we critique and attempt to extend distinctions Zuboff articulated between "automating" and "informating" technologies, highlighting important social relationships and tendencies that influence the shape of communication and communication processes. We offer a potentially profitable rethinking—and necessary complication—of the relations among work environment, technology, writer, and reader, as those concepts are embodied in hypertexts being produced and used in corporate settings.

Waiting for the Revolution:
A History and Survey of Hypertext

New technologies are commonly integrated into cultures in conservative ways, strengthening rather than defying existing relations of social and political force (Sproull & Kiesler, 1991; Marvin, 1988; Kanter, 1989). But the contemporary state of hypertext contrasts sharply with the revolutionary potential prophesied by some of its originators. Although hypertext has gained popularity in the last ten years, its history goes back to at least the 1940s. In the pages of both the *Atlantic Monthly* and *Life* in 1945, Vannevar Bush wrote enthusiastically about his design for the proto-hypertext "memex," a machine the size and shape of an office desk.[2] To Bush, the memex represented a powerful tool for drastically improving human communication and, therefore, society in general: "Presumably man's [sic] spirit should be elevated if he can better review his shady past and analyze more completely and objectively his present problems" (p. 1/54).

Like Bush, later hypertext pioneers such as Ted Nelson and Douglas Englebart sensed the failure of traditional print media to accommodate the ever-increasing and ever-diverging tide of interrelated information, as well as the restrictions print media placed on research and scholarship. Although Ted Nelson's Xanadu remains more of a conceptual than actual product, the influence of Nelson's vision of hypertext remains strong: a worldwide "docuverse" holding the interconnected web of all the world's literature—a category in which Nelson includes not only traditional works of high culture but also popular literature, scientific work, and informal communication; the system is designed to encompass any type of text (Nelson, 1982). In many ways, the growing Word Wide Web begins to approximate some of the functions and features of such a docuverse. Nelson (1990) envisions a simple royalty system for writers and publishers (p. 2/33); because readers have the same authoring privileges as writers, "publishers" can mean any users of the system interested in placing their own text in the network (p. 2/42–43). And Englebart, speaking of the NLS/Augment system he designed in the 1960s, characterized his version of hypertext as "the biggest revolution you had ever seen for humanity, in the sense of people being able to connect their brain machinery to the world's problems. And it was going to go on for many, many decades" (cited in Englebart & Hooper, 1988, p. 27).

What is most notable about these original visions of hypertext are the ways in which the medium pointed toward a revolution in not only ways of writing and reading, but also—and more important—profound *social* shifts. Although there are certainly numerous theorists and designers today who remain committed to exploring the use of hypertext in revolutionary ways, such uses are largely relegated to computer-oriented research and development facilities (e.g., NoteCards at Xerox PARC; gIBIS and rIBIS at MCC) or in some educational sites (e.g., the use of Storyspace, Intermedia, and some Hypercard stacks). In general, hypertext has been designed—and perceived—as a tool for increasing the simple, technical efficiency of existing print-based tasks rather than as a forum for transforming tasks in a broader, social sense—not only making a task easier or faster, but reconstructing communication and work environments as well.

One obvious presupposition of such a conservative approach is that hypertext versions of paper-based documents should be little more than faster, electronic versions of original source text. Thus, these systems tend to encourage, in terms of design, hierarchical indexing of topics mapped politically and cognitively to book technologies. In terms of use, for example, these systems encourage browsing of indexes and existing connections between author-generated links (see, for example, online help in Microsoft Word or PageMaker), as opposed to less traditional, but perhaps more valuable, user-generated associative trails. Certainly, such traditional use of hypertext provides a valuable addition to the growing repertoire of technological aids that modern workers draw upon: more efficient retrieval of information represents an important investment for business and industry, especially as workers and users contend with increasingly large amounts of available information. But the capability of hypertext to virtually emulate other literacy technologies and dominant cultural forms can mold specific instances of this technology into well-worn channels of hierarchical control.

Shoshana Zuboff's critique of computerization in industry offers one important perspective in examining the reasons for technical communication's concentration on making efficient, rather than transforming, traditional work practices. Zuboff (1988) defines two main methods of computerization in corporate sites: automating and informating. Automating technologies act to speed up the pace of work by translating repetitive, predictable human activities (such as turning pages or locating cross-referenced material) into machine instructions. According to Ritchie (1991), such computerization strategies may tend to reinforce the traditional "logic of bureaucracy." Informating technologies, in contrast, produce new information based on automated tasks. For example, a hypertext-based procedures manual for equipment maintenance might *automate* a maintenance person's navigation of an online text. Henderson (this volume) provides the useful distinction between improving on *processes* and on *by-products:* the types of automation frequently found in hypertext improve on the by-products but do not encourage users to rethink the fundamental processes in question. In this case, the user's task has not changed in a substantial way. Informating texts provide users with new possibilities, but they do not (at least in theory) require specific uses of the new information they provide. Informating texts oscillate between cycles of automation and user control. So, in the hypothetical maintenance manual, the text could not only automate communication processes but also *informate* by offering the user additional information—suggesting alternate procedures for maintenance, allowing users to communicate with other users in similar situations, providing historical tracking of the performance of the equipment in question compared with similar technologies or contexts, etc.

A more specific example of an informating technology comes from the aerospace industry, which is currently converting many of the paper-based technical manuals associated with its attack helicopters into electronic technical manuals (ETMs). Although strictly automated paper manuals are, arguably, less useful during military operations than paper-based manuals—they represent additional electronic equipment that is not easily deployed or maintained in combat environments (Schnell, 1992)—informating versions of such manuals might prove useful. The new Comanche attack helicopters (the RAH-66) will contain ETMs that provide various access paths for maintenance or operational tasks. For example, "if a soldier's request is in the form of a trouble code from the onboard diagnostics, the actual corrective measures will appear on the screen along with the related logistics procedures to update the aircraft logbook and requisition parts" (Schnell, 1992, p. 25). As this example illustrates, such an ETM could be considered informating in that it highlights, for users, related information and suggested tasks. Notably, the system merely poses secondary activities instead of completely automating the process and removing control away from the user.[3]

Despite the seeming usefulness of informating hypertexts, current workplace structures tend to mitigate against the dispersal of control encouraged by such technologies (Schrage, 1990). As Zuboff (1988) notes, informating technologies seem to threaten traditional hierarchical organizations because they encourage decision-making capabilities and skills to move outward from centralized control; in other words, they foster networked, rather than hierarchical, relationships (see also Kanter, 1989; Drucker, 1988; Reich, 1991; Hansen, this volume). Although scholars and researchers have provided numerous examples of and arguments for informating-class hypertexts (VanLehn, 1985; Johnson-Lenz & Johnson-Lenz, 1992; Selfe et al., 1992; Johnson-Eilola, 1992; Selber et al., 1996), such systems are largely relegated to corporate research and development sites and educational institutions. Even World Wide Web browsers often act only to automate activities such as looking up entries in a library card catalog. For the most part, developers and users seem comfortable automating traditional tasks in order to realize immediate and easily distinguishable increases in simple, technical efficiency. Such tendencies—which are understandable but should not be unquestioningly accepted—have channeled the development of hypertext along relatively limiting and limited paths. To more fully understand the reasons behind this uneven development, we can examine the parallels between hypertext and other technologies that were shaped by (and exerted shaping forces upon) the social environments from which they emerged.

Critiquing Categories: Problems with Automate versus Informate

Some of the difficulty in classifying hypertexts as either auto-mating or informating stems from the fact that our distinctions between these two types appear, at this stage, to be a feature of the technology disconnected from social use. Such a flaw hints at a vague sort of technological determinism: the technology seems to determine its own use regardless of how a person uses the tech-nology. To a degree, this is true: a hammer embodies certain pos-sibilities, significantly different possibilities than does a screw-driver. For each technology there exists a range of possible uses. These possibilities are not completely determined by the technol-ogy but are mutually constructed in the nexus of both the tech-nology and the social situation (which are, themselves, complex and often contradictory constructions). A simple technology such as a mirror encourages one type of use in dressing rooms and quite another in high-energy optics. But in neither situation is the user able to freely substitute any other technology. The computer offers a particularly ambivalent technology, a "virtual" machine that can be easily molded to emulate a wide variety of mecha-nisms (Feenberg, 1991; Bolter, 1991). Zuboff (1988), in discussing the ways in which computers can either empower workers or alienate them, depending on how the specific types of uses are constructed in differing environments, notes that

> In many cases, organizational functions, events, and pro-cesses have been so extensively informated—converted into and displayed as information—that the technology can be said to have "textualized" the organizational environment. In this context, the electronic text becomes a new medium in which events are both observed and enacted. As an automat-ing technology, computerization can intensify the clerk's ex-ile from the coordinative sphere of the managerial process. As an informating technology, on the other hand, it can pro-vide the occasion for a reinvigoration of the knowledge de-mands associated with the middle-management function. (p. 126)

The case appears more complex for technologies such as hypertext. The purely automating features of hypertexts are apparently the simple substitution of one technology (the computer) for another (the book). But, as we have already illustrated, some uses and designs of computer technology begin to include an informating component differently from that of most books. The nature and shape of this transformation—technological and social—is not frequently reflected upon in the use of hypertext as an automating device. As Zuboff (1988) warns, "It is quite possible to proceed with automation without reference to how it will contribute to the technology's informating potential" (p. 11). Likewise, Carolyn Marvin (1988), in her historical analysis of electronic communication, argues that "[e]arly uses of technological innovations are essentially conservative because their capacity to create social disequilibrium is intuitively recognized amidst declarations of progress and enthusiasm for the new" (p. 235). Frequently, especially in hypertext, both automating and informating aspects coexist. However, because the informating aspects are often not reflected upon or articulated, their shape and function can become absorbed by the current social situation. That is, the automating features are touted and discussed, while the informating features are ignored or dismissed. The inertia of automation restricts the informating capacities to an invisible development along lines of preexisting forces. In addition, even in cases where hypertext informates work processes, the use of that new information may be restricted (used, for example, by management to track worker productivity and learning).

The importance of context becomes apparent when we attempt to classify technologies such as style-analysis or grammar-checking programs commonly included with word processors. For some users and contexts, these programs informate by analyzing text and offering numerous possibilities that users can act on as they wish. Other users in different contexts, however, may not possess the required skills, confidence, or motivation to do anything but accept the program's advice as correct. As many writing teachers have found, users who are not already knowledgeable about mechanical, stylistic, and rhetorical issues in a variety of discourses may use such programs in automating ways. In the same technology there exists the possibility for both informating and automating uses. Similarly, the procedures software tool (PST) described by Wieringa et al. (this volume), for example, would both automate and informate the process of writing procedures.

The possibility for both types of use with this technology does not mean that the technology is itself neutral, only that there are multiple forces involved in the construction of specific uses.

From the standpoint of management, a primary difficulty that stems from informating aspects of a technology is the degree to which that technology might require or even encourage skilled decisions on the part of workers. An automating technology commonly represents an attempt to remove not only "drudge work" but also the skill located in any one worker. For example, consider Harley Shaiken's (1986) discussion about the introduction of numerical-control technology in machine shops and an automatic turret punch press designed to stamp sheet metal parts based on computer-tape instructions. The manufacturer of the punch press offered free training courses to shop staff. Despite the interest in these courses expressed by the machine crew, shop management allowed only "an engineer, a foreman, [and] an electrical shop supervisor" to attend the free classes (p. 115). "As one worker commented later, 'The work program is of great concern because it is being used as a basis for justifying a removal of work . . . away from the sheet metal shop and into the hands of draftsmen and engineers'" (p. 115). Even when the work crew surreptitiously trained themselves in programming the machine—a capability resulting in higher-quality work—management, sensing the encroachment of worker control into the technology, installed an override switch on the machine that prevented the workers from entering or modifying machine instructions (p. 116).

On the surface, cases of automating hypertext seem very much different from the numerical-control machines discussed above; hypertext does not appear to de-skill workers in any substantial way.[4] What has been automated are tasks such as turning pages, retrieving manuals from bookshelves or distant sites, and discussions with colleagues sometimes necessary in troubleshooting or learning new procedures. In this view, hypertext has improved the efficiency of day-to-day tasks in ways that most workers would applaud. What has happened with common introductions of hypertext, however, is a general limitation of the informating aspects that are also possible with this technology. In general, hypertext has been framed in strictly automating terms, without reminders that the technology might also be articulated in ways that can support technical communication of a different kind, working to expand rather than contract processes of communication.

Rearticulating Influences: Contractions and Expansions of Communication

At this point, it might be useful to rethink Zuboff's terminology in a way that allows us to get at not merely the functional characteristics of an isolated technology, but also at the social and political contexts in which technologies are developed, used, maintained, and reconstituted. Instead of categorizing hypertexts as either one type or another on the basis of only concrete technological determinants, we need to broaden our scope and take apart the technology as it is used in order to look at the relations among the various elements. Although the automating/informating distinction offers a useful starting point, what becomes primary (from our perspective) is not the specific characteristics of any one technology but how those characteristics are taken up, channeled, defined, and defied by people. Because most hypertext applications possess at least some degree of informating capacity, our point is not that a certain type of hypertext generates information while another merely automates processes. For those technologies that informate, what is done with that information becomes central. In other words, *does a specific hypertext primarily contract or expand communication processes?* Framed this way, we can rethink how this technology is used in social situations, noting the influences that traditional corporate structures can exert over such uses. First, however, it may be useful to more fully define our terms.

The distinction we want to make is based on two opposing views of writing and reading (activities that, in hypertext, sometimes begin to resemble one another). Technical communication theorists frequently construct similar categories (Dobrin, 1989; Katz, 1992; Slack, Miller, & Doak, 1993). In the first view, something we will call *contraction*, technical communication is a process of information transfer from sender to receiver based on the classic Shannon and Weaver model of communication (1949). Communication in a contractive technology shrinks in conceptual/visual size so that the link between sender and receiver is constructed as a frictionless, noise-free, and if possible, completely invisible wire. In this model, communication technologies are designed to increase accuracy of information reception and the raw speed at which information moves—in discrete, ideally unambiguous chunks—from writer to (relatively passive) reader.

At the opposite end of the spectrum lies the *expansion* view, in which writing and reading are themselves modes of thinking, less information transfer than a continual process of constructing and deconstructing multiple, often contradictory meanings. Communication in this view is a social and political process rather than a mechanistic transfer of information packets.

The contraction/expansion view represents a broad range of social and technological possibilities rather than easy pegs on which to place specific hypertexts. An important difference between Zuboff's automate/informate and our own contract/expand is the idea that the production of information is *continual* in most work contexts (even if not apparently emanating from a specific piece of computer technology). We are attempting to widen the sphere of concern to include not only the discrete technology (e.g., a specific database) but also the social construction of that information—a construction that, in part, determines how information can be used by specific workers. Thus, "information" is not only object delivered to an end-user, but also recursive process taking in user, designer, technology, and context. In a different but related context (that of groupware), Johnson-Lenz and Johnson-Lenz (1992) have observed the polarization that often develops between "mechanistic" and "open" systems of computer-based communication. As they warn, "[I]t is tempting to grasp for easy answers—either tighter mechanisms of social control or its polar opposite—refusal to make responsible choices. . . . [T]he way forward reveals itself as a dynamic balance . . ." (p. 291).

At the most contracted extreme, a text cuts off discussion and reflective thinking—the text offers, perhaps instantly, one, and only one, "correct" chunk of information. At the most expanded extreme, the text offers no unqualified answers and a huge number of navigational choices (but few hard and fast rules for users to distinguish which choice to make); an expansion medium encourages users to play out and construct possibilities. The distinction here lies, however, not merely in the quantity of data produced, but primarily in the *social* options opened for the circulation and reconstruction of that data by user-workers. We cannot equate the number of explicitly available paths through a text space with the degree of "freedom" people have in using the text. The actual experience of reading the hypertext may still be relatively contracted if a user's current social situation requires or even strongly suggests a specific path. Consider, for example, someone using a phone book to look up a single, predefined name and corresponding number: the phone book itself, as a concrete technology, offers thousands or even tens of thousands of differing paths, but the current user's context contracts those numerous possibilities to a single one. (This is not to say that phone books are oppressive, only that if someone claimed they represented a general technological breakthrough with profound social and political implications, we should be skeptical.) It is important to note that this contraction happens *prior* to reading experiences rather than during the moment-by-moment process of navigation that must occur in a temporal stream of reading and thinking. Thus, the distinction between contraction and expansion lies in the dynamic convergence of both social and technological forces.

Currently, the more open type of text is most frequently found in experimental fiction such as Michael Joyce's *Afternoon* or Carolyn Guyer and Martha Petry's *Izme Pass,* texts that continually challenge readers to navigate and reconcile the postmodern territories of collapsing subjectivity, indeterminacy, and complicity (see, e.g., Moulthrop, 1989; Landow, 1992; Douglas, 1991; Johnson-Eilola, 1994). We also see examples in hypertext-based collaborative writing environments designed to support both developmental and design work (Selber et al., 1996) and in some areas of the World Wide Web (although, at least currently, the Web encourages browsing rather than authoring for users in most contexts). Although few nonfictional texts reach the extreme of experimental fiction, one might consider Jay David Bolter's *Writing Space* hypertext an example that tends toward expansion. Bolter's text, based on an accompanying print text, integrates both a hierarchical structure and abundant extra-hierarchical material. On the one hand, readers are encouraged to expand on the reading patterns suggested by print texts, moving in and out of the structure in order to gain a fuller (but never completely unified) perspective on the implications of Bolter's arguments. On the other hand, the text contains some elements that encourage an automated use—the hierarchy, for example, connotes hypertext as an automation of the book. More important, although many theorists claim that hypertext readers should always be able to also become writers, Bolter's text is relatively closed, presenting a situation that may signify to readers that the information is traveling in one direction, from Bolter to reader (Johnson-Eilola, 1992; Amato, 1991; Tuman, 1992). *Writing Space* offers a mixture of contracting and expanding capacities that emerge differently, depending on specific actions of users. The importance of such oscillations suggests that automation can and should be a crucial—but not sole—element of communication.

As we have highlighted throughout, contracting/automating texts are the most popular applications of hypertext in technical communication. A naive explanation would claim that expanding texts are inefficient and offer little value to corporate users. But in conceptually and functionally contracting the processes of writing and reading—decreasing time spent in these activities as well as diminishing a sense of personal responsibility for the construction of meaning in both activities—corporate users face difficulties immediately evident on the surface. As we have already mentioned, the contraction of writing and reading purchases much of its foundation from the outdated "conduit" theory of communication: that information passes, in packets, from sender to receiver. In this view, more efficient media—implicitly, "better" media—are those that transfer the information packets with as little "noise" and as much speed as possible. Although this theory has been replaced by a host of more complex communication theories, the commonsense view of the conduit model continues to exert great influence over day-to-day operations in technical communication environments: the popularity of hypertext that emulates the book (and also attempts to construct virtual books as a transparent medium) testifies to its continuing survival.

From the perspective of readers, the drawbacks to the conduit model seem significant. For example, little responsibility is given to the reader's role in constructing meaning. Because the information in this view is actually constructed by the author, only "carried" by the medium and "received" (passively) by the reader, only the author can bear responsibility for the effectiveness of a message—a situation highlighted in the term often used for this model, "the magic bullet theory." The writer constructs a bullet and shoots it at the reader; if the bullet misses its mark, it is because the writer constructed an ineffective bullet, chose a poor weapon, or aimed sloppily or at the wrong target. The violent nature of this model aside, readers are implicitly discouraged from assuming any real responsibility or credit for their readings in a contracting medium. This perspective is supported by the current Society for Technical Communication's Code for Communicators, where writers are mandated to make meaning of texts for readers.

In contrast to this view is perhaps the most unique potential of hypertext as it was defined by early thinkers: it increases the power of users because they actively make navigational decisions in the act of reading. This tension is resolved, however, in automatic uses of hypertext when readers internalize another system of control, that of their work. Although information is being produced, the social context of the information production constructs a very contracted range of possibilities. In an expanding medium, however, readers might be encouraged to consider such matters as the possibility of multiple (even conflicting) interpretations or views in the text, the accuracy of the information, or the ideological agendas of the technology, the author, or the task.

In addition, the contraction inherent in the information transfer model is distributed unequally across job classes. As Harry Braverman (1974) argues,

> The recording of everything in mechanical form, and the movement of everything in a mechanical way, is . . . the ideal of the office manager. But this conversion of the office flow into a high-speed industrial process requires the conversion of the great mass of office workers into more or less helpless attendants of that process. . . . The number of people who can operate the system, instead of being operated by it, declines precipitously. In this sense, the modern office becomes a machine which at best functions only within its routine limits, and functions badly when it is called upon to meet special requirements. (p. 348)

Historically, automation has displaced work at the lowest levels of responsibility and social class: the forms-processing tasks normally completed by office clerks (Zuboff, 1988, pp. 133–159; Machung, 1988); the sewing and mending performed by women (Kramarae, 1988); the hands-on skills of the pulp-mill operator (Zuboff, 1988; Hirschhorn, 1984); and the traditionally female task of housework (Leto, 1988). Frequently, when workers are not completely displaced from their work in such situations, they find that they are now both isolated from co-workers and also expected to substantially increase their output (normally without corresponding increases in pay). The association of automating or contracting tasks with decreased responsibility and increased stress is not guaranteed, but often constructed by hierarchical, efficiency-driven structures of many workplaces. Thus, hypertext takes its place in this history of technological efficiency as a way of streamlining the processes of reading and writing, contracting the activities to the point of disappearance or, at best, low significance.

Our critique to this point may appear overly pessimistic: currently, hypertext does not seem to portend the massive automation and de-skilling that accompanied technologies such as the automotive assembly line. But as hypertext becomes more popularly conceived of as a technology that transfers information and contracts communication, it becomes less likely that hypertext will be developed along expansive lines, especially for those classes of workers (such as the claims clerks discussed by Zuboff or many writers in corporations) whose tasks often fall under the totalizing goal of easy efficiency.[5]

Reasserting Responsibility: Opportunities for Technical Communicators

Despite frequent claims for hypertext in general, the popular online documentation form of this technology (often the epitome of the contracting class) does not necessarily move control from author to reader, but may in fact begin moving control away from both parties and into the machine/technology itself. In this way, hypertext follows in the footsteps of other de-skilling technologies that were used by managers to translate operator knowledge into computers in order to exercise more complete control over information processes and products (Shaiken, 1986; Zuboff, 1988; Hirschhorn, 1984). Paradoxically, then, from the perspective of technical communicators, the activity of writing is not the construction of meaning but often the attempt to render their own positions transparent—functional texts should ideally transmit meaning directly from technology to user. Even more complex views of communication, such as the translation theory of communication, in which writers translate technical material into lay terms, tend to ignore the fundamentally political nature of the balance of power inherent in the relations among writer, reader, technology, and work environment (Slack, Miller, & Doak, 1993).

In recognition of this diminution of importance, we call on technical communicators to begin reconceiving the broadly political influence exerted through their role in the process of communication. Although assuming such a responsibility is never simple or expedient—and often, given the traditionally low status of technical writers in industry relative to scientists and engineers, such an assumption is potentially dangerous—technical communicators must begin to slowly, but purposefully, recognize both contracting and expanding forms of hypertext. Technical communicators might, for instance, begin offering end-users the capability to not only "receive" information from the hypertext, but also to become full-fledged authors capable of adding their own links and nodes to texts. (Tentative forms of these capabilities can be found in the bookmarking facilities of recent online help documents and in World Wide Web browsers such as Netscape and Mosaic.) Such a facility would not only increase the importance

of both writers' and readers' interactions with the text, but, perhaps more important, can be connected to management's concerns for efficiency and flexibility. Users can customize systems
so that they are more effective (in the broad sense of the term) in
their specific situations.

Other approaches to thinking about text and meaning provide
technical communicators with possibilities for increasing their
own responsibilities in the communication process. Articulation
theory, a movement generally attributed to the cultural criticism
of Stuart Hall (1985), represents an attempt to explain and act upon
the complex political/power relationships between language and
culture. In this perspective, meaning is constructed in varying
ways, depending on both object and social situation; differing
environments engender different articulations. The concept of
articulation offers technical communicators a powerful method
for reconstituting the shape and relevance of communication in
corporate and industrial sites, giving new importance and responsibilities to the roles and activities involved in writing and reading (Slack, Miller, & Doak, 1993). As a brief example, consider the
case of a technical writer who might define her position of "writer"
as "the creator of documents that make technology easier for novices to use." In this articulation, the term *writer* is connected or
articulated to a number of culturally powerful concepts that affect and partially construct the meaning of the term: "writer" can
be easily seen as articulated to terms such as "transparency," "in-
formation/knowledge transfer," "efficiency," and "clarity."

Dominant articulations such as these frequently organize or
reinforce social relations as hierarchical structures; those at the
top of these structures are frequently able, through various coer-
cive and ideological means, to enforce articulations that more
deeply entrench unequal power relations. As such, participants
continually struggle over the dominant and subordinate articulations (Hall, 1985; Grossberg, 1986; Grossberg & Slack, 1985;
Hebdige, 1988). As our foregoing discussion has shown, the automating or contracting orientation of many functional hypertexts
tends to articulate both "reader" and "writer" to positions of low
power—readers being passive receivers of information, and writers, at best, being possessed with the knack for allowing some
"true" meaning of a technological problem to flow through them-

selves, into computer memory, from there to the reader's brain. The process of communication contracts, in this articulation, to become a mere function, a component necessary for technological use but not of great importance (except when it fails). From this perspective, engineers and scientists—those who actually created the concrete technology—have the most power; technical communicators, as well as readers and users, are somewhat like acolytes.

But, as Jennifer Slack, David Miller, and Jeff Doak (1993) argue, "technical communicator" can also be articulated, with some effort, as "author"—a person of relatively greater prestige, responsibility, creativity, and power. The approach of the articulation view itself also suggests a much stronger articulation for reader—no longer a box into which meaning is put, but now the person who constructs meaning (albeit under some strong constraints). This transformation in many ways parallels the distinctions we have made between contracting and expanding forms of hypertext: by articulating hypertext to this new, empowered relationship, both writers and readers might be able to resist efficiency as an *overriding* articulation (although probably it will always be one of many articulations exerting force). Hypertext can be articulated in an expansive way to embrace the active construction of meaning in communication by a whole environment of interconnected agencies: "From sender through channels and receivers, each individual, each technology, each medium *contributes* in the ongoing process of articulating and rearticulating meaning" (Slack, Miller, & Doak, 1993).

The difficulty for writers and readers of hypertext in corporate settings lies in the tenacity of the dominant articulation, efficiency (which is itself complexly articulated in terms of simple, technical/mechanical expediency). As we have shown, it is more likely that upper and middle management will integrate hypertext in a conservative way, one that not only resists change but, in fact, deepens the articulation of communication as contraction by speeding up the frames of access and the ease with which information can be "received" instead of "constructed." But the opportunity exists for a different articulation, one of mutual activity and influence, especially if technical communicators can discover ways in which expansive hypertexts might construct a different meaning for their own positions, perhaps one of increased responsibility and power within an organization.

Finding Common Ground: Convergent Goals for Technical Communicators and Corporations

Even though corporations and their employees sometimes work at cross-purposes, expanding hypertexts can be productively articulated to each group. Technical communicators might find that this form of hypertext grants them a higher degree of responsibility and prestige, but these increases do not necessarily come at the expense of the corporation. The major impediment to getting corporations to understand the benefits (of what is obviously a more complex approach to text and communication) is in convincing managers and administrators to recognize the need for new corporate structures and strategies. Robert Reich (1991), for example, notes the ways in which organizations are shifting from high-volume enterprises (prioritizing hierarchical managerial structures and automation) to high-value enterprise (encouraging networked social structures and flexibility and mobility). Overly rigid hierarchical structures, one-way communication, and simple efficiency may be detrimental to deeper concerns such as innovation, market growth, and long-term financial (if not structural) stability. According to Peter Drucker (1988) and many others, old ways of doing business are no longer adequate within today's and tomorrow's global market.

In this light, contracting hypertexts represent what might be a limiting holdover from print technologies, automated factories, and rigid corporate structures. Designers who construct hypertexts that primarily automate or contract existing paper-based activities presuppose that users want an online text that operates identically to its print-based counterpart, only faster; what is missing is the idea that such a text might offer a completely new range of textual possibilities. Hypertext as informating or expanding—the original vision of Bush, Nelson, and Englebart—may become more common as the social and political situations in which it is used and developed begin to change. As work processes and products become increasingly integrated and collaborative, hypertexts may begin to resemble Nelson's Xanadu or Englebart's oN-Line System (NLS).

The need for such an expanding construction of hypertext is being expressed in projects such as the Virtual Notebook System (VNS) at Baylor College of Medicine. In the VNS project, the architecture of the system is specifically designed to "enhance information sharing among scientists" (Burger et al., 1991, p. 395). And for engineers and systems designers at Boeing, the need arises as workers collapse the common distinctions that programs such as Hypercard make between writers and readers (or authors and browsers) into interdisciplinary teams. Collapsing such categories is important at Boeing because "[e]ach engineer contributes a unique perspective to the design of a product and its processes. The information they create is interrelated and these interrelationships must be represented in the data" (Malcolm et al., 1991, p. 14).

Hypertexts that primarily contract communication processes often mirror conservative corporate structures and practices and reinforce hierarchical business operations; those that mainly expand (and there are fewer of these) hold the potential to make qualitative changes within a corporation, down to the level of individual worker. We might assume, therefore, that as corporations begin adopting new structures and strategies for competing in the global marketplace, parallel shifts will occur in their use of technologies such as hypertext. The move from "data" to "information" projected by Drucker (1988, p. 46) parallels what Kanter sees in "postentrepreneurial" corporations, corporations responding to competitive pressures by implementing the following five changes in how they organize and conduct business (1989, p. 88):

1. A greater number and variety of channels for workers are available to take action and exert influence.

2. Relations of power shift from vertical to horizontal (from chains of command to peer networks).

3. Distinctions between managers and those managed diminishes.

4. External relations are increasingly important sources of internal power and influence.

5. As a result of the first four changes, career development of workers is less intelligible but also less circumscribed.

These changes within modern organizations may encourage more expanding, as opposed to contracting, uses of hypertext. In addition, these changes may allow technical writers to take more active roles in corporate communication processes, as proposed by the articulation model previously discussed.

One difficulty with much of the writing on postentrepreneurial approaches is the way in which they frame causality: Frequently, corporations such as Boeing come to recognize the value of new approaches to technology because the corporate structure and strategies have already shifted and now require new ways of communicating. We argue that such transformations can occur in parallel, new visions of the technology driving corporate development and vice versa. However, management is not often situated in a position that encourages seemingly radical changes. From a conservative standpoint, it appears there is little to gain. But technical communicators have a higher stake in this potential transformation: expanding hypertext not only places more value on the roles of writer and reader, but also might help drive shifts in corporate structure at large that also increase the perceived value of new, expanding methods of communication, not merely in documentation but in all phases of corporate life. As Henrietta Shirk (1988) argues, even the shift from paper to online documentation, which arose from efficiency-based needs,

> requires changes in how technical communicators function in organizations that produce successful online documentation and perhaps even in how these organizations are internally structured. These changes in turn raise important issues about the professional preparation and development of online documentors. (p. 321)

The next stage of hypertext may afford technical communicators with opportunities to address these issues. Certainly, no single technical communicator can initiate sweeping changes in a multinational conglomerate. But possibilities exist, particularly in corporations that might already be considering change but are not completely convinced. By articulating hypertext as supporting both contractions and expansions in hypertext use, technical communicators can construct all aspects of communication as constructive, social activities.

Notes

1. For discussions, see Burke and Devlin (1991); Horton (1990); and Barrett's edited collections on hypertext (1988; 1989; 1992).

2. For a fuller discussion of Bush's career, see Nyce and Kahn's edited collection (1991).

3. The notion of agency remains problematic—but still productive—here because in one sense every user's decision takes place in a specific context and in a specific historical sequence. We do not want to assert that any of the forms of text we discuss here ever offer a mythical high ground divorced from ideology. We are interested in locating and complicating some of the forces that silence other concerns.

4. Admittedly, one might complain that hypertext users may lose (or never gain) important skills related to using printed texts, but the loss of aptitudes such as dog-earing pages is of dubious importance.

5. We would argue, somewhat egotistically, that academic and especially humanistic uses of hypertext frequently break free of these constraints because of the community's relatively greater emphasis on increasing personal development and acceptance of postmodern positions on unity, truth, and subjectivity. As we describe elsewhere (Selber et al., 1996), theoretical and pedagogical positions from fields such as composition offer an important perspective on the use of writing and reading technologies in corporate sites.

References

Amato, J. (1991). Review of writing space: The computer, hypertext, and the history of writing. *Computers and Composition: A Journal for Writing Teachers, 9*(1), 111–117.

Barrett, E. (Ed.). (1988). *Text, context, and hypertext: Writing with and for the computer.* Cambridge, MA: MIT Press.

Barrett, E. (Ed.). (1989). *The society of text: Hypertext, hypermedia, and the social construction of information.* Cambridge, MA: MIT Press.

Barrett, E. (Ed.). (1992). *Sociomedia: Multimedia, hypermedia, and the social construction of knowledge.* Cambridge: MIT Press.

Bernstein, M. (1988). The bookmark and the compass: Orientation tools for hypertext users. *ACM SIGOIS Bulletin, 9,* 34–45.

Bolter, J.D. (1991). *Writing space: The computer, hypertext, and the history of writing.* Hillsdale, NJ: Erlbaum.

Brand, S. (1987). *The media lab: Inventing the future at MIT.* New York: Viking/Penguin.

Braverman, H. (1974). *Labor and monopoly capital: The degradation of work in the twentieth century.* New York: Monthly Review Press.

Brown, P.J. (1987). Turning ideas into products: The guide system. In *Hypertext '87 proceedings* (pp. 33–40). Chapel Hill: University of North Carolina, Association for Computing Machinery.

Burger, A.M., Meyer, B.D., Jung, C.P. & Long, K.B. (1991). The virtual notebook system. In *Third ACM Conference on Hypertext proceedings* (pp. 395–401). San Antonio, TX: Association for Computing Machinery.

Burke, E., & Devlin, J. (1991). *Hypertext/hypermedia handbook.* New York: McGraw-Hill.

Bush, V. (1945/1987). As we may think. In T. Nelson (Ed.), *Literary machines* (pp. 1/39–1/54). South Bend, IN: The Distributors.

Carlson, P.A. (1988). Hypertext: A way of incorporating user feedback into online documentation. In E. Barrett (Ed.), *Text, context, and hypertext: Writing with and for the computer* (pp. 93–110). Cambridge, MA: MIT Press.

Charney, D. (1994). The impact of hypertext in processes of reading and writing. In C.L. Selfe & S.J. Hilligoss (Eds.), *Literacy and computers: The complications of teaching and learning with technology* (pp. 238–263). New York: Modern Language Association of America.

Cohen, N.E. (1991). Problems of form in software documentation. In T.T. Barker (Ed.), *Perspectives on software documentation: Inquiries and innovations* (pp. 123–136). Amityville, NY: Baywood.

Conklin, J. (1987, September). Hypertext: An introduction and survey. *IEEE Computer, 17*–41.

Davies, M.W. (1988). Women clerical workers and the typewriter: The writing machine. In C. Kramarae (Ed.), *Technology and women's voices: Keeping in touch* (pp. 29–40). New York: Routledge.

Dobrin, D.N. (1989). *Writing and technique.* Urbana, IL: National Council of Teachers of English.

Douglas, J.Y. (1991). Understanding the act of reading: The WOE beginner's guide to dissection. *Writing on the Edge, 2*(2), 112–125.

Drucker, P.F. (1988, January/February). The coming of the organization. *Harvard Business Review*, 45–53.

Eisenstein, E. (1983). *The printing revolution in early modern Europe.* New York: Cambridge University Press.

Englebart, D., & Hooper, K. (1988). The Augmentation System Framework. In S. Ambron & K. Hooper (Eds.), *Interactive multimedia* (pp. 15–31). Redmond, WA: Microsoft.

Feenberg, A. (1991). *Critical theory of technology.* New York: Oxford University Press.

Grossberg, L. (1986). History, politics and postmodernism: Stuart Hall and cultural studies. *Journal of Communication Inquiry, 10*(2), 61–77.

Grossberg, L., & Slack, J.D. (1985). An introduction to Stuart Hall's essay [Essay introduction to Hall, "Signification."]. *Critical Studies in Mass Communication, 2*, 87–90.

Hall, S. (1985). Signification, representation, ideology: Althusser and the post-structuralist debates. *Critical Studies in Mass Communication, 2*, 91–114.

Hebdige, D. (1988). *Hiding in the light: On images and things.* New York: Routledge.

Hirschhorn, L. (1984). *Beyond mechanization: Work and technology in a postindustrial age.* Cambridge, MA: MIT Press.

Horton, W.K. (1990). *Designing and writing online documentation: Help files to hypertext.* New York: Wiley.

Johnson-Eilola, J. (1992). Structure & text: Writing space and STORYSPACE. *Computers and Composition: A Journal for Teachers of Writing, 9*(2), 95–129.

Johnson-Eilola, J. (1994). An overview of reading and writing in hypertext: Vertigo and euphoria. In C.L. Selfe & S.J. Hilligoss (Eds.), *Computers and literacy: The complications of teaching and learning with technology* (pp. 119–219). New York: Modern Language Association of America.

Johnson-Lenz, P., & Johnson-Lenz, T. (1992). Postmechanistic groupware primitives: Rhythms, boundaries, and containers. In S. Greenburg (Ed.), *Computer-supported cooperative work and groupware* (pp. 271–293). San Diego: Harcourt Brace Jovanovich.

Kanter, R.M. (1989, November/December). The new managerial work. *Harvard Business Review*, 85–92.

Katz, S.B. (1992). The ethic of expediency: Classical rhetoric, technology, and the holocaust. *College English, 54*(3), 255–275.

Kramarae, C. (Ed.). (1988). *Technology and women's voices: Keeping in touch.* New York: Routledge.

Landow, G.P. (1992). *Hypertext: The convergence of contemporary critical theory and technology.* Baltimore: Johns Hopkins University Press.

Leto, V. (1988). 'Washing, seems it's all we do': Washing technology and women's communication. In C. Kramarae (Ed.), *Technology and women's voices: Keeping in touch* (pp. 161–179). New York: Routledge.

Machung, A. (1988). 'Who needs a personality to talk to a machine?': Communication in the automated office. In C. Kramarae (Ed.), *Technology and women's voices: Keeping in touch* (pp. 62–81). New York: Routledge.

Malcolm, K.C., Poltrock, S.E., & Shuler, D. (1991). Industrial-strength hypermedia: Requirements for a large engineering enterprise. In *Third ACM Conference on Hypertext proceedings* (pp. 13–24). San Antonio, TX: Association for Computing Machinery.

Marvin, C. (1988). *When old technologies were new: Thinking about electronic communication in the late nineteenth century.* New York: Oxford University Press.

Moulthrop, S. (1989). In the zones: Hypertext and the politics of interpretation. *Writing on the Edge, 1*(1), 18–27.

Nelson, T.H. (1982). A new home for the mind. *Datamation, 28,* 168–180.

Nelson, T.H. (1987). *Computer lib/dream machines.* 2nd ed. Redmond, WA: Microsoft.

Nelson, T.H. (1990). *Literary machines 90.1.* Sausalito: Mindful Press.

Nielsen, J. (1990). *Hypertext and hypermedia.* Boston: Academic Press.

Nyce, J.M., & Kahn, P. (1991). *From memex to hypertext: Vannevar Bush and the mind's machine.* New York: Academic Press.

Parsaye, K., Chignell, M., Khoshafian, S., & Wong, H. (1989). *Intelligent databases.* New York: Wiley.

Raymond, D.R., & Tompa, F.W. (1987). Hypertext and the new *Oxford English Dictionary.* In *Hypertext '87 proceedings* (pp. 143–153). Chapel Hill: University of North Carolina, Association for Computing Machinery.

Reich, R.B. (1991). *The work of nations: Preparing ourselves for 21st-century capitalism.* New York: Knopf.

Ritchie, L.D. (1991). Another turn of the information revolution. *Communication Research, 18*(3), 412–427.

Schnell, W.J. (1992). Automated technical manuals. *Army aviation, 41*(2), 24–25.

Schrage, M. (1990). *Shared minds: The new technologies of collaboration.* New York: Random House.

Selber, S.A., McGavin, D., Klein, W., & Johnson-Eilola, J. (1996). Issues in hypertext-supported collaborative writing. In A.H. Duin & C.J. Hansen (Eds.), *Nonacademic writing: Social theory and technology* (pp. 257–280). Hillsdale, NJ: Erlbaum.

Selfe, R.J., et al. (1992). Online help: Exploring static information or constructing personal and collaborative solutions using hypertext. In *SigDoc '92 Conference proceedings* (pp. 97–101). Ottawa: Association for Computing Machinery.

Shaiken, H. (1986). *Work transformed: Automation and labor in the computer age.* Lexington, KY: Lexington Books.

Shannon, C.E., & Weaver, W. (1949). *The mathematical theory of communication.* Urbana: University of Illinois Press.

Shirk, H.N. (1988). Technical writers as computer scientists: The challenges of online documentation. In Edward Barrett (Ed.), *Text, context, and hypertext: Writing with and for the computer* (pp. 311–327). Cambridge, MA: MIT Press.

Slack, J.D., Miller, D.J., & Doak, J. (1993). The technical communicator as author: Meaning, power, authority. *Journal of Business and Technical Communication, 7*(1), 12–36.

Sproull, L., & Kiesler, S. (1991). *Connections: New ways of working in the networked organization.* Cambridge, MA: MIT Press.

Tuman, M. (1992). Rev. of Bolter, "Writing space." *College Composition and Communication, 43*(2), 261–263.

VanLehn, K. (1985). *Theory reform caused by an argumentation tool.* Report ISL-11. Palo Alto: Xerox PARC.

Walker, J.H. (1987). Document examiner: Delivery interface for hypertext documents. In *Hypertext '87 proceedings* (pp. 307–323). Chapel Hill: University of North Carolina, Association for Computing Machinery.

Zuboff, S. (1988). *In the age of the smart machine: The future of work and power.* New York: Basic Books.

Chapter 7

Automating the Writing Process: Two Case Studies

Douglas R. Wieringa, Marvin C. McCallum,
Jennifer Morgan
Battelle Seattle Research Center

Joseph Y. Yasutake
Electric Power Research Institute (EPRI)

Hachiro Isoda
Central Research Institute of Electric Power Industry
(CRIEPI)

Robert M. Schumacher Jr.
Ameritech

As the technology used by the writer becomes more sophisticated, the potential to both help and complicate the writing process increases. This chapter will present two case studies of industrial efforts in which sophisticated writing technology has been considered or developed. The first case study describes a software tool for nuclear power plant procedure writers. The second describes an effort at a telecommunications company to rewrite hard-copy documentation as online documentation. These case studies will illustrate the potential benefits, as well as the costs, of automation.

Although the nuclear power and telecommunications industries are quite diverse, their automation efforts share several similarities in the effects on writers.[1] This chapter will discuss those effects. We will begin by presenting a brief summary of each effort, and then we will draw some common lessons that can be applied by companies considering changes to writing technology, and by teachers, who will be able to better prepare their students to participate in this type of change in the workplace.

Automation in Nuclear Power Plants: Procedures Software Tool

Although commercial nuclear power plants in this country have a distinguished safety record, the industry is always looking for ways to further improve safety and increase efficiency. Efforts in these areas are directed toward engineering solutions, or human factors solutions, or some combination of both. In other words, researchers, engineers, and workers are constantly striving to improve the design of the plants and to reduce the likelihood that the people operating the plants will make an error.

In 1989, the United States' Electric Power Research Institute (EPRI) and the Japanese Central Research Institute of Electric Power Industry (CRIEPI) embarked on an effort to reduce errors in the area of maintenance and testing in nuclear power plants. EPRI and CRIEPI sought to identify areas associated with relatively high error rates and relatively low productivity, and to identify interventions that would reduce errors and increase productivity.

One such intervention was specialized procedure-writing software. In nuclear power plants, procedures are written documents that specify a sequence of actions necessary to accomplish a task. It is not unusual for a nuclear power plant to have several thousand procedures that collectively govern all aspects of plant operation, including plant administration, normal and emergency operations, health physics (i.e., control of personnel exposure to radiation), and maintenance. Several factors complicate the procedure writer's task of producing accurate, usable procedures[2]:

- A nuclear power plant is a complex system. Procedure writers must document this system accurately.

- A nuclear power plant is also a complex organization. Procedure writers must deal with a host of other individuals, including other procedure writers, technical experts, managers, reviewers, training personnel, and procedure users (Sturdivant, 1988a, 1988b). The difficulties in coordinating so many people complicate and often delay procedure development.

- A procedure writer's job is never done because the documents that he or she produces are "living documents" that are subject to constant revision. Revision requests can come from users, managers, or regulators. Revisions can also be driven by changes in the equipment that a procedure describes.

EPRI and CRIEPI recognized that procedure writers in this environment could benefit from an automated procedure writing aid. They also realized, however, that the introduction of automation into an industry as technically complex and highly regulated as nuclear power was not a simple undertaking. Procedures are highly integrated with all aspects of the day-to-day operation of a nuclear power plant, and changes in the ways procedures were written and distributed could have far-reaching effects that might not be apparent without further study.

Accordingly, EPRI and CRIEPI commissioned Battelle to undertake further study. Specifically, they initiated a five-step process to examine the feasibility of a "procedures software tool" (PST):

1. *Identify the functional requirements for PST.* The first step was to determine what functionality should be incorporated in the software to reduce errors and increase efficiency. In other words, what software features would help procedure writers, procedure reviewers, procedure distributors, and—ultimately—procedure users?

2. *Assess the capability of current software systems to meet those requirements.* Once potential areas for improvement were identified, we examined whether they could be successfully addressed by available software tools. For example, we might consider whether a commercially available word processor could be modified to provide PST's functionality or whether it would be necessary to develop specialized software.

3. *Develop a functional description for PST.* This functional description could be used to write a detailed system specification should EPRI and CRIEPI decide to proceed with the development of PST.

4. *Estimate the costs of PST development.*

5. *Estimate the costs and benefits associated with implementation of PST.*

The PST functional description was driven by needs; that is, we identified various procedure characteristics that could contribute to errors and then specified PST features that could improve those characteristics. We surveyed by mail a nuclear power plant's maintenance supervisors, asking them (1) how often specific procedure-related problems were encountered and (2) to estimate the typical effect of those problems on safety and productivity. We also reviewed the requirements placed by the Nuclear Regulatory Commission (NRC) on procedures, recommended standards for procedures, and relevant research on procedures.

In addition to defining these general needs, it was important to talk with potential users of PST to ensure that we would specify a tool that would meet *their* needs. Accordingly, we interviewed procedure writers, their supervisors, word-processing staff, and computer professionals from selected nuclear power plants. From these interviews, we developed a formal description of the procedure development process (see McCallum et al., 1995).

A broad set of potential functions emerged from this effort and were documented in our report. PST features would include, among many others, templates that would automate formatting; style and syntax checking (made possible by the limited syntax that may be used in procedures); access to an online style guide; links to external databases of technical information; and electronic routing of review copies. (A full discussion of PST's capabilities is beyond the scope of this chapter. If you are interested in other information on PST, please see our project report [McCallum et al., 1995].)

The PST developed by EPRI and CRIEPI has laid the crucial groundwork that will enable individual utilities in the United States and Japan to move forward with automation in procedure writing as deemed necessary.

Automation in Telecommunications:
Reference Delivery Automation

Ameritech is one of the seven regional operating companies formed by the breakup of AT&T. In recent years, telecommunications companies such as Ameritech have been subject not only to increasing competition, but also to a range of new telephone services that have become technologically and economically possible. Such services currently include voice mail, caller identification, distinctive ringing, call forwarding, and so on. In the future, telecommunications companies may be offering services that are even more sophisticated, such as interactive television.

Because of these changes, Ameritech realized that it was moving into the future with an outmoded method of documenting its products of pages of hard-copy manuals. The system was breaking down because of the sheer number of pages required to document the increasingly complex products being offered. Users had difficulty finding the information they needed, and the costs of duplicating, distributing, and filing the manuals was high.

The decision was made to move the product information online; however, Ameritech personnel involved in this effort, known as "reference delivery automation" (RDA), knew that moving hard-copy documents directly online, with no change in organization or delivery, was a certain recipe for failure (Horton, 1995). The material would have to be rewritten for the online environment, where users would be reluctant to read long blocks of text and where hypertext links and automated searching could help users quickly locate the information they needed.

Ameritech personnel further realized that they weren't simply facing problems of document format. Over the years, Ameritech documentation had become rather lengthy. Authors needed to "essentialize"—to decide what information was truly essential to readers and include only that information in the manuals. Without this fundamental change, the electronic documentation would grow to the same difficult-to-use proportions as the existing hard-copy documentation.

Moving in a methodical, thorough manner, Ameritech attacked the problem on several fronts:

- It researched the situation, documenting the problems with the existing system, the work habits users had developed to compensate for these problems, and the costs and savings associated with the move to online documentation.

- It selected software. RDA authors would write in a popular word-processing program. Their documents would be converted to standard generalized markup language (SGML),[3] which could be read by the software used to present the documents online.

- It established a support structure. An editorial staff was assigned exclusively to RDA, and the position of information manager was developed to assist with training and conversion of the documents to SGML.

- It provided documentation and training for authors. Battelle's role in this project is to prepare a style guide and present a training course.

As this chapter is being written, this new set of protocols is being piloted at various Ameritech locations. The RDA software, the RDA documents, and the process used to write the documents will be revised as necessary, as RDA moves toward the goal of moving Ameritech documents online.[4]

Address a Genuine Need

Several lessons can be drawn from these efforts. One is that a company devoting the time and resources to developing an automated writing system should do so only in response to a genuine need. Automation is expensive—there are costs of developing an automated system and ongoing support costs once the system is in place. Ongoing costs include installation, training of new users, enhancements to the system, and modifications required by upgrades to the hardware or operating system. The benefits of the system must outweigh these costs.

There are nonmonetary costs as well. Automation on a large scale, such as PST and RDA, can also change business processes, changing or perhaps even eliminating jobs. Clerical staff may be particularly affected. One issue related to PST involved document-control personnel. Their job was to duplicate, distribute, and track procedure copies—a task that could be performed by PST.

Ameritech has developed RDA in response to a legitimate need—its current documentation system could not move Ameritech into the future. EPRI saw a potential for improvement in nuclear power plant procedures and commissioned the PST functional description to assess that potential. A decision to develop PST can now be made on the basis of that information.

PST and RDA are major efforts that demonstrate that the costs of automating the writing process in a large organization, and doing it *well*, are high. The resulting benefits must be high as well.

Do Your Homework First

Once you have determined that there is a need, do the research necessary to determine what must be done to address that need. The entire PST effort to date has consisted of such research. Ameritech embarked on similar research before beginning work on RDA.

Because the driving force behind PST was the potential to further reduce maintenance errors, we developed a formal methodology for assessing the effect of PST on maintenance errors. First, we developed a list of the problems that could occur in procedures and assessed the potential effect of each problem on maintenance errors and productivity.[5] We then assessed the effectiveness of various PST features for reducing each procedure problem and the consequent effect on error rates and productivity. The final step was to develop three levels of sophistication for PST, intermediate, and full. The base level gave the greatest effect for the money by including those PST features that showed the greatest promise for reducing error rates and increasing productivity. The intermediate and full levels provide additional features that produce less incremental benefit.

Similarly, Ameritech conducted extensive research prior to the development of RDA. It documented the business case for RDA and also talked to writers and users of the current hard-copy manuals to determine the essential characteristics of RDA. The results of this comprehensive task analysis influenced the design of the RDA interface, the RDA workflow (i.e., the process a document follows from conception to completion), and the organization and format of RDA documents.

One particularly interesting technique RDA developers used was the desk audit. In a desk audit, they examined the materials that future RDA users actually used at their desks. RDA developers found that users highlighted information in manuals, used Post-It™ notes to mark pages, and developed "cheat sheets." By seeing what people actually used, RDA developers were able to learn more about the documents they should be delivering.

It is important to talk to the writers as you conduct this research (and listen to what they have to say), of course, as they will be most affected by the automation of the writing process. But it is equally important to listen to others who are involved or who will be affected. In the course of developing the PST functional description, we interviewed procedure writers, their supervisors, procedure users, computer professionals, and document-control personnel. Remember that the automation effort must address their needs, as well as the needs of users.

Be Sure That Automation
Will Solve the Problem

Once the research is completed, take another look at the problem to determine whether automation will solve it and whether automation *alone* will solve it.

Ameritech realized that the RDA software could contribute only part of the solution to the problems it was facing; it was also important to change the way that some writers wrote. The concept is crucial to RDA's success, and the RDA software cannot essentialize. Essentializing is a skill that must be taught to those writers who do not understand it or do not understand how important it is. Accordingly, the training class and style guide for RDA emphasize essentializing. An editorial group was also developed to assist the authors and to review RDA documents and suggest improvements. This is one aspect of an integrated effort to move documents online. The software alone is not the answer.

Keep the System as Simple as Possible

Automated systems should be kept as simple as possible. In the specification phase, it is easy to brainstorm features, but those features take resources to implement and increase the complexity of the software and its effects on the organization.

For example, one potential feature for PST was a means of linking information in the procedure to an external database and automatically updating procedures when the database changed. A piece of information tolerance for a pump seal, for example, could be stored in a central database and accessed by the procedure. If the seal tolerance changed, it would be necessary to update it only once, in the central database, and the change would be propagated throughout all procedures pertaining to that pump. It would not be necessary to change every procedure, a time-consuming task. However, there were substantial administrative and practical hurdles to making this system work, and the feature had to be modified so that updates were performed explicitly by writer request. It is an example of an idea that is theoretically possible but not feasible in actuality.

Similarly, RDA uses a relatively simple grid structure to organize information, where one axis of the grid lists the various products and the other axis lists common topic headings, such as features or cost. It does not use the free-form web that hypertext allows, where hypertext nodes are linked to each other without adhering to a specific structure, although some cross-linking is allowed.[6] Some authors (e.g., Brockman, Horton, & Brock, 1989) argue that the web structure is the most expressive of the hypertext structures (although others would argue its benefits [e.g., Raskin, 1987; Landow, 1987]). Documents with the web structure are also the most difficult to write well and to write consistently. RDA designers thus decided to implement a simpler grid structure and, in fact, have developed a template for each RDA document that enforces the grid. Any cross-linking is done with the assistance of the editors.

By simplifying RDA in this manner, Ameritech has reduced the demands on RDA authors and editors and increased the consistency of RDA documents. Consistent organization is important because RDA users will be able to find information more quickly if all documents in the RDA set are organized in the same way.

Realize That Writers Are Customers

Another common thread in EPRI and Ameritech's documentation efforts is that both recognize the key role played by the authors. Writers are busy people who will be hesitant to use a system they do not believe is helpful. If the system fails, or, just as important, if writers believe it will fail, productivity and morale will suffer. Ameritech explicitly realizes that RDA success hinges on acceptance by the many authors who will write RDA documents. Similarly, procedure writers' acceptance of PST will be a crucial factor in its success. A major aspect of the PST effort to date has been to determine procedure writers' needs so that the PST specification would meet those needs.

Ameritech, in fact, has gone to some effort to internally sell RDA. Its designers have produced a video on RDA's benefits and have held numerous meetings where they have described the benefits of RDA to writers and other involved parties. They have even commissioned novelty items such as RDA T-shirts and mouse pads. Ameritech also realizes the importance of the training class associated with RDA—the class will be many writers' first exposure to RDA. A poorly presented class could lead to word-of-mouth reports that could undermine the RDA effort.

Conclusion

Examination of the PST and RDA efforts shows that efforts to automate the writing process in large organizations are complex undertakings that affect people throughout the organization. Writers, of course, are affected, but other effects can ripple through the organization if the documentation is tightly linked to the way the organization does business. Automation efforts should begin with an assessment of the problem and the effects of the proposed solution. It is also important to assess the effects on writers and to specify a system that suits their needs. Automation must acknowledge the crucial roles played by the humans in the system, including writers.

Notes

1. An additional similarity that made this chapter possible was that the Battelle Seattle Research Center was involved in both efforts.

2. Wieringa and Farkas (1991) provide a more detailed discussion of the characteristics of nuclear power plant procedures.

3. SGML is the emerging standard for document format. SGML allows the structure of the document to be coded in a manner that can be read on various types of hardware. For more information, see *Society for Technical Communication* (1993a; 1993b).

4. For more information on RDA, see the proceedings that will be published of the 39th Annual Conference of the Human Factors and Ergonomics Society, held October 9–13, 1995.

5. It should be noted that, in the spirit of continuous improvement, these reductions in errors would occur from an impressive initial baseline. Error rates were low initially, and there are safeguards and redundancies built into nuclear power plant operation that prevent the errors that do occur from having safety consequences.

6. Horton (1995) discusses these various hypertext structures.

References

Brockman, R.J., Horton, W., & Brock, K. (1989). From database to hypertext via electronic publishing: An information odyssey. In E. Barrett (Ed.), *Society of text: Hypertext, hypermedia, and the social construct of information* (pp. 162–205). Cambridge, MA: MIT Press.

Horton, W. (1995). *Designing and writing online documentation: Hypermedia for self-supporting products*, 2nd. ed. New York: Wiley.

Landow, G.P. (1987). Relationally encoded links and the rhetoric of hypertext. *Hypertext '87 proceedings* (pp. 331–343). Chapel Hill: University of North Carolina, Association for Computing Machinery.

McCallum, M.C., Morgan, J., Wieringa, D.R., Kinghorn, R.A., & Kantowitz, B.H. (1995). *Procedures software tool requirements analysis and functional description* (EPRI Research Project RP3111-03). Palo Alto, CA: Electric Power Research Institute.

Raskin, J. (1987). The hype in hypertext: A critique. In *Hypertext '87 proceedings* (pp. 325–330). Chapel Hill: University of North Carolina, Association for Computing Machinery.

Society for Technical Communication. (1993a). Special issue: Standard generalized markup language. *Journal of the Society for Technical Communication, 40,* 208–229.

Society for Technical Communication. (1993b). Special issue: Standard generalized markup language. *Journal of the Society for Technical Communication, 40,* 376–409.

Sturdivant, M.H. (1988a). An integrated procedures system as a management tool. In *IEEE International Professional Communications Conference* (October 5–7, 1988, Seattle, WA). New York: International Association of Electrical and Electronics Engineers.

Sturdivant, M.H. (1988b). Upgrading procedure production and delivery systems. In *IEEE International Professional Communications Conference* (October 5–7, 1988, Seattle, WA). New York: International Association of Electrical and Electronics Engineers.

Wieringa, D.R., & Farkas, D.K. (1991). Procedure writing across domains: Nuclear power plant procedures and computer documentation for Computing Machinery. In *9th Annual International Conference on Systems Documentation* (pp. 49–58). Salem, MA: Association for Computing Machinery.

Chapter 8

Online Editing, Mark-up Models, and the Workplace Lives of Editors and Writers

David K. Farkas
University of Washington

Steven E. Poltrock
Boeing Corporation

Although editors make extensive use of computers in their work, most editors still mark changes on paper, using traditional editing symbols despite compelling reasons for editors to begin marking copy on the computer. After considering online editing from the perspectives of both editors and employers, this chapter explores the various mark-up models embodied in current online editing software. Demonstrating ways that mark-up models can affect the quality of edited material and the work life satisfaction of editors, the authors discuss ways to encourage the development and adoption of online editing tools that editors will find congenial.

Significant writing projects in the workplace are generally carried out by a group of people working together (Ede & Lunsford, 1990). Typically, a team of writers will contribute components of the eventual whole. In the process, they are likely to informally edit each other's contributions. The draft may also undergo review by higher-level subject-matter experts, whose focus will be the technical accuracy and appropriateness for the intended audience (Paradis, Dobrin, & Miller, 1985; Kleimann, 1993). Very often, a professional editor will apply his or her communication expertise to the document.

Today's computer technology can provide impressive support for many group-writing activities. Writers can easily share fully formatted drafts over computer networks, either within their building or across continents. The computer can also serve as a project librarian, keeping track of who has (and has had) each section of the document and controlling who can change certain components. The review process is also reasonably well supported: features such as hidden text, pop-up notes, and special annotation footnotes allow reviewers to comment on the author's draft. Soon it will be commonplace for reviewers to embed audio and even video clips anyplace in the author's document where they want to comment.

There is, however, one part of the review process in which computer support is considerably less effective: editing. Consequently, although almost every stage in the preparation of typical workplace documents is digital, most editors, as we shall see, continue to work with paper and pencil. This situation and the prospects for change are the starting point for this article. We review the role of the editor in workplace writing and the status of both general computer use and online editing. Then we consider how organizations and editors view online editing, concluding that online editing will gradually take hold in the workplace. If this is so, the nature of both online editing tools that will be used becomes important both for editors and the writers who work with them. Therefore, we show some of the ways that the fundamental operation and features of these tools can affect both the quality of edited material and the workplace lives of editors and writers, and we suggest that the technical communication community should take an active role in determining the character of the tools that will be developed and adopted.

The Editor's Role in Creating Documents

Editors serve a variety of roles in preparing documents, including helping to plan the document, coordinating the work of writers, and supervising production; however, their fundamental and defining role is to improve the document by marking changes in the draft they receive from the author (Rude, 1991; Haugen, 1990). These changes include making large-scale organizational changes and rewriting whole passages, but editors—unlike reviewers—are responsible for style, grammar, usage, and mechanics, and so they mark a large number of small-grained changes. For this reason, a key characteristic of any online editing tool is how the markup process is handled. As we shall see, there are major challenges in creating software that can effectively deal with large numbers of small-grained changes.

In addition to marking changes, editors—much like reviewers—must write messages to the author. These may be queries for more information, justifications for what they have done, or proposals setting forth how the editor plans to deal with some difficulty in the document. In most cases, the author has ultimate responsibility for and intellectual "ownership" of the document. Authors therefore reject some changes and make new changes. Also, they will send their own messages back to the editor, messages that the editor may reply to. Editing, then, entails a dialogue between editor and author, a dialogue that may continue through several cycles. After the completion of the editor-author dialogue, the editor (or an editor's assistant) will incorporate the agreed-upon changes into the document in preparation for final formatting and printing. Or the author or person doing the production work will incorporate the changes.

Authorial review can be a difficult and troublesome part of the editor's job. Many editors establish excellent relationships with authors; on the other hand, there are inherent tensions stemming from one person's making corrections in the work of another. Indeed, this relationship is often characterized by suspicion, disrespect, and antagonism. From the author's point of view, the sins of editors include making unnecessary and arbitrary changes, introducing errors and unintended meanings, and not adequately explaining why changes were made (Rude, 1991, pp. 338–345; Tarutz, 1992, pp. 47–64). Editors, of course, do not defend the introducing of errors or the changing of the meaning in the document without querying, but they expect to be recognized as the project's communication experts (Gerich, 1994). Tarutz's book on technical editing provides numerous glimpses of writers' frequent suspicion of and antagonism toward editors. She notes, for example, that most writers "approach editors cautiously and skeptically" and "have a lingering bad taste from previous edits" (1992, p. 54). She portrays an editor (p. 47) who asks, "Why do writers hate me?"

In Duffy's survey of twenty-eight expert editors, the ability to establish a collaborative relationship with the author ranks as number six in a list of the thirty-nine most important editorial skills—more important than the ability to find and correct errors in grammar, syntax, and punctuation (Duffy, in press). Speck's (1991) bibliography of the literature of professional editing shows that relations with authors is a constant theme. Because relations with authors is an important and problematic aspect of the editor's work, an important consideration in the design or selection of an online editing tool is how that tool is apt to affect editor/author relationships.

How Editors Use Computers

Most editors make some use of the computer in their work. A survey of "writer-editors" by Rude and Smith (1992) shows that 63 percent of the respondents use the computer as part of their editing work. Duffy's survey shows that 78 percent of his expert editors use the computer. The computer tasks performed are varied, including formatting, checking spelling and grammar, performing search and replace operations, generating an index, and sending and receiving drafts. Most likely, the amount of computer use by editors will continue to increase.

Editors work differently in different settings and have individual habits and preferences; therefore, there are innumerable specific scenarios for how editing is carried out. Following is one scenario that entails significant use of the computer. It is not, however, complete online editing because the editor is still marking changes on paper. In this scenario, the editor

1. Receives a draft from the author over a computer network or on disk.

2. Prints a copy and skims or reads to become familiar with the material. The editor may take some notes at this stage.

3. Performs a computerized spelling check (and perhaps a grammar check) and makes changes in the online version. (Here we assume that the editor has been authorized to make minor changes "silently"—without marking them for the author to review.)

4. Makes any necessary major organizational changes online and writes a message to the author, explaining these changes. It is easier to rearrange large sections of an online document than to mark these changes on a printed copy. Also, the author is better able to visualize the restructuring when he or she sees the changes executed.

5. Prints a copy of the document and makes one or more major editing passes, marking the changes with a pencil on the printed copy. This is the heart of the editing process.

6. Returns the paper copy to the author and negotiates the final changes.

7. Keyboards the changes into the computer in preparation for final formatting and book building or gives the paper copy to a formatting/production person, who will keyboard the changes while doing the production work.

This scenario shows that an editor can use computer technology while marking changes on paper. This fact, no doubt, helps to explain the loyalty of many editors to the red pencil. On the other hand, the use of the pencil, the only nondigital part of the entire publications process, is a return to an earlier era, and, as we shall see, is inefficient in some important respects.

Neither Duffy's survey nor Rude and Smith's provides a precise view of the prevalence of online editing; clearly, however, online editing is atypical among these respondents. Of Rude and Smith's respondents, about 15 percent edit online. When Duffy's twenty-eight expert editors were asked to list the computer tools they employ, only two listed an online editing tool (DocuComp from Advanced Software, Sunnyvale, CA), and one of these editors commented that DocuComp was usable only for documents that contained few editorial changes.

Alred, Oliu, and Brusaw (1992) offer a negative assessment of online editing, an assessment we believe is widely shared: "The potential advantages that online editing offers cannot compensate at this time for its liabilities" (p. 293). In this comment, they are referring primarily to difficulties in marking copy on the computer and in visualizing and navigating an online document, issues we address later. Princeton University Press is seeking to widely implement online editing, but nonetheless "red pencils still rule in the editorial department" (Kincade & Oppenheim, 1994, p. 235). Boeing and Microsoft are two large, technologically sophisticated organizations that have been looking at online editing for quite a few years, but hard-copy editing remains the rule at both companies.

While online editing has achieved only limited acceptance, there clearly is interest in it and pressure for its adoption. In the following sections, we look more closely at this situation by examining both the perspective of organizations and the perspective of editors on the use of online editing. We believe that, from both perspectives, the advantages of online editing are considerable, although the benefits accrue more assuredly and directly to organizations.

The Organization's Perspective on Online Editing

Online editing potentially offers organizations greater speed in preparing documents, better version control, better archiving, increased productivity, improved systems integration, and other benefits. Online editing, however, must not degrade quality and must fit within the organization's overall operation.

Speed

The speed with which a proposal, product catalog, or manual update can be prepared is often crucial. Formerly, when deadlines were tight, and collaborators were physically separated, paper drafts were often sent back and forth among authors, reviewers, and editors by Federal Express or even courier. In the era of the fax, the physical distance separating collaborators is a less important issue, but even now, valuable time is lost, and errors may be introduced when agreed-upon changes marked on the paper copy are keyboarded into the digital version. Online editing in its most current implementations makes it possible to incorporate agreed-upon changes instantly and without introducing errors. In fact, with currently available tools, such as Aspects (Group Logic, Arlington, VA), authors, reviewers, and editors can simultaneously enter changes to the document and view a continuously updated version of the document.

Version Control to Prevent Mistakes

One major difficulty in creating complex documents is simply keeping track of where the various parts are in the writing, review, and editing cycles and controlling who is working on what. At times, organizations mistakenly assign writers and editors to work on sections of a document that managers have already decided to delete from the final version. Worse yet, draft chapters containing serious factual errors are inadvertently included in a printed document; and occasionally, writers or editors, following a personal agenda, make surreptitious changes that appear in the published version. In paper environments, project librarians check drafts out, check them back in, and in general, attempt to maintain version control. As noted earlier, in an all-digital environment, the computer can be employed to provide effective version control: the computer can keep track of who has (and has had) each section of the document, limit the distribution of certain sections, withhold all but "read-only" access to parts of the document an individual is not authorized to change, and display the changes made by each individual.

Efficient Archiving

Organizations must often archive the complete life histories of documents. They must archive not only all published versions, but all drafts, review comments, and even personal notes. Such archiving may be necessary to support an old version of a product, trace responsibility for a mistake, or determine the date on which a patentable idea was conceived. Archiving paper material is time-consuming, requires expensive storage space, and still leads to serious problems of information retrieval. Archiving and retrieving digital material is much easier and cheaper.

Increasing Productivity while Maintaining Quality

Naturally, organizations are concerned with the productivity of individual editors and the efficiency of the editing process. An online editing tool that significantly slows down the editors or the authors who review edited copy is not acceptable. Similarly, while organizations might not have the same sensitivity to document quality that editors do, serious quality-control problems caused by a clumsy editing tool will likely be unacceptable. Some online editing tools have failed in the marketplace for these reasons; newer tools may prove superior to current tools, and to paper editing as well, in regard to both productivity and document quality.

The Requirement of Overall Systems Integration

Necessarily broad, *systems integration* refers to all the ways in which a particular online editing tool fits the organization's existing technologies and operations, including the kinds of documents they prepare and their writing and publishing processes. It also includes issues such as staffing, training, and budgets. The need for systems integration within an organization can easily lead to the rejection of a particular online editing tool and possibly of all available online editing tools. For example, an organization may reject tools that cannot be tightly integrated into its electronic publishing system or electronic mail system, that cannot gracefully handle elaborately formatted documents, or that cost too much. For all these reasons, editors cannot simply assume that tools they like and that authors like will automatically be adopted by their organizations. Editors may have to make a strong case for preferred tools within their organizations and encourage the commercial development of tools that both satisfy themselves and fit the needs of their organization.

Other Values

Organizations should inherently value the quality of workplace life and want their employees to work comfortably, feel pride in their work, and enjoy positive human relations. In any case, deficient workplace quality ultimately hurts productivity. Another priority valued in organizations is respect for the environment; online editing reduces the amount of paper and toner consumed in large organizations, thereby both protecting the environment and reducing costs.

The Editor's Perspective
Regarding Online Editing

Because editors have a stake in their employers' success, they share an interest in efficiency, accuracy, and cost reduction. Presumably, they support technologies that protect the environment. Editors, however, also have their own concerns. They are naturally concerned with the comfort and healthfulness of their work environment. Also, they care about the operation of their tools—whether these tools make possible high-quality editing, and whether they make the job more complex and difficult.

Comfort and Health

Online editing increases the number of hours each week that the editor spends at the computer, raising questions about health and comfort. Back pain, carpal tunnel syndrome, eye fatigue, and (in the opinion of some) monitor emissions are major societal problems. These should be and are being addressed through means such as ergonomic office furniture and keyboards and low-emission monitors with more legible displays. Ergonomic problems associated with computer use persist, of course, and this makes editors understandably wary.

The computer is nevertheless the center of the professional workplace, and many kinds of workers spend long hours staring at the screen. If online editing tools become highly efficient, editors (like newsroom journalists a decade or more ago) will probably have little success citing increased time at the computer as a reason for rejecting these tools. Fortunately, editors are apt to engage in professional activities, such as interviewing and project management, that limit time at the computer. Also, editors can significantly reduce time at the screen by reading from a print copy when they first familiarize themselves with a document and switching to the computer screen when they begin marking up the document. Paper thus becomes a useful temporary interface but is not really part of the main flow of the process of preparing a document.

Typos and Reading Errors

It is also possible that the screen's inferiority to paper in regard to resolution and other viewing factors can cause editors to miss typos and make other character-level errors. Evidence of reduced performance is mixed. Horton (1994) reviews a variety of conflicting studies and concludes that "with careful design of screen displays, reading speed and accuracy can approach those of paper" (p. 13). No doubt the quality of displays will continue to improve. Furthermore, an important but often unnoticed point is that the editor is not restricted to a particular set of font and display variables when reading from the screen. Contemporary word-processing software allows the editor to zoom screen text (effectively increasing font size), view text in ultra-readable screen fonts, change the text color, and in general, create a customized reading and editing environment. Most editors, we assert, would miss fewer typos working in their preferred environment than they would reading a document in 9-point Times Roman type produced by an ink-jet printer on both sides of low-quality, show-through paper. The ability to create a custom on-screen reading environment also alleviates part of the comfort and health problem discussed earlier.

Visualization and Navigation

Visualization refers to how well an editor can visualize the structure of a document; *navigation* refers to how easily an editor can find a portion of the document (e.g., the editor needs to look quickly at the fourth section of Chapter 11). Without adequate visualization and navigation, online editing becomes impractical.

Like many other editors, the editors surveyed by Rude and Smith cite superior visualization and navigation as major reasons for working on paper. This belief is certainly not surprising: we are all comfortable with print elements such as tables of contents, running heads, and page numbers; furthermore, the heft and physicality of paper help people gauge the size of the whole document, sense their current location within it, thumb through it readily, and keep several pages open at once.

On the other hand, because the navigation and visualization issue pertains not just to professional editors, but also to all those who use computers to prepare documents, the visualization and navigation capabilities of word processors and electronic publishing systems have improved greatly in the last decade. For example, contemporary word-processing software provides means for visually gauging the approximate size of the document and one's location in it, can display different portions of the document in separate windows, and offers special views of the document such as the outline view and thumbnail images of multiple pages. Editors, moreover, can instantly jump to any word, phrase, or page and can easily find every element in a manuscript that shares a certain formatting characteristic (boldface, a certain heading level, etc.). Finally, monitors that can display a full $8 \frac{1}{2} \times 11$ page (or larger) are not rare. It may well be that some of Rude and Smith's respondents were not considering the capabilities of the best word-processing products when they judged in favor of paper, and significant improvements have occurred since that survey.

Those who laud the heft and physicality of paper almost always assume a document that is very manageable in size, not a physically cumbersome document requiring multiple volumes. We assert that, objectively considered, visualization and navigation in the best word-processing programs clearly exceed visualization and navigation in paper when documents are even moderately long. Furthermore, there is at least one study in the research literature that lends strong support to this view (Egan et al., 1989).

Marking Copy

The way the editor marks copy is crucial. It bears upon productivity, document quality, and job satisfaction. It has major implications for editors' relationships with authors. Consequently, in assessing any online editing tool, editors will doubtless give much weight to this aspect of the tool. (We examine mark-up in the next section.) For now, we can say that editors will make rigorous demands of mark-up, both because of its importance and because the mark-up model embodied in traditional paper editing is efficient in four important respects:

1. The traditional symbols are fairly easy for editors and authors to learn, and a workable subset (e.g., the symbols for deletion, insertion, transposition, and other basic operations) is both familiar and highly intuitive.

2. The traditional editing symbols represent a rich repertoire of editing operations, enabling editors to mark changes rapidly.

3. There is no difficulty in distinguishing the editor's hand-entered work from the author's printed draft. The author easily sees what has been changed.

4. Because of the rich, well-designed symbology, the careful editor can make fairly extensive changes without making the marking so complex that the author will have difficulty reviewing the changes. At some point, however, it is best for the editor to simply rewrite a passage and ask the author to compare the new one with the original.

Prospects for the Future

Editing is almost always an organizational activity, performed within or for companies. Consequently, the organization's perspective is apt to be influential. We expect that the organizational agenda will result in a gradual but steady increase in the amount of online editing. Furthermore, although many editors are wary of (or even hostile toward) online editing, the benefits, we believe, of editing online and working entirely in a digital environment should continue to win over more editors. There is certainly anecdotal evidence of editors who have become enthusiastic proponents of online editing. For example, Lynnette Porter, who works actively as a freelance editor, reports positive experiences using a range of online editing techniques; and Joann Een, an editor for the Seattle-based training company Catapult, endorses online editing tools in Microsoft Word and declares online editing to be "more efficient than manual editing."

If online editing is apt to become prevalent (and perhaps dominant), an important question is, what will the tools be? Will there be many tools or just a few? Will they be stand-alone tools, or will they exist as part of word-processing and electronic publishing applications? Will some tools become optional add-ons, possibly created by third-party developers? Most important, what will be the features of these tools, and how well will the features fit the work of editors and writers, as well as the agendas of their organizations?

Editors and writers certainly have a stake in the nature of these tools, and if they are to influence the tools they use, they will first need to understand the key differences among these tools and the implications of these differences. Clearly, the nature of a tool significantly affects the user of the tool, but the nature of this relationship is not easy to determine. In the next section, we look at what is perhaps the most fundamental characteristic of any online editing tool: the mark-up model it embodies.

Implications of Mark-up Models

It is hard to overestimate the importance and centrality of mark-up in any online editing tool. It is how the editor works and how the document is changed. Michael Shrage (1990) observes that "all collaboration relies on a shared space" (p. 153) and writes about the computer's potential to create better shared spaces among collaborators in many domains. The mark-up model embodied in any online editing tool, the particular implementation of the model, and the features associated with it collectively make up much of the shared space between editors and writers.

To provide a full survey of mark-up models or online editing tools is beyond our scope. Rather, our goals here are simply to delineate the concept of a mark-up model, illustrate the most important models, and argue that the choice of a mark-up model and, more generally, the choice of an online editing tool have many important, subtle, and hard-to-predict implications. Also, please note that the names of particular products are used only as examples of the models these products embody; we have made no attempt to discuss all product features or to evaluate these products. Finally, we assume that any useful online editing tool will enable two-way messaging between editor and author, although these may lie outside the mark-up model. In most instances, whatever means reviewers use to send comments to writers (e.g., hidden text or an annotation feature) will serve for messaging between writers and editors.

The Silent Editing Model

Silent editing means simply that the editor works on the author's draft by using the normal features of a word processor. This is the simplest model—almost the lack of a model. It requires no special tool or technique. This model is effective when the author fully trusts the editor (or has limited concern for the manuscript). This model, however, causes frustration and, likely, antagonism if the author wishes to check the editor's work against the original carefully, for doing so requires the author to read both versions sentence by sentence, an excruciating task.

Editors may enjoy working in this untrammeled manner, but the practice is dangerous, even when authors will permit it. First, this model causes the editor to work in the manner of an author and likely results in less regard for the author's original text and, hence, overediting. Second, because this model is "destructive," the editor cannot readily recover the author's wording once it has been changed.

Silent editing is routinely and effectively used in a very limited form and in conjunction with some other model. The editor is authorized to make minor, utterly unarguable changes silently, thus simplifying the workspace shared by editor and author and reserving this workspace for weightier issues. Even here, however, the author must trust the editor's judgment about which changes to make silently.

The Comment Model

The comment model is embodied in pop-up notes, temporary footnotes, hidden text, and special symbols placed within the text. It was also the basis for the unsuccessful product MarkUp (Mainstay Software, Agoura Hills, CA), in which the editor marked changes on a virtual "acetate" layer created by the editing tool.

In its most rudimentary form, such as pop-ups and hidden text, the editor is simply writing brief notations indicating desired changes, as in Figure 1. The notation indicates the editor's intention to delete "savage." This model can work reasonably well, especially for editing manuscripts that are short and in need of few changes, but it is too labor intensive for many settings.

In its more sophisticated form, software can execute the marked changes. Online editing is performed in this manner at the Princeton University Press (Kincade & Oppenheim, 1994) by using the XyWrite word processor and custom programming. Even in this more sophisticated form, however, a significant amount of extra keyboarding is required to mark the proposed changes.

The Edit Trace Model

The edit trace (or "compare") model is the dominant model in current online editing software. It has been implemented in DocuComp and in various word processors.

In the edit trace model, the editor works like an author, deleting, adding, and moving text by using all the usual features of the word-processing software. The computer, however, can compare the editor's new version to the author's original version and so permits the author to view the draft with the editor's changes juxtaposed on it by means of typographic attributes such as strikethrough to show deletion, and underlining (or boldface) to show

> ## Mary had a savage <del little lamb.

Figure 1. A typical implementation of the comment model.

> A ~~little lamb~~ Mary had <u>a little lamb</u>
> whose fleece was white ~~like~~ <u>as</u> snow.
> <u>And everywhere that Mary went</u> ~~T~~<u>t</u>he
> lamb~~, moreover,~~ was sure to go
> ~~everywhere that Mary went~~.

Figure 2. The edit trace model.

insertion. The edit trace model is shown in Figure 2. Microsoft Word includes a useful feature that enables the author to jump from one of the editor's mark-ups to the next. In a less sophisticated variation of this model, only a change bar appears in the margin where the editor has changed the text. The author must look at the original version to see the unedited passage.

The edit trace model could easily win favor among editors because of the ease of making changes. On the other hand, this mark-up model is apt to encourage heavier editing and less regard for the author's original text. If this is indeed the case, there may be significant implications for the quality of edited documents, the editor's standing within the organization, and the editor's relationships with authors. In this way, the edit trace model is like the silent model but far more feasible because the editing is not destructive.

There are three different ways that editors can view the "trace" made by the computer. In the first, the editor stops and begins a distinct compare operation. In the second, the trace appears in real time as the editor works. In the third, a second scrolling window continuously shows the trace. The second and third options are apt to limit heavy editing and are therefore more desirable than the first.

Because this mark-up model uses typographical attributes rather than a complete, highly refined symbology, changes are not economical or easy to interpret. For example, in Figure 2 there is significant visual complexity just to show the change from an uppercase "T" to a lowercase "t." With traditional paper editing, only a single slash mark would be drawn over the uppercase "T."[1] This difficulty may hinder editors, and it can be quite difficult for authors. Conceivably, it can make authors careless about reviewing their edited drafts or less willing to work with editors. An implementation that used traditional editing symbols rather than typographical attributes would be better.

Most implementations of the edit trace model have another deficiency: they show that a block of text has been deleted, and they show that a block of text has been inserted, but they do not communicate the concept of moved text. Hence, when text is moved beyond the confines of a paragraph or page, the editor must provide messages to indicate the move. Otherwise, the author is apt to see the deletion and ask, "Why did the editor take that out?" Seeing an insertion, the author might say, "Why is the editor putting this in twice?"

The Traditional Model Adapted for the Computer

The traditional paper mark-up model can be adapted for the computer screen. One approach is that of Red Pencil, a clever DOS product that allows the editor to apply a nearly complete set of traditional editing symbols directly to a document. Using the mouse or keyboard, the editor highlights a word, phrase, or passage and issues a command to add new editing marks to the document. Once marked in this way, the text can be transmitted to the author for review. The author can then remove and add new editing marks to the document. When the process is complete and the final changes have been made, all the marked changes are executed with a single command; and so, as with the edit trace model, there is no manual keyboarding of editing changes.

Red Pencil has not been successful in the marketplace. This is partly because Red Pencil was never designed to deal with elaborately formatted text and partly because the Capsule Codeworks (Redmond, WA), the very small software company that developed Red Pencil, has had trouble keeping up with changes in computer hardware and software environments, leading to limitations in the area of systems integration.

Another implementation of the traditional model is becoming feasible thanks to the advent of a technology that lets the computer recognize both human handwriting and basic editing symbols: the editor uses "digital ink" to mark a simple subset of the traditional editing symbols, along with the words the editor means to insert into the draft. The digital ink looks like a simple bitmap but is much more powerful (Mezick, 1993); for, when the author has reviewed the editor's changes, the editing symbols (known to computer scientists as "gestural commands") can be executed. The editor can also enter messages to the author, such as "Please improve this passage." These comments remain as digital ink and are ultimately deleted.

MATE is a research prototype that uses digital ink, although the editor writes with a stylus on a pressure-sensitive tablet rather than directly on the screen (Hardock, Kurtenbach, & Buxton, 1993). One excellent feature of MATE is a second window, which scrolls in conjunction with the main window and shows what the document looks like with the changes executed. This second window is a major benefit to both editors and authors, especially when text has been heavily edited. The two windows are shown in Figure 3. One capability that is not present in MATE, but that can be implemented with digital ink, is the automatic "neatening" of editing symbols.

PenEdit (Advanced Pen Technologies, Upper Saddle River, NJ) is a promising new online editing tool that emulates many aspects of traditional paper editing. In PenEdit, the editor uses an electronic pen to place the traditional deletion symbol and certain other editing symbols directly on the computer screen. Text can be inserted either with the pen or with a keyboard; text appears on the same line as the author's text but in a distinctive "handwriting" font. Text marked by PenEdit is shown in Figure 4. This process encourages restrained editing, and in one published account, a pencil-and-paper editor describes the new process favorably (Hilts, 1994). If authors have computers that run PenEdit, they can view the editor's changes and respond to them on the computer; the less expensive procedure is for editors to

Annotation View	Edit View
This is a sample document with several annotations mark on it. (ed marked above)	This is a sample document with several annotations marked on it.
Note some that annotations correspond to ~~specific~~ editing commands.	Note that some annotations correspond to editing commands.
Whereas others are more general comments. *Reword*	Other annotations are simply comments to the author.

Figure 3.   A passage edited in MATE. One window shows the
changes marked in digital ink; the other shows the
passage with the editing commands executed.

Much of the ~~background~~ knowledge & ~~and~~ guidelines for
structure ~~kiosk~~ **plan** ~~design~~ comes from the field of exhibit **plan**
~~design~~ (e.g., Klein, 1988; Konikow, [Au: Spell 1] 1984; Miles & Alt,
1988). [Au: Date 1] Indeed, a major principle of exhibit **plan** ~~design~~ is to
create displays that attract attention & ~~and~~ invite
participation. However, the many technology components &
~~and~~ the nature of the interaction possible with interactive
systems poses many new challenges even for experienced
exhibit designers [FN: 2].

[End Page 1]

Figure 4.   Copy marked with PenEdit. The rounded rectangle
indicates a footnote. The squared-off rectangles
indicate queries to the author.

ask authors to review printouts of the marked copy. Editors and authors can also view a "clean" version of the manuscript, in which all the changes have been executed.

Because PenEdit currently runs in a special pen-based operating system, and because manuscripts need to be imported into PenEdit, organizations using PenEdit must address some systems-integration issues. This product, however, is under active development by people who are attuned to the needs of professional editors.

A special issue of *Byte* magazine (1993) that discusses digital ink is notable for emphasizing that digital ink and voice recognition are complementary technologies. In the scenario that emerges from this section, editors use both digital ink and voice commands. Crane and Rtischev (1993) offer this example: "While editing on the screen, you might say the following: Move this sentence [indicating what 'this sentence' refers to by simultaneously circling the sentence] to the beginning of this paragraph [simultaneously circling the paragraph] . . ." (100). Assuming that the oral "move" command would also create some traceable record of the move, the combination of pen and voice input might be a very efficient implementation of the traditional mark-up model.

Whether implemented on paper, in Red Pencil, or with digital ink (possibly augmented by voice commands), the traditional mark-up model encourages restrained editing. Editing changes take more time to mark than they do with the edit trace model, and the editor is always reminded that he or she is altering another person's document. Restrained editing is favored by most experienced editors and reduces conflicts with authors. Furthermore, to the degree that the rich vocabulary of traditional editing symbols is retained, authors and editors can interpret the editor's markings more readily than they can in the edit trace model.

The Role of the Technical Communication Community

No one can know just how editing will be performed in the future. We believe, however, that online editing will be prevalent, if not dominant, and we have tried to show that in regard to just one design issue (albeit a central one), the number of design options is great and the differences among them significant.

A key question is whether online editing will improve the quality of edited documents and the work lives of both editors and the writers who work with them. There is, at least, the potential for a "win-win" situation in which these tools will please editors, writers, and their employers. To ensure that good tools will be developed and to ensure that the best of these are adopted, editors, and the technical communication community in general, should try to exert some influence. We can, for instance, help software developers understand the work of editors (as well as informal editing) and make clear which features are necessary and useful and which will create problems. We can also influence the technology planners in our own organizations.

The basis of this influence is our own understanding of the still-uncertain issues surrounding online editing. Therefore, we have a great need for research such as the survey of Rude and Smith (1992) and that of Duffy (in press), which had the explicit goal of contributing to the development of better tools for editors. Also important are detailed and sensitive case studies, such as that of Kincade and Oppenheim (1994). We hope as well that this analysis focuses attention in a useful manner.

Finally, we note that editing is just one of an enormous number of collaborative activities that are moving online (Baecker, 1993). Online editing, however, is a relatively early and fairly challenging test case for computer-supported collaboration. If effective tools for online editing emerge and are accepted, the prospects for computer support of collaborative work in many other domains brighten, and there may be lessons to share with others whose work is moving online.

Note

1. Complex changes in formatting may, in fact, surpass the capabilities of an edit trace tool or result in typographic markings that are too complex for anyone to deal with. Therefore, when an editor wishes to show complex formatting changes in a text element—for example, a list

or table—the best procedure is often to duplicate the element, reformat the new instance, and let the author simply compare the two.

References

Alred, G.J., Oliu, W.E., & Brusaw, C.T. (1992). *The professional writer: A guide for advanced technical writing.* New York: St. Martin's.

Baecker, R.M. (Ed.). (1993). *Readings in groupware and computer-supported collaborative work: Assisting human-human collaboration.* San Francisco: Kaufmann.

Crane, H.D., & Rtischev, D. (1993, October). Pen and voice unite. *Byte,* 98–102.

Duffy, T.M. (In press). Designing tools to aid technical editors: A needs analysis. *Technical Communication, 42.*

Ede, L., & Lunsford, A. (1990). *Singular texts/plural authors: Perspectives on collaborative writing.* Carbondale: Southern Illinois University Press.

Egan, D.E., Remde, J.R., Gomez, L.M., Landauer, T.K., Eberhardt, J., & Lochbaum, C.C. (1989). Formative design-evaluation of superbook. *ACM Transactions on Information Systems, 7*(1), 30–57.

Gerich, C. (1994). How technical editors enrich the revision process. *Technical Communication, 41*(1), 59–70.

Hardock, G., Kurtenbach, G., & Buxton, W. (1993). A marking-based interface for collaborative writing. In *Proceedings of the ACM Symposium on User Interface Software and Technology* (pp. 259–266). Atlanta, GA. Nov. 3–5.

Haugen, D. (1990). Coming to terms with editing. *Research in the Teaching of English, 24*(3), 322–333.

Hilts, P. (1994, January 3). I sing the editor electric. *Publisher's Weekly,* 43.

Horton, W. (1994). *Designing and writing online documentation.* 2nd ed. New York: Wiley.

Kincade, D., & Oppenheim, L. (1994). Marking it up as we go along: Into editorial production's electronic future. *Journal of Scholarly Publishing, 25*(4), 233–242.

Kleimann, S. (1993). The reciprocal relationship of workplace culture and review. In R. Spilka (ed.), *Writing in the workplace: New research perspectives* (pp. 56–70). Carbondale: Southern Illinois University Press.

Mezick, D. (1993, Oct.). Pen computing catches on. *Byte*, 105–112.

Paradis, J., Dobrin, D., & Miller, R. (1985). Writing at Exxon ITD: Notes on the writing environment of an R&D organization. In L. O'dell & D. Goswami (Eds.), *Writing in nonacademic settings* (pp. 281–307). New York: Guilford.

Rude, C. (1991). *Technical editing.* Belmont, CA: Wadsworth.

Rude, C., & Smith, E. (1992). Use of computers in technical editing. *Technical Communication, 39*(3), 334–342.

Shrage, M. (1990). *Shared minds: The new technologies of collaboration.* New York: Random House.

Speck, B.W. (1991). *Editing: An annotated bibliography.* New York: Greenwood.

Tarutz, J.A. (1992). *Technical editing: The practical guide for editors and writers.* Reading, MA: Addison-Wesley.

Chapter 9

Who "Owns" Electronic Texts?

Tharon W. Howard
Clemson University

New information technologies make it increasingly difficult for authors and corporations to claim that ideas and information are property which can be sold. To understand the problems of authorship in electronic environments, this chapter examines the historical development of U.S. copyright and three historically distinct theories of ownership upon which it is based. The author ultimately argues that a revised social constructionist perspective best addresses the challenges of ownership created by new technologies.

The Congress shall have the power . . . to Promote the Progress of Science and useful Arts, by securing for limited Times to Authors and Inventors the exclusive Right to their respective Writings and Discoveries.

—U.S. Constitution, Art. 1, Sec. 8

Notwithstanding the provisions of section 106, the fair use of a copyrighted work, including such use by reproduction in copies or phonorecords or by any other means specified in that section, for purposes such as criticism, comment, news reporting, teaching (including multiple copies for classroom use), scholarship, or research, is not an infringement of copyright.

—17 U.S. Code, Sec. 107

For most people, including a large number of practicing professional writers and professional writing teachers, the issue of intellectual property isn't something they usually consider particularly problematic. Most writers today, particularly those of us who spent a lot of our academic careers in and around English departments, tend to subscribe to the view that authors "own" their texts. We tend to believe (as is implied by the excerpt from the Constitution, above) that we have the right to expect remuneration for "our" writing and, furthermore, that we ought to be able to have some control over how our texts will be used.

However, recent trends toward more collaborative writing projects in the workplace, along with the use of online computer conferences, electronic discussion groups, hypertexts, multimedia presentations, groupware, and other computer technologies aimed at enhancing and promoting collaboration, are all seriously challenging the popular, romantic view that an author owns his or her text. More and more frequently, professional writers are finding themselves confronted with intellectual property and copyright issues which result from the increased reliance on computers in the workplace, and, in many cases, writers are finding themselves unprepared to deal with these issues. Consider, for example, the following scenarios:

Scenario 1

You work in the document design department of a large corporation, and, traditionally, your department has made it a point of pride to produce dramatic covers for the company's annual report. One of your co-workers finds a reproduction of a famous photograph in a popular magazine, and the image would be perfect for the theme of this year's annual report with some cutting, pasting, and a few other modifications.

Since the photograph is famous, since you're going to use only part of the image, and since you're going to modify the image in order to produce something which is essentially a new image, should you go ahead and scan it? Or do you first have to have permission from the magazine which first reproduced it, the publishing house which sells reproductions of it, or the photographer who originally took the photograph?

Scenario 2

You've just been hired to do some desktop-publishing work for a large consulting firm. The office manager bought you a new computer system to use, but the system came with a new software package that is incompatible with the old version of the software used by the rest of the office. As a result, you can't share files with co-workers and do your job effectively. Fortunately, however, the office still has the installation disks for the old version of the software, and the office manager tells you that, since these disks were purchased by the company, you can install the old software on your system.

Should you go ahead and copy the software since the office has already paid for it?

Scenario 3

You're doing research on an article about usability testing for *Technical Communication*, and, as part of your research, you join an electronic discussion group on the Internet, where people doing human-factors research exchange e-mail messages about their works-in-progress. As you're writing your article, someone posts an e-mail message to the group describing the results of her unpublished research project. These results are central to your article's thesis and force you to completely revise your thinking about the subject. Since these results haven't been published elsewhere, you wish to quote from the e-mail message in your article.

Can you legally and ethically quote from an e-mail message? Indeed, are you obligated to cite the message since it has had such a profound impact on your own thinking? If so, does anyone own the copyright on the message? Do you need to seek the author's permission? Or, since the message was electronically "published" by an electronic discussion group, do you need to have the permission of the person(s) who created and operate the discussion group or the university or company which owns the computer that hosts the group?

Scenario 4

You work for a large corporation in which e-mail is the primary means of communication. Instead of using informal notes, memos, short reports, or phone conversations to contact each other, people in your company use e-mail. In keeping with this "paperless office" milieu, you have maintained an electronic correspondence with a co-worker in another department for some time. You and your co-worker (who happens to be of the opposite sex) are careful to keep your electronic interaction limited to your breaks and lunch periods so that it does not interfere with your work. Your supervisor knows what you're doing and has said that she actually prefers that you correspond via e-mail on your breaks since that way, you're not tying up the office telephone. How-

ever, one afternoon, you discover that your electronic exchanges are being monitored and even shared as jokes among
people in the computer operations department. You're furi-
ous at this violation of your right to control how your texts
will be used, but your supervisor tells you that the company
owns the computer and, therefore, has the right to monitor
its use.

Can you stop this monitoring of your e-mail? Who actually "owns" the messages you've been sending? Do you, as
the author, own the messages? Does the addressee who received them? Or does the owner of the system on which the
messages were produced? Furthermore, what rights does
ownership of the messages entail?

Scenario 5

You're a faculty member in a professional writing program
at a large university, and one of your responsibilities is to
serve as the placement director for the program. In order to
help your graduates find information about companies which
routinely hire writers, you decide to create a Hypercard stack
which will allow students to click on a map of the United
States. Then, depending on the state students select, students
would receive information about specific companies located
in that state. You construct your stacks on the university's
computers, and from a book which provides an alphabetical
list of national corporations, you select data on companies
which you think might routinely hire technical writers. The
resulting hypertext is so popular among your students that
several publishers learn of it and are interested in publishing
it.

Can you publish your hypertext? Have you infringed on
any copyrights by providing your students with your
hypertext in the first place? If you can publish your text, are
you legally obligated to pay any royalties to your university
or to the publisher or author of the book from which you
selected your data?

As these scenarios illustrate, the new electronic environment
in which professional writers must now function makes intellectual property and copyright issues more and more a part of their
everyday experience in the workplace. Indeed, these sorts of issues are becoming so commonplace that we may well wish to
make an understanding of intellectual property in an electronic
environment a criterion of "electronic" or "computer literacy." As

I will show when we return to these scenarios at the end of this essay, even a relatively clear understanding of the principles of copyright law may not allow writers to answer the questions posed in these scenarios.

However, not only do professional writers need to have a better understanding of copyright issues because they are more likely to encounter them than ever before, but they also need to better understand questions about intellectual property in an electronic environment because new information technologies are forcing us to reshape traditional notions about authorship and ownership. In a world where, for example, a software package can reorganize and rewrite the information in databases (thereby "virtually" creating or authoring texts without human intervention), colloquial ideas about authorship and ownership may no longer be enough. In fact, these sorts of technological challenges to traditional ideas of ownership are particularly troublesome to writers in the workplace because (a) they may diminish writers' claims to remuneration for their work, and (b) they may strip writers of the right to control how their texts will be used.

In order to better understand the problems of ownership in the electronic workplace, I will offer a brief historical examination of the origins of U.S. copyright law since it is through copyright laws that the rights of individual authors and corporations have come to be defined. Furthermore, by examining the evolution of current copyright law, I will explore why electronic publishing, electronic discussion groups, computer conferences, and other new information technologies represent such a challenge to current copyright law. A historical examination of another new publishing technology, i.e., the printing press, will show that then, as now, the introduction of new technologies challenged existing systems for owning and controlling texts. Furthermore, this examination will show that, although many people are not aware of it, current copyright law reflects an interesting struggle among at least three historically distinct and competing theories of textual ownership. First, there is, of course, the romantic and commonplace notion that authors have a "natural right" to the fruits of their intellectual labors. Second, there is the assertion that the public has a right to all knowledge since "Laws of Nature" and absolute truths cannot be the property of any one individual. And third, there is the view that all knowledge is socially constructed, that a text is a product of the community the writer inhabits, and that the text must therefore be communal, rather than individual, property. These three theories have tended to compete when the question has been whether a copyright is a natural right of private property or whether a copyright is a privilege granted to individuals by the public's representatives.

A Historical Overview

When I've taught my professional writing students about the history of copyright laws, and even when I've discussed the subject among some of my faculty colleagues, one of the things that always seems to surprise them is the fact that the original impetus to develop copyright laws did not come about through a desire to protect the "natural property rights" of authors. Indeed, most people I've encountered tend to have the same misimpressions about copyright issues that they have about driving their cars. Most people tend to think that it's their "right" to operate any motor vehicle they care to purchase. Similarly, they tend to believe that, since they also own the texts they write, they ought to be able to control how those texts will be used and ought to be able to profit from that use. And, of course, in actual practice, there are few things in our day-to-day experiences to challenge these notions. Today, the use of an automobile is so pervasive in our society that we just expect everyone to have access to them.

And yet, those unfortunates who either fail to receive or somehow lose their driver's license serve to remind us that operating an automobile is not a right we can expect; rather, it is a privilege we are granted by the government under certain specific circumstances. Similarly, as legal historians such as Joseph Beard are quick to point out, a copyright or (literally speaking) the right to reproduce copies of a particular text was not and, indeed, is not a "natural unlimited property right." Instead, it was and is a "limited privilege granted by the state" (Beard, 1974, p. 382). As with a driver's license, the government gives writers license to "operate" texts in the public domain. What's more, it makes the license so easy to obtain that we seem to forget that we're dealing with an issue of privilege rather than of natural right. Yet, if we consider the origins of English and American copyright laws in the sixteenth century, we can quickly see that protecting an author's natural right was never really an issue then either.

During the fifteenth and sixteenth centuries, the great new technological development was the printing press, and, just as today's "computer revolution" is stimulating the growth of new industries in information technology and electronic publishing, the printing press was producing tremendous growth in the book-publishing industry. Prior to the introduction of printing-press technology, the book trade depended on an excruciatingly slow and tremendously expensive publishing technology. Scribes, illustrators (then called limners), and book binders worked laboriously to produce each single copy of every book. Because of the enormous expense involved in this technology, most book-publishing efforts required the funding of either the Church or the Crown, a situation which made it easy for those in power to control the kinds of texts which would be produced and consumed.

Of course, the printing press changed all this. The radical reduction in production costs meant that texts could be produced and marketed cheaply and easily; yet, with a limited number of popular and lucrative texts available for publication, there was a dramatic increase in competition among book publishers. Two significant developments resulted from this increased competition. First, people involved in various aspects of the book-publishing industry (i.e., limners, book binders, printers, etc.) banded together into a cooperative organization which came to be known as the Stationers' Company. As Patterson and Lindberg (1991) point out, the Stationers were essentially a "group of businessmen who agreed to allow one of the[ir members] the exclusive right to publish a specific work in perpetuity" (p. 22). Thus, the Stationers created a voluntarily enforced form of copyright, which (though it did not carry the force of law and said nothing about the "natural rights" of authors) still offered book publishers limited protection against competition. In other words, the increased competition which brought about the development of the Stationers' Company clearly established the need to protect a publisher's (though not an author's) copyright. Indeed, as Martha Woodmansee (1984) points out, it wasn't until the eighteenth century that writers were able to realize any real profits from the competitive book trade in the form of royalties. In fact, even in the eighteenth century, copyrights were valuable properties:

> ... a flat sum remained customary, upon receipt of which the writer forfeited his [sic] rights to any profits his work might bring. His work became the property of the publisher, who would realize as much profit from it as he could. (pp. 435–436)

The second result of this increased competition was that the Church and the Crown lost what had been their de facto control over the production and consumption of texts. Because of its new, more economical printing technology, the book-publishing industry no longer needed to depend on Church or State subsidies, and, consequently, publishers were free to produce texts which would not have received the economic sanction of the Church or Crown. Indeed, given that the public is always fascinated with controversial texts and is therefore going to purchase more of them, it seems likely that sixteenth-century publishers found new economic incentives to publish texts which, ironically, challenged the same religious and governmental authority which had been their chief means of support before the introduction of the printing press.

As a result of these two developments (i.e., the Stationers' desire to protect themselves from competition and the Crown's inability to control the publication of subversive books), in 1556 Mary Tudor and Philip of Spain granted the Stationers a royal charter, which stated in its preamble that it had been issued in order "To satisfy the desire of the Crown for an effective remedy against the publishing of seditious and heretical books" (Beard, 1974, p. 384). Furthermore, the Stationers' royal charter "limited most printing to members of that company and empowered the stationers to search out and destroy unlawful books" (Patterson & Lindberg, 1991, p. 23). As a result, modern copyright law finds its origins not in the recognition and protection of an author's natural property rights, but, rather, in the "ignoble desire for censorship" and in the greedy lust to "protect profit by prohibiting unlicensed com-petition" (Beard, 1974, p. 383). And yet, despite the disturbing motives behind this early form of copyright law, the Stationers' royal charter is significant because it firmly established the prin-ciple that a copyright is not the natural, absolute, or unlimited property of any individual or company. Instead, to the degree that a copyright can be considered a form of property at all, the Statio-ners' charter made it clear that to own a copyright is essentially to own a limited license or a privilege which the state grants in or-der to promote intellectual activities that are deemed to be in the best interests of the state and its citizens.

Although Mary Tudor, Parliament, and the U.S. Congress prob-ably had very different views of the desirability of censorship and book burning, the same principle of privilege that Mary estab-lished in the Stationers' charter can be found in Parliament's 1709 passage of the Statute of Anne, the statute which in turn provided the basis for Article I, Section 8 of the Constitution. Unlike the Stationers' charter, both the Statute of Anne and the Constitution recognize the rights of authors. In fact, Article I, Section 8 of the Constitution provides that authors shall have the "exclusive Right to their respective Writings and Discoveries," thereby offering writers the kind of protection which the Stationers' charter gave only to publishers. However, this provision does not assert that texts are the exclusive property of their authors; instead, what the Constitution does is to give Congress the legal authority to grant authors limited copyrights in order "To promote the Progress of Science and the useful Arts." In other words, as was the case with the Stationers' charter, copyright is still a privilege or license granted by the government for a limited period of time in order to promote not only the right of authors to profit from their la-bors, but also the enhancement of the public's collective welfare. Hence, just as the State of South Carolina makes laws which give me the right to profit from certain uses of my car for four years and under specific circumstances which are intended to protect and benefit my fellow citizens, the Constitution empowers Con-gress to make laws which give me the right to profit from certain uses of my texts for seventy-five years from their publication or for a hundred years from their creation (whichever is shorter) and under specific circumstances which are intended to promote the economic and intellectual well-being of the American public.

Major Principles of U.S. Copyright Law

Now the upshot of all this law-making, privilege-granting, condition-making legal-speak is that the Constitution has come to represent a delicate balance between the rights of an individual and the good of the public. It represents a sometimes uncomfortable compromise, "balancing an author's interest against the public interest in the dissemination of information affecting areas of universal concern, such as art, science, history, and business" (Van Bergen, 1992, p. 31). Copyright law in the United States recognizes that in order to encourage authors to produce the texts which will lead to the artistic, scientific, and technological discoveries that drive business and industry, it is essential that authors be allowed to realize a profit from their texts. Obviously, without the hope of profit, there is little incentive for a software developer to invest in the research required for the production of new computer applications, nor is there sufficient cause for a publishing house to pay large sums of money to photographers and writers in order to produce books which they cannot sell because the articles and photographs can be obtained more cheaply through some other means. In short then, U.S. copyright law is based on the simple principle that one has to spend money in the short term in order to make money in the long term; we have to pay for intellectual and economic progress by first investing in the mechanisms of research and development.

On the other hand, copyright law doesn't give authors and publishers the legal right to prevent the public from the "fair use" of texts. Indeed, I have already shown that individual authors are granted copyrights not because authors have a natural property right, but because such protection is in the public's best interests. Thus, as Pierre Leval (1990) notes, "Fair use is not a grudgingly tolerated exception to the copyright owner's rights of private property, but a fundamental policy of copyright law" (p. 1107).

The public's right to the fair use of texts is provided for in Statute 17, Section 107 of the U.S. Code, and essentially what it does is to place limitations on the "exclusive Right to their Writings and Discoveries" that authors and inventors received in the Constitution. Section 107 grants the public the right to copy a work "for purposes such as criticism, comment, news reporting, teaching (including multiple copies for classroom use), scholarship, or research." Thus, the doctrine of fair use allows the use of texts for noncommercial purposes which are in the public's best interests. However, this does not mean that, for example, teachers can freely make photocopies of entire textbooks for their classes or that a textbook publisher developing a multimedia presentation on the Vietnam War for high school history classes could freely use sequences from Apocalypse Now and *The Deer Hunter* in its stacks. Beyond granting the right to copy a work for educational purposes, the law further states that in determining whether the use made of a work in any particular case is a fair use, the factors to be considered shall include the following:

- the purpose and character of the use, including whether such use is of a commercial nature or is for nonprofit educational purposes;
- the nature of the copyrighted work;
- the amount and substantiality of the portion used in relation to the copyrighted work as a whole; and
- the effect of the use upon the potential market for or value of the copyrighted work. (17 U.S. Code, Sec. 107)

Thus, even though the two parties mentioned here (teacher and publisher) are using copyrighted texts for teaching purposes, they would both be considered guilty of copyright infringement because, in the first case, the teacher is copying the whole text and is interfering with the "potential market for" the textbook; and in the second case, the publisher of the multimedia presentation would be profiting from the commercial sale of its product to schools. Hence, in the doctrine of fair use, the balance between individual rights and public needs can once again be seen.

In addition to the "fair use" of texts, the copyright statute imposes other limitations on the exclusive rights of copyright holders, and one of the most important of these restrictions is on those features of texts which are copyrightable. According to the copyright statute in the U.S. Code, only the tangible expression of ideas belongs to the copyright holder. Ideas are not copy protected. This limitation is of particular interest because it gives perhaps the clearest articulation of the ways in which authors can be said to own their texts, and clearly this limitation undermines the commonplace and romantic notion that a "person's ideas are no less his property than his hogs and horses" (Woodmansee, 1984, p. 434). Instead, there are two principles of ownership being advanced here: first, that ideas are like universal laws of nature which, because they obtain for everyone, cannot be owned by any single person; and second, that a new discovery, even though it may be the product of one individual's intellectual labor, owes its origins to the realm of public knowledge and should therefore be considered communal property.

In terms of actual practice, current copyright law does grant authors the right to demand remuneration for their intellectual labors, and it does this by protecting the ways authors express ideas. However, it does not allow them to claim ownership of the ideas they express; authors cannot expect to have and maintain a monopoly on truth. According to copyright law, since truths are either universal absolutes or social constructions, they cannot be owned. Hence, if I write a piece of software that uses the mathematical equation $2 + 2 = 4$ as part of its code, I don't have to pay anyone for its use, nor can I expect to receive an honorarium every time someone in the United States calculates the sum of $2 + 2$, because mathematical principles and algorithms are thought to be universal truths. On the other hand, if people copy the way I used an algorithm in my software, if they borrow my code's structure or organization, then they are using my expression, and that expression is copyrighted. Consequently, while authors can't expect to profit from ideas and truths, they can expect to receive remuneration for the labor required to un/cover and to form/ulate those ideas and truths. Although it's important to remember, as the doctrine of fair use makes clear, there are still certain public uses even of an author's form of expression for which the copyright holder cannot expect to be compensated.

Copyrights in the Electronic Environment

This examination of the historical origins and principles which inform modern U.S. copyright law reveals that the commonly held belief that authors own the texts they produce does not accurately reflect the actual legal status of textual ownership. Although it is correct to say that authors do indeed own a copyright as soon as a text is produced and that they therefore enjoy the rights of copy protection, it is important that both the producers and consumers of texts understand that those rights exist in the form of a limited privilege granted by the State and that those rights obtain only under certain conditions specified by the State.

And yet, while professional communicators need to understand the general principles upon which current copyright law is based in order to function effectively in the electronic workplace, it's also important to understand that those same principles don't always yield clear answers when we have to deal with electronic texts. A professional writer may know that copyright is only a privilege, that the public has the right to certain "fair uses" of texts, and that only the form of expression is protected in a work; yet, this knowledge may still leave the writer unsure as to the exact copyright status of a particular electronic text in a particular situation. As Marilyn Van Bergen (1992) has noted, "there is good reason why the law is often symbolized by scales used as weighing instruments" (p. 31), and this is particularly true for copyright law since, as I have shown, it seeks to balance the rights of the individual against the needs of the public, since it represents a compromise among three competing theories of intellectual property, and since technological changes have, historically, represented challenges for existing forms of copy protection.

Still, in spite of the fact that the nature of copyright law makes it difficult to say for certain that a particular situation does or does not represent a copyright infringement, an understanding of copyright principles can still serve as a useful guide for professional communicators. To show how this is the case, I wish now to return to the scenarios with which I began this essay in order to illustrate how these principles can at least help writers either avoid litigation or recover the remuneration they are due.

Scenario 1

In this scenario, a member of a document-design team is planning to scan a famous photograph from a popular magazine in order to manipulate a portion of it for the cover of the company's annual report. The central questions here are (1) does such a reproduction fall under the doctrine of fair use and (2) who owns the copyright on the image?

As far as the question of fair use is concerned, it seems highly probable that this would not be considered a fair use of the original work. Since the reproduction is not being made for educational, news reporting, or critical purposes, its use is still copy protected. Furthermore, as Brad Bunnin (1990) points out in his extremely informative article "Copyrights and Wrongs," even though an image has been manipulated, it may still be "legally considered a derivation of an original work" (p. 77), and therefore its reproduction will require the permission of the copyright holder. In his article, Bunnin also reproduces an electronically manipulated version of Munch's famous painting *The Scream;* yet, in spite of the fact that *The Scream* is a famous painting in the public domain, and in spite of the fact that Bunnin's derivative reproduction is a new image, Bunnin received permission from the museum which owned the painting "and paid a $250 fee to manipulate it" (p. 77). Similarly, the member of the document-design team should receive permission before reproducing and manipulating the photograph.

As to the question of who should be contacted in order to receive permission to reproduce the image, the issue is a bit more complicated. Probably the safest course for the document designer is to purchase and receive permission to reproduce a copy of the photograph from the publishing house which owns the copyright on the original photograph rather than using the magazine's reproduction. The reason for this is that derivative works are also copy protected. As Nicholas Miller and Carol Blumenthal (1986) observe, "Copyright laws protect an author's rights in his own expression even when that expression makes use of nonoriginal information" (p. 229). For example, were I to copy Bunnin's manipulated version of *The Scream,* I would be responsible to Bunnin's publisher. Thus, in order to avoid infringing on what may be considered a derivative work in the magazine's reproduction of the photograph, the document designer should obtain a copy of the original photo from the original copyright holder.

Scenario 2

In this comparatively straightforward scenario, a writer is instructed by the office manager to copy desktop-publishing software which the company had previously purchased for use on another employee's computer. Here, the central question is whether purchasing a copyrighted work gives one the right to copy it.

There is an unfortunate, though common, misconception that, when individuals or companies own a copy of a book or a piece of software, they can use their property as they see fit. However, as the privilege principle makes clear, "owning" a text or even a copy of a text is not the same as having the right to copy a work. Typically, when I purchase a text, the only "property" that I "own" is the actual physical copy of the book, computer disks, photograph, painting, compact disk, etc. However, ownership of this physical property doesn't give me the right to copy the text. In order to copy the work, I also have to have purchased a license to copy it.

Today, most software publishers do, in fact, sell consumers limited licenses to copy their software. Usually, diskettes are sold in shrink-wrapped or sealed packages so that opening the package constitutes an acceptance of the conditions of the limited license to copy the software. Exactly which copyrights are granted in these licenses varies from software package to software package; however, the most common form of licensing agreement allows consumers only to make backup copies for protection and to install (i.e., copy) the software on one system for use by one individual.

In terms of the scenario, if this is the sort of license which was purchased by the company, then it would be a violation of copyright law to install the desktop-publishing software on a second system.

However, before the writer in this scenario refuses the office manager's instructions to copy the software, it would be a very good idea to check the exact terms of the license agreement. It may well be that the company purchased a "site license" for the software, in which case the software might legally be copied onto the second system. Companies often purchase site licenses which allow them to copy software on several machines or to install software on their local-area networks so that the software can then be copied into the memories of a number of individual computers at the site, the exact number of copies possible being specified by the terms of the site's licensing agreement.

Scenario 3

In this scenario, a writer is preparing an article for the journal *Technical Communication* and wishes to quote a passage from an e-mail message that had been posted to an electronic discussion group. The central questions here are (1) whether such a use is protected by the fair use clause and (2) whether the author of the message, the owner of the discussion group, or the university which owns the host computer for the group is the copyright holder for the message.

Currently, it would probably be considered legal for the writer to quote a short passage from such an e-mail message. The doctrine of fair use allows the reproduction of short passages for the kinds of news reporting and critical purposes typical of articles found in *Technical Communication*. However, the situation here is clouded by the technology involved and the lack of specificity in the fair use clause. The fair use clause requires that, in addition to considering the purposes for and the amount of the work being copied, "the effect of the use upon the potential market for or value of the copyrighted work" should also be taken into consideration (17 U.S. Code, Sec. 107). Thus, the author of the e-mail message may feel that her copyright has been violated since she has not been given the opportunity to publish the work through more traditional means, where the potential for remuneration is greater. In other words, the author of the e-mail message may be able to argue that her right to report on the research has been "upstaged," and therefore its potential value has been diminished.

However, although there is some validity to this argument, it seems more likely that sending an e-mail message to a discussion group would be considered a form of publication, so the author of the e-mail message can't really argue that the work has been upstaged. Indeed, while the exact copyright status of texts sent to and distributed by electronic discussion groups is still unclear and can vary widely from group to group, more and more groups are operating as electronic publications. In fact, groups like PACS-L, PMC, and E-Journal have received ISSN numbers, giving them the same copyright status granted to more traditional print publications. In other groups where discussions are open and unmoderated, the groups' owners may explicitly state that the copyrights belong solely to the authors of the messages sent to the groups. And in yet another type of group, members of the group may have a more or less tacit agreement not to quote or cite each other's messages at all, making it unethical (though not necessarily illegal) to quote their messages. Thus, even though quoting from the e-mail message sent to the electronic discussion group would probably be considered fair use regardless of the type of group, the writer of the article in this scenario should first contact the discussion group's owner for more information since the owner operates as an agent for the university and would be able to describe the quoting practices of the group. If the group has an ISSN number, then quoting from the message is acceptable under the conditions specified by the doctrine of fair use. If the group does not have an ISSN number, then the safest and most ethical course is to attempt to secure the permission of the e-mail message's author before quoting from the message.

Scenario 4

In this scenario, an employee discovers that his personal e-mail messages to a fellow employee are being monitored and redistributed by managers in the company. The central question here is whether copyright laws offer the employee any protection against this use of his messages.

Although the employee may have some legal means of preventing the management from monitoring and redistributing his messages in this case, it is unlikely that this problem can be best solved through an appeal to copyright laws because the privilege principle upon which copyright law is based does not give authors a "natural unlimited property right" to their texts (Beard, 1974, p. 382). Because a company pays for an employee's time and provides the resources the employee uses to produce texts, the company has certain rights to the use of the texts created. Usually, in fact, the company is the sole copyright holder of the texts its employees produce while in the company's employ. However, in some cases (particularly in university settings), an institution may receive only a percentage of the remuneration due to the copyright holder since part of the work was accomplished with the institution's resources and part of the work was done on the writer's own time. In this scenario, since the company's resources were used to produce and distribute the e-mail messages, this does give the company some limited rights in the use of those messages. Consequently, the issue here is probably not one of copyright infringement; rather, it is one of privacy.

In a similar case at Epson America, an employee was allegedly fired because she questioned her supervisor's right to read employees' e-mail messages. The employee is currently suing Epson not for copyright infringement, but because monitoring and redistributing employees' private e-mail messages "violated a California law that makes it a crime for a person or company to eavesdrop or record confidential communication without the consent of both the sender and receiver" (Branscum, 1991, p. 63). Similarly, in this particular scenario, the employee should probably seek appeal to either state or federal privacy laws rather than claiming copyright infringement.

Scenario 5

In this scenario, a university employee is attempting to publish a Hypercard stack which was produced on the university's computers and which reorganizes the job information compiled from a copyrighted source. The central questions here are (1) whether the university is entitled to some portion of the royalties received for the stack's publication and (2) whether using the data but not the organization or expression from another work constitutes a copyright infringement.

As was discussed in the previous scenario, since the university's resources were used to develop the stack, the university has the right to expect some remuneration for the use of its facilities. Thus, the faculty member should make arrangements to share a percentage of the profits with the university.

The question of whether the reorganization of data compiled in another source constitutes a copyright infringement is much more difficult, however. As was previously discussed, copyright law protects only an author's expression. Yet, in the case of reference materials and databases such as business lists, telephone directories, bibliographies, or indexes, virtually the only form of tangible expression is the way the data are organized. Furthermore, as Miller and Blumenthal (1986) have pointed out, with the recent developments in information technologies, "computer databases contain randomly stored information which can be retrieved by a computer program in a wide variety of ways. There is no 'organization' to protect" (p. 229). Consequently, two fundamental principles of copyright law come into conflict in this scenario. On the one hand, there is the principle dating all the way back to the Stationers' charter, which recognizes that publishers and authors must be able to expect a profit from their labors if they are going to continue to have the incentives required to produce valuable new texts. On the other hand, there is the principle that ideas and knowledge cannot be the property of any one individual and that only the expression of the ideas belongs to the author or copyright holder.

As is the case with most electronic texts today, it is not yet clear how Congress or the courts will decide to deal with these kinds of challenges to the fundamental principles of current copyright law. It may well be that, because hypertexts and electronic databases allow users rather than authors to determine the ultimate organization and shape of these electronic texts, future copyright laws will need to find radical new foundations. In fact, in a 1976 act, Congress did make a number of changes to the copyright statute in the U.S. Code precisely because of technological developments in the television, music, and computer industries. One of these changes was to Section 103, which now "provides that copyright may be had for compilations, but protection extends only to the material contributed by the author, not to preexisting material that is used in the compilation" (Patterson & Lindberg, 1991, p. 93; see also 17 U.S. Code, Sec. 103). In terms of the scenario here, then, this suggests that the faculty member's use of the information would not be a copyright infringement because the original compiler's expression has been avoided and also because Section 103 seems to reaffirm the notion that data are part of the public domain.

However, law courts are conservative institutions, and it seems likely that a scenario like this one will also be resolved according to precedents such as *Leon v. Pacific Telephone and Telegraph Co.* In this 1937 court case, the defendant essentially changed the alphabetical organization of a telephone directory to a numerical order based on telephone numbers, thereby using the data but not the plaintiff's mode of expression. Yet, in spite of the fact that the defendant did not encroach upon the plaintiff's expression, the court ruled that this was, nevertheless, a copyright infringement. As Miller and Blumenthal (1986) point out, the effect of this decision has been that "some of the recent cases which follow Leon have explicitly stated that the compiler's labor is what should be protected" (p. 229). In other words, when the courts have been required to choose between protecting a publisher's incentives to produce texts and consumers' rights to use a work's content but not its mode of expression, the courts appear to believe that protecting a producer's incentives is in the best long-term interests of the public. Thus, in this scenario, the safest and most conservative course would be to negotiate some kind of financial arrangement with the persons holding the copyright on the reference materials used in the stack.

Conclusion

As these scenarios have illustrated, the new electronic environment in which professional writers must now function makes intellectual property and copyright issues more and more a part of their everyday experience in the workplace. Today's professional communicators need to have a more thorough understanding of the principles upon which modern copyright laws are based than ever before. As the discussion of the scenarios has shown, an understanding of these principles may not allow a writer to predict with any degree of certainty how a court of law will rule in a particular case; however, I would argue that such an understanding can at least offer professional communicators some sense of how to avoid copyright infringements. And given the enormous cost of litigation, both in terms of actual dollars and potential damage to a career, I would argue that knowing how to navigate through the intellectual property minefield is a tremendously valuable skill.

References

Beard, J. (1974). The copyright issue. *Annual Review of Information Science and Technology, 9*, 381–411.

Branscum, D. (1991, March). Ethics, e-mail, and the law: When legal ain't necessarily right. *Macworld, 63*, 66–67, 70, 72, 83.

Bunnin, B. (1990, April). Copyrights and wrongs: How to keep your work on the right side of copyright law. *Publish*, 76–82.

Leval, P. (1990, March). Toward a fair use standard. *Harvard Law Review*, 1105–1136.

Miller, N., & Blumenthal, C. (1986). Intellectual property issues. In A.W. Branscomb (Ed.), *Toward a law of global communication networks* (pp. 227–237). New York: Longman.

Patterson, L.R., & Lindberg, S.W. (1991). *The nature of copyright: A law of users' rights.* Athens: University of Georgia Press.

Van Bergen, M. (1992, July/August). Copyright law, fair use, and multimedia. *EDUCOM Review, 27,* 31–34.

Woodmansee, M. (1984). The genius and the copyright: Economic and legal conditions of the emergence of the 'author.' *Eighteenth-Century Studies, 17*(4), 425–448.

Part Three

Contrasts and Crossovers between Electronic Literacy Efforts in the Academy and the Workplace

Chapter 10

Networking Technology in the Classroom: Whose Interests Are We Serving?

Craig J. Hansen
Metropolitan State University

Computer-networking technology has been eagerly embraced by communications disciplines as a means to facilitate engaged inter- action and to encourage egalitarian discourse. Yet the roots of net- working technology lie in control and management—both of infor- mation and of those who use it. In the workplace, those values often predominate over more progressive goals envisioned by scholars. This chapter explores this tension, notes that it can have very real implications for students, and suggests that we, as instructors, employ these technologies with an awareness of their role in mul- tiple value systems.

This chapter compares two surprisingly divergent views of computer networking, views that reflect differing purposes, goals, and value systems. One view, suggested by writing researchers, emphasizes the potential of computer networks for engaged, egali- tarian communication. The other view, as evidenced by industry and government, emphasizes computer networks as tools for employee productivity and managerial control. The goal here is to highlight the fundamental differences between these two views and examine the implications when the two worlds converge— that is, when the writing student assumes the role of worker and citizen—and to suggest that those who use computer networks in the classroom should think carefully about the ethical and po- litical consequences of this technology. It is also important to note that computer networking serves as a case in point: the argument presented here might well apply to the use of other computer technologies in the classroom.

Computer Networking and the Writing Classroom

Why has the use of computers and computer networks become so widespread in the writing classroom? It might be attributed to several factors. One is convenience: asynchronous networks allow students to collaborate on writing projects or to take part in peer review away from class time, outside of the classroom. They permit students to turn in work electronically, and they allow instructors to review student work online, providing, in some cases, much more immediate response. The use of computer networks to support group work and class discussion increases student writing: discussions that would otherwise be face-to-face become written. Also, I think many instructors have a sense of inevitability, that computer use is pervasive throughout the professional workplace and the writing classroom must "evolve" to remain relevant.

But beyond these largely practical considerations, those who have studied the use of computers and computer networks often identify more profound reasons for encouraging their use and do so with remarkable enthusiasm. For example, Duin and Hansen (1994) observe that, with networking technology, people "can form unique, self-contained discourse communities, bounded by common tasks, interests, and technology . . . [where they] gain insight from the computer-networked microcosm into the cultural macrocosm where they will read, write, collaborate, and construct" (p. 34). Other scholars have recorded interesting observations of student interaction in network-mediated environments as opposed to face-to-face or classroom-based communication environments, particularly in regard to students' task focus or engagement with discussion (see, e.g., Bump, 1990; Sirc & Reynolds, 1990; Cooper & Selfe, 1990; Hartman, et al., 1991; Boiarsky, 1990; Greif, 1988; Mabrito, 1991; and Olaniran, 1994, in an experimental setting). Many researchers have also noted that text-based network communications mask differences based on gender, race, ethnicity, and other factors, reducing the marginalization of participants (see, e.g., Hawisher & Selfe, 1991; Flores, 1990; Selfe, 1990; Sproull & Kiesler, 1991). Finally, as Barker and Kemp (1990) have noted, the networked environment's ability to foster egalitarian participation extends beyond individuals and into the social context that surrounds communication. In networked classrooms, the traditional teacher-based hegemony becomes decentered as all participants tend to interact as peers, creating an ideal medium for the postmodern classroom.

In the studies cited above, instructors have carefully adapted technology to support specific goals. In these examples, the network becomes an extension of the context of the classroom. Capable composition instructors create a classroom environment that supports and empowers individual students; they encourage students to explore, to question, to grow. Indeed, the reward system in the writing classroom may well be based on students' sincere efforts in these directions, including their willingness to interact over networks. In this setting, teachers view technology, at best, as a benevolent collaborator in their effort, or at worst, as a transparent means of text distribution. This generally positive attitude is reflected in much of our field's research on computer networks, despite a number of works that sound cautionary notes (see, e.g., Hawisher & Selfe, 1991, who evoke Bentham's Panopticon in relation to computer networks).

Computer Networking and the Workplace

Computer networks in industry and government reflect very different value systems. To understand the depths and significance of this difference, I think it is necessary to digress very briefly to examine the history of computer networking as it has developed in these sites.

The vision of the paperless information system—i.e., vast networks of interconnected users, huge centralized databases—began in the 1960s. A pioneer in this effort was the Central Intelligence Agency. Although processors and storage media were primitive by current standards, the CIA launched an ambitious and cleverly designed system in 1972 called SAFE (Support for the Analyst File Environment). Its goal was to help steer an overwhelming flood of intelligence data to those who needed it, while keeping it out of the hands of those without the requisite security clearance (Lancaster, 1978, pp. 17–47; for a more recent treatment of the same idea, see Malone et al., 1988). It is useful to pause for a moment and examine some of the assumptions behind this system. A basic assumption is that data accumulation is important. The only way a computer system can accomplish this is if information within the system consists of discrete, objective, Cartesian facts. Any constructive process ends when the data hit the database. These systems privilege historical information, not change. Another assumption is that while computer networks can effectively distribute information, they are equally valuable as a means of controlling this information—its entry, storage, secure distribution, and retrieval. For the CIA and many other large institutions, networking is clearly and cleanly tied to the goals of the organization.

Throughout the next decade, huge networks, like the CIA's but bigger, faster, and more geographically dispersed, proliferated among large organizations. Hierarchical networks with tens of thousands of users employed increasingly powerful mainframe computers to centralize information gathering and dispersal. When sketched out on paper, the design of these networks (one or more mainframes on top, cascades of connected peripherals and terminals below) mirrors the pyramidal power hierarchies of the organizations they support; these are, after all, "management information systems" (MIS). Organization theorists such as Gareth Morgan (1986) have tied MIS to the mechanistic view of corporate organizations, where management acts as a gatekeeper for highly structured, vertical information pathways, mediating requests for information between different organizational subunits. MIS supports these kinds of "controls" (p. 29).

The explosive growth of personal computers in the 1980s, however, created an upheaval in MIS. The importance of networked, mainframe-based systems that controlled the flow of information, that tracked and recorded every transaction through the network, that reinforced the power of management, eroded due to pressure from an unanticipated competitor. The popular metaphor for this (in the computer industry trade press, such as *Datamation* and *Communications Week*) is the growth of "islands of computing," and it is tied to the growth of personal computers. Management initially saw personal computers as tools for productivity enhancement. They permitted workers to more efficiently create documents and to perform mathematical calculations without waiting to submit and receive mainframe "batch" jobs; however, personal computers initially lacked file-sharing capabilities. Local-area networks, networks of personal computers that interconnected users within and between departments, met this need. Because employees grew accustomed to personal computers (they are much more flexible and user-friendly than nonintelligent, "dumb" terminals and could be customized for individual needs), local-area networks, despite haphazard growth and many architectural incompatibilities, became, and continue to be, the preferred means for data communication in many large organizations (Forsythe, 1991). The huge centralized networks seemed outmoded, becoming secondary pathways for information, and MIS in many corporations had no idea who was talking to whom or what information was going where. There simply was no longer any way to track it.

This trend has had a variety of interesting side effects. Some, like the redundancy (i.e., layoffs) of middle management as information gatekeepers, are not relevant here. Others, like the reactions of upper management to regain control of information flow, are worth exploring. Beginning in the late 1980s, the concept of "open systems" became very popular among large network users and the vendors that supply them. It is still the current controlling metaphor for network development among most large organizations. Open-systems standards, now embraced by many standards organizations that define computing architectures (e.g., IEEE, International Standards Organization), seek to connect the islands of computing into large, centralized, cohesive—and controllable—networks. A driving force behind the open-systems movement has been the United States Department of Defense, which has published a variety of procurement specifications that mandate the implementation of open-systems network architectures. Indeed, the industry that has grown around interconnecting incompatible networks with hardware devices is expected to have sales in the area of $5 billion by 1997 (Panettieri,

1993). The term "open" means, to industry, the ability to connect disparate types of network hardware and workstation software; the effect of this openness, viewed from another perspective, is closure, as these protocols reintroduce centralized network control. The technical challenges of reestablishing control over networks are daunting. One model has emerged for accomplishing this: "metacomputing," advocated by the supercomputer industry and some academics and touted as the next significant direction in open systems, proposes the use of artificial intelligence to route and track information flow among disparate networks (Schatz, 1992). To summarize, networks of interconnected personal computers created new pathways for information flow in corporations and new informal horizontal networks among employees, but the drive to control, to manage communications, seems to be reasserting itself in the open systems guise (cf., the essays in Siefert, Gerbner, & Fisher, 1989, which trace this trend in society at large).

The context of networked computing in a corporate setting, then, may be quite different from the context in the academy. In both situations, the network reflects local values, local goals. In the classroom, those goals facilitate the exchange of ideas, even if at times some tension exists between a teacher-centered hegemony and a computer-mediated hegemony. In the workplace, tension arises from different factors. First, the scale of networking can be vastly different, creating the possibility of multiple networking cultures, some closely tied to formal power structures, some perhaps resistant to them. Indeed, networking technology itself may introduce tension at an institutional level when new pathways for information conflict with those already established and formally defined. Second, networks in corporations may be far from neutral, far from transparent carriers of information: they may be used to reinforce practices of management and control, some of which may be oppressive.

Computer Networks and Society

But networks are not confined to educational institutions and the workplace of large organizations. Indeed, they have become almost ubiquitous. And while I cannot begin to address all of the implications of computer networks and society, it is important to describe some of the significant trends, such as the information superhighway. Promotion of a national information superhighway based in computer networks has been in the political arena for a number of years. Politicians from both liberal and conservative camps identify networks with the well-established rhetoric of stronger educational systems and increased national competitiveness. Networks have made prime time, presented as an inevitable next step in our heritage of technological progress. Much is already in place. Thousands of electronic bulletin boards daily connect millions of people. The Internet, in 1992, connected 8,000 computer networks, 1.3 million computers, and about 8 million users. Since then, the size of the Internet has at least quadrupled: the World Wide Web alone, at the time of this writing, consists of more than 27,000 "pages," with that number doubling every fifty-three days (Cortese, 1995). Industry and government have pushed forward in the development of a national backbone network, relying on fiber-optic and frame-relay technologies, not waiting for other kinds of funding and endorsements (Thyfault, 1993). When fully implemented, the information superhighway will interconnect business, education, and government. Branching off the superhighway, single digital links will serve homes, providing access to distance education, to enhanced communication services, and to greatly expanded options for entertainment.

As it moves from private to public spheres, computer networking looks like an "escaped" technology. The printing press, a communications technology developed primarily to meet contemporary demands for religious publications, introduced a new industry with explosive growth in the fifteenth and sixteenth centuries, forever changing legal systems, literacy rates, concepts of authorship, and a host of other factors (Eisenstein, 1979). The telephone, another communications technology characterized by very limited anticipated uses (see, e.g., Lockwood, 1891, pp. 16–17, who suggests their use within a business as speaking tubes and burglar alarms), also anchored a new industry, grew with tremendous speed, and had a wide variety of unanticipated social and cultural consequences, especially for women; interestingly, telephony was seen at the turn of the century as a technology that would encourage egalitarian communication, a force that could help level and democratize an increasingly stratified society (Rakow, 1992). These technologies created or intensified profound, often surprising, social changes; it seems likely that the entire computer age is another such revolution in the making.

Future Computer Networking Scenarios

If one takes research on computer networks from writing scholars and applies it to the vision of an entire networked society as described above, a compelling picture emerges. Networks become a site for meaningful exchanges of ideas, exchanges unbounded by gender, ethnicity, or visual or dramaturgical cues that might marginalize the communicators (assuming text-only communication). People using networks exhibit a special engagement in their discussions. New network-mediated discourse communities form, free of the constraints of geography and time zones, encouraging a fluid, dynamic, responsive society. Massive horizontal communication—communication among people anywhere—decenters political power, undermining the ability of centralized government to channel popular thinking and of mass media to select information and shape its consumption. Electronic democracy consists of thousands of well-connected interest groups, of millions of well-informed citizens. Concepts of authorship fundamentally change in a shift toward nonlinear, interactive texts. Text itself becomes a problematic concept as it incorporates (as it can now) increasingly sophisticated elements of sight and sound. Expand this picture to global interconnectivity, and a web of distributed processing and instant messaging renders traditional geographic and political boundaries obsolete. It is interesting to speculate about the consequences of this on our self-conception, when interconnectedness and distributed processing replace the solitary processor as the operational metaphor for cognitive activity. If this were to be the future, I would have no reservations about computer networking in the classroom. But the reality is likely to be more complex.

Networking technology does not exist in a contextual vacuum. Networks, on whatever scale, have been developed and supported by institutions that have a stake in their use. The origins and much of the current use of networks revolves around information control as much as distribution. Networks are designed to support the productivity and efficiency that strengthen existing organizations; recent efforts to recentralize control of computer networks supports traditional hierarchy rather than decentering it. In this sense, computer networks support maintenance of the status quo, not change.

The importance of preexisting power distribution can even be seen in classroom use of computer networks. Use by students of computers is strongly affected by the kind of environment created by the writing instructor (see Greenleaf, 1994); in one study, students made limited use of a computer network when the instructor dominated the conversation (Thompson, 1988). To students, the teacher can be an authoritative presence on the network, someone who could always be watching what students say, a constant reminder of the institutional reality of evaluation and assessment. This is what Hawisher and Selfe (1991) warn of when they raise the image of the Panopticon: on a network, you never know who is watching. It can become a tool of discipline.

Writing instructors can do much to combat this perception by creating an environment of openness and trust and by modeling positive use of the computer network. In the workplace, however, where there is generally less concern about maintaining a supportive environment than in the classroom, surveillance over networks can have real consequences. In a study of technology use in one large corporation, I found that few employees used e-mail to convey anything more than routine types of messages (e.g., time cards due, notice of department meetings). Feelings of uncertainty permeated this corporation, due to market reversals and lay-offs, and in this unpredictable environment, employees feared surveillance by management if they communicated over computer networks; they did actively communicate, but they chose to use the telephone or face-to-face conversation (Hansen, 1992). In this case, it was not clear whether surveillance actually took place. Nonetheless, its perception alone affected network use. In fact, corporate employees have no legal right to privacy in computer networks, unless that particular network is tied to a public computer network (Bing, 1990). However, there are some legislative efforts under way to change this ("Legislation," 1991). Surveillance ties in with network security: a large body of literature in computer science journals and the computer industry trade press deal with network security. An employee's right to privacy is seldom, if ever, an issue.

Privacy and surveillance are also significant factors in considering computer networks outside the classroom or outside the organization. Networks with public access—like the information superhighway—could be susceptible to surveillance by the various organizations that support and implement them, namely, the government, business, and educational institutions. At the same time that networks introduce new possibilities for communication, potentially giving voice to those who might otherwise be silenced, they also introduce a new potential for violation of privacy rights. This is not simple paranoia. The federal government has endorsed the adoption of "clipper chips" in all telephone and computer equipment. The chips, developed by the National Security Agency, contain a component that can facilitate law enforcement agencies (with special access codes) in intercepting and decoding computer communications ("U.S. Adopts Chip," 1994; Vaughn-Nichols, 1995). Knowledge of this potential may have a dampening effect on network use or even shape computer networks as a means for political suppression. Acknowledging trends like these, Cynthia Selfe and Richard Selfe still advocate seizing network resources for resistance, as the "virtual landscapes" of massive networks may prove too complex for anyone to control (Selfe & Selfe, 1996).

Other factors besides privacy and surveillance may undercut the potential benefits of networked communication. One major factor with many dimensions is access. Access may well be affected by gender. It has become a truism that men tend to use computers more than women (and boys more than girls). Although some have applied feminist theory to networks in the classroom and viewed this use favorably (Selfe, 1990; Flores, 1990), others, when looking at the use of these technologies in society at large, are far, far more critical (e.g., Jansen, 1989; Greenbaum, 1990, who notes that computer systems themselves are gendered in important ways). A tendency for computer networks to become another forum for men to speak may be reduced in the closed world of the classroom, but might be a significant issue in larger settings. The importance of entertainment as a goal for the information superhighway should also give pause in this regard: one aspect of this is likely to be growing participation in interactive gaming, and many current computer games perpetuate destructive images of women as victims or sexual objects.

Another factor affecting access on a societal scale is tied to resources: Who can afford connection to the information superhighway? Without strong, progressive policies to ensure that lower-income families and individuals have the same access to the expanding horizons of available information, computer networks may help cement, rather than ameliorate, existing inequities in society. Rather than promote diversity and egalitarian communication, networks may further solidify the bonds of the dominant culture. Indeed, the status quo interests of the powerful institutions necessary to implement far-flung networks may be realized in access restrictions that overwhelm the positive tendency for networks to engender constructive, critical communication. On a global scale, network access may be economically determined, with networks interconnecting the commercial enterprises and governments of powerful, wealthy nations and excluding developing nations as unprofitable and unproductive. Consequently, access may be doled out to developing cultures—carefully defined access—in return for interests in natural resources or political considerations. In this scenario, computer networks enable technological colonialism.

Finally, I think it is a fair question to ask, who wants computer networks in the classroom? Who provides the equipment? Who encourages its use? There are many responses to this, and only one requires reflection. When computer vendors provide equipment, when corporate foundations provide grants for educational technology, they may have two goals (among others) in mind. One is to develop consumer markets for computer equipment— once trained in using computers for writing and other activities, students are far more likely to acquire their own. The other is to allow students who are computer literate (and network literate) to move seamlessly into the productivity- and control-oriented corporate workplace, accepting the use of these technologies as unavoidable, essential, and beneficial.

Conclusion

My point in writing this, as I stated at the beginning of this chapter, is to convey some of the many purposes and points of view that surround this technology and to connect networks clearly to the social contexts that affect and often define their use. I want to conclude by noting that I am actually an enthusiast (if a cautious one) about the potential of computer networks for accomplishing many of the benefits discussed above—whether used in classrooms or in society at large. I am less sanguine about their use in large organizations such as corporations. In general, corporate management is not interested in sites for social construction, in postmodern dissolution of traditional authority, in personal exploration through communication. If a computer network in a corporation were left unmonitored, over time, perhaps some of these elements would emerge. But networks are monitored, if only haphazardly, and corporate employees always feel the appraising eyes of upper management. These are the workplaces that will employ many of our students. Will we have given them a false sense of security concerning the use of computer networks? Will they view these technologies as neutral or transparent? As we plan to integrate computers and computer networks into our writing classrooms, we need to keep in mind that they are designed to play a role in supporting the organizational hierarchy, that the "bottom line" for their use is reduced costs from increased worker productivity and control. These are goals that are antithetical to those of the writing classroom. Some of these goals may well affect the configuration of computer networks on a societal level as well.

I do not mean to advise that we turn our backs on this technology. I share a sense of inevitability in regard to the growth of computer networking and a sense that we can employ networks for our own purposes, as Selfe and Selfe suggest. What we also need to do as instructors is address the many social issues surrounding technology with our students, to encourage not fear, but self-conscious, critical use. Students themselves, given the opportunity, will raise many of the issues suggested here, and these issues provide fruitful ground for class discussion or written explorations. Students can—should—emerge from writing classes that include the use of technology with an understanding of its benefits, a certain level of comfort in its use, and, perhaps most important, a realization that technology cannot be separated from the dynamics of society or students' responsibilities as human beings.

References

Barker, T., & Kemp, F. (1990). Network theory: A postmodern pedagogy for the writing classroom. In C. Handa (Ed.), *Computers and community: Teaching composition in the twenty-first century* (pp. 1–27). Portsmouth, NH: Boynton/Cook-Heinemann.

Bing, G. (1990, February). The e-mail privacy dilemma and some solutions. *Network Computing*, 10.

Boiarsky, C. (1990). Computers in the classroom: The instruction, the mess, the noise, the writing. In C. Handa (Ed.), *Computers and community: Teaching composition in the twenty-first century* (pp. 47–67). Portsmouth, NH: Boynton/Cook-Heinemann.

Bump, J. (1990). Radical changes in class discussion using networked computers. *Computers and the Humanities, 24*, 49–65.

Cooper, M., & Selfe, C. (1990). Computer conferences and learning: Authority, resistance, and internally persuasive discourse. *College English, 52*(8), 846–869.

Cortese, A. (1995, February 2). Cashing in on cyberspace. *Business Week*, 80–86.

Duin, A., & Hansen, C. (1994). Computer networks as social construction and social interaction: An overview. In C.L. Selfe & S. Hilligoss (Eds.), *Literacy and computers: The complications of teaching and learning with technology* (pp. 89–112). New York: Modern Language Association of America.

Eisenstein, E. (1979). *The printing press as an agent of change: Communications and transformation in early modern Europe.* New York: Cambridge University Press.

Ferrara, K., Brunner, H., & Whittemore, G. (1991). Interactive written discourse as an emergent register. *Written Communication, 8*(1), 8–34.

Flores, M. (1990). Computer conferencing: Composing a feminist community of writers. In C. Handa (Ed.), *Computers and community: Teaching composition in the twenty-first century* (pp. 106–117). Portsmouth, NH: Boynton/Cook-Heinemann.

Forsythe, J. (1991, August 5). A decade of PCs. *Information Week*, 24.

Greenbaum, J. (1990). The head and the heart: Using gender analysis to study the social construction of computer systems. *Computers and Society, 20*(2), 9–17.

Greenleaf, C. (1994). Technological indeterminacy: The role of classroom writing practices and pedagogy in shaping student use of the computer. *Written Communication, 11*(1), 85–130.

Greif, I. (Ed.). (1988). *Computer-supported cooperative work*. San Mateo, CA: Kaufmann.

Hansen, C. (1992). Flow, form, context, and technology: A model for understanding communication in a business setting. Unpublished doctoral dissertation, University of Minnesota.

Hartman, K., Neuwirth, C., Kiesler, S., Sproull, L., Cochran, C., Palmquist, M., & Zubrow, D. (1991). Patterns of social interaction and learning to write: Some effects of network technologies. *Written Communication, 8*(1), 79–113.

Hawisher, G.E., & Selfe, C.L. (1991). The rhetoric of technology and the electronic writing class. *College Composition and Communication, 42*(1), 55–65.

Jansen, S. (1989). Gender and the information society: A socially structured silence. In M. Siefert, G. Gerbner, & J. Fisher (Eds.), *The information gap: How computers and other new communication technologies affect the social distribution of power* (pp. 196–215). New York: Oxford University Press.

Lancaster, F. (1978). *Toward paperless information systems*. New York: Academic Press.

Legislation could restrict bosses from snooping on their workers. (1991, September 24). *Wall Street Journal*, B1.

Lockwood, T.D. (1891). *Practical information for telephonists*. New York: Johnston.

Mabrito, M. (1991). Electronic mail as a vehicle for peer response. *Written Communication, 8*(4), 509–532.

Malone, T., Grant, K., Lai, K., Rao, R., & Rosenblitt, D. (1988). Semistructured messages are surprisingly useful for computer-supported coordination. In I. Greif (Ed.), *Computer-supported cooperative work* (pp. 311–331). San Mateo, CA: Kaufmann.

Morgan, G. (1986). *Images of organization*. Newbury Park, CA: Sage.

Murray, D. (1991). The composing process for computer conversation. *Written Communication, 8*(1), 35–55.

Olaniran, B. (1994). Group performance in computer-mediated and face-to-face communication media. *Management Communication Quarterly, 7*(3), 256–281.

Panettieri, J. (1993, September 20). Out for a LAN speed record. *Information Week,* 15.

Rakow, L. (1992). *Gender on the line: Women, the telephone, and community life.* Urbana: University of Illinois Press.

Schatz, W. (1992, August 3). Computing without boundaries: In metacomputing, use terminals mask a supercomputing universe. *Information Week,* 22–28.

Selfe, C.L. (1990). Technology in the English classroom: Computers through the lens of feminist theory. In C. Handa (Ed.), *Computers and community: Teaching composition in the twenty-first century* (pp. 118–139). Portsmouth, NH: Boynton/Cook Heinemann.

Selfe, C.L., & Selfe, R. (1996). Writing as democratic social action in a technological world: Politicizing and inhabiting virtual landscapes. In A.H. Duin & C. Hansen (Eds.), *Nonacademic writing: Social theory and technology* (pp. 325–356). Hillsdale, NJ: Erlbaum.

Siefert, M., Gerbner, G., & Fisher, J. (Eds.). (1989). *The information gap: How computers and other new communication technologies affect the social distribution of power.* New York: Oxford University Press.

Sirc, G., & Reynolds, T. (1990). The face of collaboration in the networked writing classroom. *Computers and Composition, 7,* 53–70.

Sproull, L., & Kiesler, S. (1991). *Connections: New ways of working in the networked organization.* Cambridge, MA: MIT Press.

Thompson, D. (1988). Conversational networking: Why the teacher gets most of the lines. *Collegiate Microcomputer, 6*(3), 193–201.

Thyfault, M. (1993, September 20). Data highway: Picking up the pace. *Information Week,* 56.

U.S. adopts chip giving it access to messages. (1994, February 5). *Minneapolis Star Tribune,* 7A. [Summarizes an article first reported in the *New York Times.*]

Vaughn-Nichols, S. (1995, February). It's alive: Clipper's still kicking. *Internet,* 62.

Chapter 11

Gaining Electronic Literacy: Workplace Simulations in the Classroom

Nancy Allen
Eastern Michigan University

Industry generally expects communicators to be skilled with electronic communications. Some debate exists, however, as to how these skills are best acquired. Focusing on three detailed examples, this chapter describes how future professionals can gain necessary skills and experience in university courses. While acknowledging that differences between classroom simulations and workplace realities can produce problems, the author argues in favor of the benefits that can accrue for both sites through classroom practices.

In today's workplace, many experienced workers have found e-mail to be a quick, easy way to communicate; they consider e-mail and other communication technologies to be part of the job and use them extensively. Unfortunately for newcomers to these technologies, the skills they need for using them don't come with appointment to a position. Those who are new to electronic literacy, whether in an office or a classroom, can find the initiation to be traumatic as they struggle with the technical and social complexities technology brings to communication. For example, on one September morning, several messages from a student new to e-mail appeared in the list of mail on my computer. The messages, most of them only subject lines, looked like this:

From: ENG479405432   23-Sep-1992   10:59.11 am
Subj: thought for the day

216

From: ENG479405432   23-Sep-1992   11:05.52 am
Subj: thought for the day revised

From: ENG479405432 23-Sep-1992 11:11.49 am
Subj: frustration and thought for the day

Sure hope this goes through. Grossmans misquote of
HL *

From: ENG479405432   23-Sep-1992   11:18.32 am
Subj: help with this stuff

From: ENG479405432   23-Sep-1992   II:23.03 am
Subj: AAArrrgh   : (

This student, who was in an upper-division technical communication course, had been given a computer account to help him learn to become a professional communicator. He was expected to gain some facility with electronic literacy by communicating with others in the class and with students and professionals on network lists set up for technical communicators. As his messages that September morning made clear, e-mail was not an easy technology to master.

The need for electronic literacy on the job has been well documented (Anderson, 1985; Caernarven-Smith & Firman, 1992; Hawisher & Selfe, 1991; Ray & Barton, 1991). The best means for acquiring these skills, however, is less clear. The process can be fraught with anxiety, as student ENG479405432 found out, and in some cases can include potentially disastrous results if important information is lost. Shirley Haley-James (1993), a former NCTE President, recently chronicled the trials and occasional shocks she encountered as she learned e-mail in order to facilitate NCTE communications. The problem for newcomers to electronic literacy, whether they be aspiring students or established professionals, is to acquire the necessary skills and conventional knowledge while keeping anxiety and disaster at bay, or at least under control.

The professional writing classroom can provide a bridge between the campus and the workplace by introducing future professionals to the complexities of electronic literacy before they arrive at an office. Within an academic setting, future professionals can learn to handle commonly used hardware and software in an atmosphere that also allows them to explore possibilities, experiment with new approaches, and question implications of the technology in ways that the constraints associated with a job can prevent. According to Ray and Barton (1991), "University English departments are in a position, both theoretically and pedagogically, to encourage institutional interaction, developing the authority of the individual over technology by analyzing the discourse of technology" (p. 281). Classroom discussions of the effects and implications of electronic media for communication allow future professionals to develop understandings that will help them control the technology rather than be controlled by it. Consequently, in the classroom, a newcomer to electronic communication has the opportunity to gain more than proficiency with particular skills. While students develop the technical skills necessary for their future work, they also become professionals who can evaluate the factors operating in a rhetorical situation and recognize their ethical implications (Couture et al., 1985; Knoblauch, 1989). As an added advantage, the explorations that develop these skills and insights occur in a relatively safe environment: a learner's misstep that brings a bomb to the screen or occasionally even "crashes" a system may create embarrassment, but it doesn't risk loss of company data or, possibly, of a job.

Attempting to meet this complex of practical and pedagogical purposes within professional writing classrooms presents teachers and students with difficult issues: they must cover both communication strategies and new technical skills within a traditional academic time frame, deal with differences between a simulation and reality, gain access to appropriate technology within the academy, and adapt to changes in the nature of classroom communications. This chapter describes situations in which these issues have occurred and the ways they have been handled within upper-division professional writing classrooms. The issues are illustrated with examples drawn from testimony by teachers and professionals, from an ethnographic study of a course I observed for one semester, and from the experiences of students in this course and my own. As the descriptions that follow show, incorporating training in electronic literacy into these classes has not been without problems, yet it has also produced some successes and provided students with a foundation of skills and knowledge upon which they can build as they join the professional world.

Adding Electronic Literacy to a Writing Curriculum—A Lesson in Time Management

An important issue related to the e-mail examples shown above is one of allocating class time to technology. Semesters and terms seldom seem long enough to cover the material traditionally included in professional writing courses; now training in electronic literacy is being added to the requirements. Learning to manipulate a computer and a word-processing program takes up class time; adding the complexities of e-mail multiplies these time requirements. Yet, as access to technology on campuses expands, classes from first-year writing through graduate-level professional communication have begun to include e-mail messages as one form of writing students are asked to perform (Susser, 1993). Training in using e-mail has clear practical value, but it takes time— time that might have to be stolen from other class writing activities. Consequently, teachers want multiple value from the electronic experiences: they want their students to gain the technical skills, but they also want them to learn more about concepts surrounding communication and to make progress on course projects.

To help reach their practical and pedagogical goals, some teachers have incorporated e-mail into class projects and made the electronic messages themselves a kind of writing to be examined. On a local-area network (LAN) in computerized classrooms, for example, students leave messages for one another concerning their projects, as they might do with a workplace project. In classes having access to a wide-area network (WAN) like the Internet, students are introduced to the complexity of a network system with its ties to people from nearly anywhere in the world and to vast stores of information while they also learn the syntax and conventions for communicating electronically.

To cite a few examples of WAN e-mail in writing classrooms, in 1992 Tharon Howard at Purdue University established an electronic bulletin board for professional writing students to discuss writing and audience issues. This exchange eventually included students from several U.S. universities and a class from France. Since 1991, Richard Selfe at Michigan Technological University has regularly maintained an electronic bulletin board for students interested in computer-aided publishing. This bulletin board included students and their teachers from four universities in three states and some professional writers. As network technology becomes available, the use of class listservs is also growing throughout the county.

Are the chunks of classroom time required for practicing and participating in network technological skills justified in meeting the combined class goals of attaining professionally useful skills and a theoretically based understanding of communication? The answer to the first part of this question is "yes." Not only does LAN electronic communication occur within offices all over the world (Olsen, 1989), but the Internet is also gaining wider use. A technical writing supervisor from Livermore Laboratories describes a project for which technical researchers and writers in the United States, Russia, Sweden, Japan, England, Italy, and other countries use the Internet to send information to an electronic storage location on the World Wide Web. Though they sometimes face problems with transporting and accessing graphics electronically, project members believe electronic network storage is the form they should be working to develop (Peterson, 1993). Training in the use of networks, then, is likely to be a skill that will be put to use.

Students also use the Internet in ways that are quite different from those usually found at work. For instance, on WAN bulletin boards they discuss issues about which they hold strong opinions with other communicators whom they have only met electronically. These discussions are valuable to the students, partly because some of the participants are professionals in the students' future fields. But such discussions are not typical of the kind of electronic communication that occurs in the workplace, where e-mail tends to be focused on particular tasks. Terri Merte (1993), a professional from a midsized computer software and services company who has also participated on student bulletin boards, found herself impatient with the student messages, many of which she felt were "writing something just to get conversation going. That's not what you use e-mail for in the workplace," Merte said.

Not only do the uses of e-mail differ from workplace to classroom, but so does the form. Merte particularly described differences in the form and content of message subject lines between student and workplace examples. Participants on the student bulletin board, she said, "weren't specific on the subject line. For instance, there were 20 or 30 messages with the subject 'Mac vs. IBM' and 20 or 30 more on 'gender.' People should say 'Costs for Mac vs. IBM' or 'Ease of Use—Mac vs. IBM.' Subjects at work are much more specific" (Merte, 1993). She suggested, for example, that a student group might leave a message with the subject line "Meeting Change," whereas a professional in an office would more likely include a subject line that said, "Tuesday Marketing Meeting Changed to Friday." Those seeing the subject line would thus know if they were affected and whether they needed to read the message for other meeting details, such as an agenda.

As these comments show, becoming a successful electronic communicator in a professional world involves mastering not only the technology but much more. When students join an electronic discussion, they are entering a discourse community and are immediately met with a set of barriers and conventional practices. Some of these barriers are electronic, as was the case with the e-mail message fragments at the beginning of this chapter. To overcome these barriers, newcomers to networks must learn the correct syntax required to communicate with the computer system in exact detail, or their messages will go nowhere. Computers are inflexible taskmasters. Having mastered the local syntax, however, students are not prepared for all future networks they will face. Systems, networks, and list setups vary; success on one does not necessarily mean immediate access to happy messaging on another. Students and professionals also often add an additional technological layer by communicating through modems and the various software packages that support them, each of which has its own syntax. It's no wonder that, after several failures in half an hour of trying, student ENG479405432 finally gave up the struggle with an "AAArrrgh : (" .

Other barriers newcomers face in entering an electronic discourse community are conventional practices that are negotiated and established by that community. Though of a different sort from electronic syntax, a community's conventional barriers are no less real nor easy to deal with. Newcomers wonder: What are acceptable topics? How is one supposed to talk about them? Will anyone care what I say? Often these issues are not as firmly established as newcomers may expect but are, in fact, continually redefined by regularly participating discussion members. Grant Hogarth, a long-term subscriber to several lists, estimates an eighteen-month cycle for questions of who should participate and what should be discussed on lists (1992). He explains that "[t]o participate, a member has to overcome a fear of failure (silence or ridicule) and then state their idea before somebody else does." He refers to those who attempt to limit discussion as "volume/content restrictors."

On an established electronic mail list, questions of topic or style appropriateness arise within a history of community precedents, and after some discussion has occurred, experienced members return the conversation to other topics of interest to the group. A difference with lists established for students is that the discussion may never get past the initial stages to a point at which participants know what is expected of them and have established areas of interest around which future exchanges can center. Discussions on student lists just get rolling nicely when a semester break or summer recess brings them to a halt; when the list resumes, many participants have changed, and negotiations must begin again with tentative new members who are just learning to cope with the technology as well as the discourse community. On workplace networks, those who receive messages related to their responsibilities must respond in some form. On established Internet lists, participants know that, for a number of reasons, there are many members who read the comments posted but don't themselves send messages for others to read. On student networks, those who read without responding can include almost everyone unless teachers help students break the technological and discourse barriers.

The discourse barriers that newcomers encounter during their early experiences with electronic communities reflect the broader culture in which the community is based (see the chapters by Selfe and by Johnson-Eilola and Selber in this volume); however, the fact that this culture is a subpart of our national culture offers little help to the new network user. Few of us, including those experienced with electronic literacy, are likely to have articulated the implications of familiar cultural features or to have explored their relationships to particular discourse practices. Classroom discussions can help fill this gap, giving students the more theoretically based view of communication they need. Students' experiences with electronic communities can serve as grounding for discussions that explore particular community conventions and the effects of community and conventions on all communication. The insights gained will prepare students to be more comfortable and successful as they enter workplace discourse communities, as well as provide them with a better understanding of the culture within which their workplace and profession are situated.

Because of insufficient time to practice technical skills or gain experience with the conventions of electronic communication, students often do not communicate electronically as frequently as their teachers might wish. Nevertheless, through the experiences they do have, students learn electronic communication skills that can be expanded on the job, and they gain firsthand understanding of how communication operates within discourse communities. Class time spent on electronic literacy thus contributes to both practical and pedagogical goals.

Workplace Simulations—A Paper Moon over a Cardboard Sea?

A second important issue surrounding uses of electronic communication in classes hovers around the use of workplace simulations. A complaint sometimes brought against such simulations is that the classroom can never replicate actual conditions that operate on the job. Certainly, classroom and workplace experiences differ, and those differences could discredit a simulation experience in terms of training students for future jobs. Strict adherence to workplace parameters, on the other hand, could undercut academic explorations that are valuable in preparing future professionals. The following example shows these conflicting processes working within a classroom simulation setting.

An upper-division course in writing computer documentation included a project designed to involve students in a writing experience similar to one they might face as professional writers: students were to revise documentation for a software package used to teach calculus through conceptual understanding rather than formula manipulation (Dubinsky, 1989). Documentation for the software was sparse, and the math students were having problems following manual instructions and using the program.

Working in teams, the writing students observed the math students using the manual; then, in groups and in class, the writers evaluated the manual for problems. For example, they noted immediately that the manual lacked both examples and an initial statement explaining the program's purpose. After two weeks during which the writing students observed users and evaluated their research results, one of the professors who used the program with his students visited the writing class to answer questions about the software and its use in the calculus course. The writing students learned about the goals and development of the software program, including the fact that the program and manual had been written and revised entirely on the basis of expert knowledge without any observations of actual users. To this point, the simulation was following a pattern appropriate to a documentation project that might occur within a professional technical communication department.

Following the background research and interview, students began the difficult task of determining what, in fact, they should propose as manual revisions. Their initial task was to prepare memos describing the problem they were attempting to solve and suggest solutions for improving the manual. In class discussions, students gradually honed their combined list of possible solutions until they arrived at a description of a proposed document. They then divided up the tasks required to prepare a finished proposal for the math professors and divided themselves into groups to accomplish these tasks, which included preparing the proposal and developing a scheme for the manual described in it. The work divisions the students established for preparing the proposal were

- choosing graphics to be used in the manual
- preparing a format template for the manual
- preparing a task list to structure the manual
- choosing screens that would need to be pictured
- drafting proposal text on a word processor
- developing the overall proposal structure (including appendixes)

Students were now three weeks into the project, and they had just gotten their project goal defined. Three and a half additional weeks passed before students had a complete first draft of their proposal, and the project was in its ninth week before students agreed that the proposal was finished and sent it to the math professors. They had not yet begun any actual manual revision.

Long, complex proposals for multimillion-dollar contracts in industry may warrant extended time to prepare—an engineer for a large chemical corporation reported a collaboration in which managers of five departments spent three to four weeks in meetings to write a goals statement for a project that would last for three years (Gaston, 1985). However, in industry, nine weeks would be an intolerable commitment of time and salary for preparing a proposal for a small project like the one in this writing class. Were the conditions for this project, in fact, appropriate, or did they give students an incorrect idea of demands they would face on the job? In other words, did this simulation fail because of a focus on pedagogical goals?

One way in which this simulation replicates the workplace is in the multiple tasking required of the student participants. Just as professionals often work on more than one project during a given time period, after seven weeks, when a first draft of the proposal had been completed, these students began initial steps for other projects that they would work on while the proposal was being revised. The value of including multiple projects in this classroom thus partially fulfilled the responsibility of preparing students for realistic work conditions; however, it also contributed to extending the time devoted to the documentation project well beyond work limits. A more realistic setting and task assignment was thus a trade-off with less realistic time requirements.

As with the e-mail experiences described earlier, the need for technical skills affected this documentation project. Many of the students in this class had never used computers like those in the classroom nor the software programs needed to prepare their proposal. After the first week, little class time was spent instructing students on these skills; instead, students gradually acquired technical abilities through experience and by learning from one another. This process offered the worthy pedagogical benefits of empowering classmates as contributing teachers and of distributing authority throughout the class, but it also meant that students worked slowly and unevenly as they gained technical skills. In the workplace, it would be unusual for several of the writers on a project to be unfamiliar with the required technology; if such were the case, formal training would likely occur so that the team could get up to speed quickly.

By far the most important difference between this classroom simulation and a workplace experience was the formal attention paid to a rhetorical understanding of this situation and of communication in general. As the students worked their way through research and drafting for the proposal, they also read about and discussed

- relationships between writers and rhetorical situations
- mythical writers and real writers
- the use of writing to solve problems
- relationships between writers and readers
- reader practices, especially with instructions
- features of good document design
- the task-oriented approach to manual structure
- various approaches to document evaluation

- strategies for engaging readers
- research methods
- proposal purposes and preparation
- document beginnings

While students gained experience with hardware and software skills needed for document production, they also learned techniques for

- working in groups
- performing user observations
- managing complex projects
- dividing and delegating subtasks
- critiquing others' work and their own

The simulation project described here provided students with an opportunity to learn principles of good technical writing as they applied them to a real project. To meet this goal successfully, the classroom setting also had to allow students the freedom to work their way through the various stages at a pace that made the learning meaningful. As a result, many features of this simulation did not faithfully replicate a workplace project. The focus here was on understanding rather than on efficiency, a goal that academe can indulge but industry must often forego. This simulation in many ways may have been unreal, only a paper moon sailing over a cardboard sea, as an old song describes. If workplace realism is the goal, then this classroom simulation failed. But if the simulation contributed to learning that would benefit both the students and their future employers, as this one seems to have done, the simulation should, indeed, be judged a success.

Access to Technology—Varied and Unequal

A third issue for learning electronic literacy in the classroom is one of gaining access to appropriate hardware and software. As technology becomes common in the workplace and on campuses, workers and students are involved with it whether or not the technology is formally included in their projects. Access to technology appropriate to assigned tasks, however, can vary widely. Workers are more likely than students to have technology available that fits their project needs and that is compatible with that of their team partners. Such availability and compatibility are important to getting jobs done efficiently. On campuses, where resources are sometimes scarce and equipment is obtained piecemeal, technology that contributes to task performance and student learning may be available to some team members but not to all or available only in an old, outdated form.

The following example from a basic technical writing course illustrates how access to technology changed the nature of the writing experience for various participants and altered the document produced. For this project, students were to write a report recommending action on a recycling plan to a local city council. Students in the class divided the research and report preparation into subtasks and then worked in small groups on different facets of the problem. The information developed and prepared by each student group was to be combined into one report that would be sent to the city council. One student group acted as coordinators and assumed much of the responsibility for editing and producing the final report draft.

Technology contributed to the successful completion of this report in various ways. First, though the course was not taught in a computerized classroom, most groups used word-processing software to prepare their sections of the report. In addition, the organizational plan developed by the coordinators took students' technical skills a few steps further. Because several of the class members were engineering or technology majors, they had computer accounts available to them. The coordinators instructed the groups on how to use these accounts to exchange report drafts via e-mail. Students who did not have computer accounts were asked to save their drafts on a diskette in generic ASCII characters that could be read by other word processors. The coordinators used these skills themselves to bring more coherence to the report by sending e-mail messages to the other groups about problems with content and format the coordinators found in report section drafts. These problems were then critiqued and resolved in class discussion. By the end of the project, members of three groups were able to master the file transfer capabilities of their e-mail accounts to send their group's section of the report to the coordinators electronically; one group provided a copy of their section on disk and as a paper copy.

Unfortunately, technology also hindered the work of some students. Because students were using computing resources outside the classroom, not all of them had access to similar facilities, nor did they all have equivalent technical skills with which to perform tasks the coordinators requested. One group was never able to overcome the technical problems and didn't provide their report section on either e-mail or disk. Though they were able to hand in a paper copy of their section for a grade, their part of the project did not get included in the combined final report that was forwarded to the city council because they lacked an electronic copy for the coordinators.

While these students were gaining technical skills, largely through the initiative of the coordinating group, they were also learning about rhetorical principles and features of document design through readings and class discussion, as had the students in the computer documentation course. Their oral progress reports revealed inconsistencies in terminology and overlaps in research and topic coverage that the students saw as threats to the success of their work. Their insights prompted spontaneous discussion of ways to develop credibility in their final report. Through this experience, the students also realized the interdependency among their groups and, by implication, other groups working on complex projects. Unfortunately, their experience also points out their dependency on access to compatible technology and electronic literacy. The kinds of writing experiences students received from this project, both formal document preparation and informal messages between group members, varied among students in direct relationship to their access to technology and their skills in using it.

The lack of appropriate and compatible technology on campuses shows up in other ways as well. For example, problems arise concerning the relationship between computers based on different platforms, such as IBM and Apple. Often students' home computers are of one type while the classroom computers are of another. Though software exists to convert between platforms, classes are often not equipped with it. Consequently, students are limited in work they can do outside of class; the inconveniences or inability to transfer between home and campus can result in their spending less time on assignments.

Lack of access to appropriate technology, such as the situations described here, raises serious impediments to students' attempts to gain electronic literacy. Fortunately, as technology becomes more widespread on campuses, these problems should become less common.

Technology and Changing Communication Patterns

An issue that affects both classroom and workplace is the way in which electronic technology changes the nature and substance of the communications that occur. These changes are particularly noteworthy in relation to technology's control over who will communicate. Electronic discussions don't include everyone who has an opinion on a particular topic; they include those who have a computer account, access to appropriate equipment, the necessary technical skills, awareness of electronic discourse practices, *and* a comment to make on the topic. And, though electronic discussions can concern virtually any subject, from the outrageous to the mundane, some of the face-to-face interactions most common today may become rare through technology's influence. These effects on communication offer advantages and challenges to all of us as communicators.

Characteristics of workplace communications related to electronic literacy are discussed in detail in other chapters in this volume (see, for instance, those by Howard, Sims, Dautermann, and Hansen). Here, I will describe one hypothetical example to illustrate how technology can change a common communication, a request to join a co-worker for lunch. Before office e-mail, an employee strolled down the hall to talk with a colleague about having lunch; while they talked, work or social issues may have become part of the conversation as well. Today, with the advent of workplace electronic communication, such interactions may become part of office nostalgia. A message about lunch, or a message along with a picture of the messenger, can appear on a colleague's computer screen as a momentary interruption. The electronic message prompts a brief reply, thus keeping the interaction focused on question and answer with little comment off-topic. Workers may be further inclined to avoid social chat on office networks because such electronic exchanges are public rather than private; companies "own" not only the networks but also the electronic messages they carry.

To carry this example further, for some workers technology also changes or eliminates the conversation that might have occurred over lunch; many professionals now work out of their homes electronically via modem, fax, and telephone, seldom appearing at company offices in person. In 1992 the number of telecommuters working in "virtual offices" through computer connections was 7.6 million, according to the research firm Link Resources (O'Malley, 1994). Colorado, with the Center for the New West in Denver and the Telluride Institute InfoZone project, is presently developing telecommunication facilities specifically directed toward the needs of these professional "lone eagles" and other electronic communicators in its communities (Taylor, 1994). Ann Arbor, Michigan, is home to forty-four executives who use telecommuting to manage 105 factories spread over a dozen states and five countries (Grantham, 1994). Telecommuters represent a clean industry: all these workers need is high-bandwidth communication lines. With today's communication options, those discussing a topic or working on a project electronically may never have met their "co-workers" or "team partners" face-to-face, adding new dimensions to our definitions of these workplace terms. If these co-workers met for lunch, it would likely be in a "virtual deli."

Electronic technology in the classroom also changes the kinds of communications that occur there—between teacher and students, students and other students, and students and writers beyond the classroom. The manual development class described earlier was held in a classroom in which computers were connected to a LAN with class folders for messages on various topics and purposes. Using this network technology, the teacher posted assignments and messages and received homework electronically; students left messages and incomplete drafts for one another concerning the projects on which they were collaborating. In one instance, each student drafted a proposal introduction and developed a structural plan for a complete proposal, which was then posted to the network. The teacher combined these openings and structural plans (without names) into one document, which each student printed at the next class; these copies became the basis for a class discussion of how to construct the final proposal. By referring to their compiled document, students first labeled each opening as "friendly," "efficient," "formal," etc. They then discussed how each of these labels focused on some part of their project (e.g., friendly = the reader; efficient = the task list) and began to determine a structural plan that would include their multiple purposes and reflect the tone they wanted to achieve. Finally, they focused on wording by looking at effective sentences in the openings and began to develop a good opening sentence for their proposal. The classroom computers and LAN facilitated in-class discussion of the proposal by providing a convenient means for collecting and compiling each student's written work and making the combined text easily available. With sufficient computer skills, students could have carried out their discussion without using paper at all by combining and scrolling through the document on-screen. With additional software, they might also have participated in an online discussion of the openings; such an "electronic" discussion could have prepared them with ideas for the "live" discussion that ensued (Langston & Batson, 1990). While technology facilitates interaction, it also influences the nature of those interactions and the identity of participants.

Computer accounts and e-mail add communication avenues to the in-class discussions and face-to-face conferences available with traditional classroom arrangements. Students needn't wait for an appointment or until they have problem grades to discuss before talking with their teacher; they can send short questions about their assignments to their teacher or other classmates as they work. Teachers, too, are more free to interact. Instead of being restricted to office hours for communicating with students, they can read their e-mail at home in the evening or early morning and send individualized responses. Some teachers have even kept in contact with students when they were away from campus because of conferences or illness (though their students may not have counted this as an advantage). In the classes described in this chapter, e-mail messages didn't eliminate face-to-face conferences; they supplemented them, increasing frequency of contact between teachers and students during the courses.

E-mail, of course, also connects students with others outside their classroom, and these interactions have a very different nature from those that occur within a classroom. On bulletin boards and message boards, students aren't seeking approval from teachers but responses from real readers, who are interested in what they have to say. The readers may be students at other institutions or professional writers on the job who subscribe to the same electronic bulletin boards. Through the Purdue-based bulletin board described earlier, technical editing students at Eastern Michigan University were able to send editorial suggestions to a group of students in France, who were practicing their English by writing about a tour of France. On the bulletin board established at Michigan Technological University, writing students from four universities received comments from professional writers in the field that contributed to definitions developed by the group to distinguish electronic publishing from desktop publishing.

Electronic discussions posted to a WAN bulletin board or a LAN class folder designated as a message board can also serve another purpose for a class: they provide an arena in which students can complain—about assignments, their work load, writing practices, and, often, the technology. Examples from the classes described here included complaints about requirements that they use nongendered language in their documents and about the injustice of plunging inexperienced computer users into a course that includes complex desktop publishing software, which more experienced students had used before. Of course, not all discussions on networks and message boards concern writing theory, practice, or pedagogy. During the campaigns of 1992, presidential politics was a frequent target as well as a platform students used to proclaim their own political stances.

Some of the complaints and proclamations on these bulletin boards received sympathetic commiseration; however, other participants on the network often had differing viewpoints and challenged assumptions. In the case of gendered versus nongendered language, for instance, many students both for and against changes in custom held strong opinions. Professionals urged taking a long view; they described the current awkwardness we notice in writing "s/he" or pluralizing to "they" as transitional and offered practical reasons for accepting the temporary inconveniences. Discussions on student bulletin boards often remain unresolved, providing an opportunity for voicing opinions without necessarily leading to consensus (Selfe, 1993). In the bulletin and message boards reported here, issues were seldom resolved, but they were sometimes defused. The negative nature of some electronic discussions, however, provided teachers with a basis for classroom discussions of theoretical issues important to rhetorical effectiveness.

As technology facilitates different forms of communication for writing students, it also presents challenges to their teachers. For example, students' complaints about having to learn technology as well as writing principles may be reflections of their fears. They see their skills with the technology as affecting their grades on writing. If one student who has access to a color printer outside of class prepares a document with multicolored graphs and diagrams, other students don't see the document as demonstrating new technological possibilities. Instead, they fear that such a document, which they have no opportunity to duplicate, may be judged better simply because it "looks" better. Because of such fears, it is especially important that teachers in computer classrooms make clear to students the criteria on which they will be judged.

Technology also changes in-class teacher/student communications in a very direct way: the teacher in a computer classroom sometimes competes for attention with a compelling screen or talks over the clack of keyboard or printer. Such potential problems related to setting can, in fact, contribute to an unexpected benefit. A computer classroom setting for writing classes lends itself to a distribution of authority between teacher and class members in various ways. First, the noise and classroom configurations that come with electronic technology encourage teachers to forego traditional lecture formats and instead to vary their teaching methods by including one-to-one advice as students write. In addition, technically skilled students can gain authority as they help others improve their technical skills and provide demonstrations of particular features. Finally, the communication opportunities of network technology allow student groups to assume responsibility for project work without step-by-step intervention by the teacher. Such arrangements can reinforce students' feelings of empowerment within the class as well as their belief in their writing and technical abilities. These effects can bolster their confidence as they enter the workplace.

Summary

The experiences recounted here demonstrate that the characteristics and uses of electronic technology in the classroom differ from those found in the workplace. Nevertheless, gaining electronic literacy skills in the classroom makes a valuable contribution to preparing future professionals. As students, writers gain practical electronic literacy skills before they enter a job, with all the complexities and hazards specific to a workplace setting. But more important, the classroom setting allows writers to gain these skills in ways that also facilitate a broader understanding of the potentials and limitations entailed in the use of technology. As Couture et al. (1985) put it, university classrooms provide a "protected atmosphere . . . where writers have the liberty to reflect on the full meaning and consequences of their communications in ways the workplace often cannot allow" (p. 421). These experiences can be quite successful in preparing professional writers who are both technically skillful and capable of analytical thinking.

Student ENG479405432, by the way, became very proficient with e-mail and his modem. As the semester drew to a close, he had engaged members of the WAN bulletin board in a wide-ranging discussion of the future of electronic publishing. The technical skills he gained, as well as the information he and others learned from the discussion, will increase his confidence and competence as he enters his profession.

References

Anderson, P. (1985). What survey research tells us about writing at work. In L. Odell & D. Goswami (Eds.), *Writing in nonacademic settings* (pp. 3–83). New York: Guilford.

Caernarven-Smith, P., & Firman, A.H. (1992). An 8-hour to 16-hour curriculum in computer hardware for technical writing programs, with reading list. *Technical Communication 39,* 175–181.

Couture, B., Goldstein, J.R., Malone, E., Nelson, B., & Quiroz, S. (1985). Building a professional writing program through a university-industry collaborative. In L. Odell & D. Goswami (Eds.), *Writing in nonacademic settings* (pp. 391–426). New York: Guilford.

Dubinsky, E. (1989, September). Interview.

Gaston, J. M. (1985, September). Interview.

Grantham, R. (1994, January 30). A2HQ. *Ann Arbor News,* E1 ff.

Haley-James, S. (1993, November). Entries from a new e-mail user's notebook. *Computers and Composition 10*(4), 5–10.

Hawisher, G.E., & Selfe, C.L. (Eds.). (1991). *Evolving perspectives on computers and composition studies: Questions for the 1990s.* Urbana, IL: National Council of Teachers of English; Houghton, MI: *Computers and Composition.*

Hogarth, G. (1992, November 27). Message I.D.: <**01GRN7UV5VS-08WX94J@ulkyvx.bitnet**>. Computers and Composition Digest (R. Royar, moderator).

Knoblauch, C.H. (1989). The teaching and practice of "professional writing." In M. Kogen (Ed.), *Writing in the business professions* (pp. 246–264). Urbana, IL: National Council of Teachers of English and Association for Business Communication.

Langston, M.D., & Batson, T.W. (1990). The social shifts invited by working collaboratively on computer networks: The ENFI project. In C. Handa (Ed.), *Computers and community: Teaching composition in the twenty-first century* (pp. 140–159). Portsmouth, NH: Boynton/Cook-Heinemann.

Merte, T. (1993, December). Interview.

Olsen, L.A. (1989). Computer-based writing and communication: Some impressions for technical communication activities. *Journal of Technical Writing and Communication 19*(2), 97–118.

O'Malley, S. (1994, January). Home sweet office. *Michigan Country Lines*, 23.

Peterson, S. (1993, March). Interview.

Ray, R., & Barton, E. (1991). Technology and authority. In G.E. Hawisher & C.L. Selfe (Eds.), *Evolving perspectives on computers and composition studies: Questions for the 1990s* (pp. 279–299). Urbana, IL: National Council of Teachers of English; Houghton, MI: *Computers and Composition*.

Selfe, R., Jr. (1993). Dissensus to what end? Technical communicators at a distance. Paper presented at the Ninth Conference on Computers and Writing, Ann Arbor, MI.

Susser, B. (1993). Networks and project work: Alternative pedagogies for writing with computers. *Computers and Composition 10*(3), 63–89.

Taylor, L. (1994, January 26). Message I.D.: <**Pine.3.05.9401262208.C8722-b100000@teal.csn.org**>.

Chapter 12

Tales from the Crossing: Professional Communication Internships in the Electronic Workplace

Robert R. Johnson
Miami University

Internships are integral to many professional communication programs and represent many students' first exposure to writing in a specific workplace. Drawing on a decade of formal internship reports required of master's-level students in his university's program, the author describes three ways students interacted with computers during their internships: writing with, writing for, and writing through the computer. He concludes that professional communication programs should include techniques of collaboration, connections with industry, as well as theoretical and historical issues in their curricula.

Internships have been a central feature of technical and scientific communication programs for at least two decades, and their presence in one form or another is probably an expectation of most present curricula (Storms, 1984; Bosley, 1988; Coggin, 1989). As Sherry Burgess Little (1993) has argued, internships are more than just pragmatic experience. They are, in fact, a source of experiential learning that, on one level, introduces a student to the practical rigors of the profession but that, on another level, can help to guide the theoretical goals of professional writing education. Put simply, internships help to enrich the education of the professional

I thank Gail Bartlett, a former student in the Master's in Technical and Scientific Communication program, who helped conduct valuable archival research into the internship reports discussed in this chapter.

238

communication student and, at the same time, provide a similar enrichment to our programs. Yet, the "return trip" of this two-way street back to those of us in the academy is often neglected. By that I mean we have been remiss in examining the experiences of our interns. This is not to say that we have totally missed this opportunity to research industry and other large organizations through the eyes of our students, but for the most part I believe we have not attached the same purpose to understanding these experiences as we have to, say, ethnographic studies of the workplace. To the end of learning something from our students' experiences, then, I offer the following portraits of a few students who have "crossed the bridge" to the nonacademic writing world and returned to tell about it in formal internship reports.

In following the focus of this collection, however, I am going to concentrate on the stories of several students who have encountered the electronic workplace: a place where the professional communicator's image, role, and status are as mutable as the computer medium. To begin, I will explain the context of internships in Miami University's Master's of Technical and Scientific Communication (MTSC) program. Following this, I will discuss three situations in which professional communicators can be found—writing with the computer, writing for the computer, and writing through the computer. The intent here will not be just to define these various situations of the electronic workplace, but to examine the social aspects of these situations. That is, I want to expose what the electronic workplace means to writers, especially those writers who are finding their way into the social strata of the workplace. Finally, I will offer some thoughts on the role of internships in professional writing curricula in light of these students' experiences.

MTSC Internships and the Formal Report

A full-time internship is a requirement of the Miami MTSC program. After completion of at least six of the eight required courses in the program, each student seeks an internship with an institution that is as close to the student's chosen technical or scientific area as possible (often in medical, environmental, computer, or manufacturing organizations). As the MTSC Regulations Governing Internships states:

> The essential feature of an internship is that the student works full-time for at least one semester (or at least fourteen weeks in the summer) in a professional capacity with the guidance of a person knowledgeable about technical and scientific communication. A student may arrange an internship with a business, government or non-profit organization anywhere in the world. ("Regulations," p. 1)

In addition, the regulations stipulate that the employer is responsible for ensuring that (1) the student will be paid; (2) the organization will share evaluations of the student's work and cooperate with the student's supervisory committee to monitor the internship; (3) the student will be allowed to share samples of her or his work; and (4) these samples can be published in a report written after the completion of the internship experience.

After completing the internship, the student is required to write a formal report based upon the experience and submit it to his or her committee for approval. The reports were originally not limited in length, but in 1988, after an external review of the MTSC program, the faculty decided to limit the report to approximately twenty-five pages. Most of the reports discussed in this article are from the post-1988 period, so let me briefly describe their form and content.

As I have already stated, these reports are formal. That is, they follow a fairly prescribed format consisting of four chapters (Chapter 1 describes the company or organization; Chapter 2 overviews the internship; Chapter 3 focuses on one major project; and Chapter 4 reflects upon the experience and relates it to what the student learned in her or his coursework at Miami). Also, the report must conform to Miami library thesis format conventions because it is ultimately published and filed in the library like a traditional master's or doctoral thesis. Once completed (which usually entails several revisions under the guidance of the committee chair), the report is read and approved by a committee consisting of two MTSC faculty and one faculty member from outside the English department.

A Note about My Method

The methodology that I have employed here is textual and qualitative. Thus, the formal reports filed with the Miami library are the primary source of information. While this method of interpreting people's experiences may be somewhat limited, I have found it to be an interesting technique because the reports themselves are highly narrative and thus they contain stories from a first-person perspective. Often rich in description and full of political and social tensions of the workplace, these texts are a significant source of information about our students, the workplace, and the often discussed "bridge" between academe and industry.

Also, because the main purpose of the internship report has obviously not been to discuss the role of electronic technologies in the workplace, I have chosen to discuss the reports in a qualitative manner. I have done this in order to focus on the cases of several individuals whose experience represents what I see as crucial problems with electronic literacy in the workplace for professional communicators. On the one hand, this is a highly interpretive methodological stance that I have taken, and I take responsibility for its limitations. On the other hand, though, I do not want to imply or mislead anyone into thinking that this research is anything akin to a survey of electronic workplace literacy.

Writing with the Computer: Using Computers to Build a Community

Using the computer as a tool is a common theme in the internship reports, and although I do not wish to imply a historical progression of these internship experiences, it is probably safe to say that this impact of the computer on workplace literacy has the longest heritage in the reports. As you might expect, the problems of learning how to use new electronic devices was a common experience, especially in the early reports, and reports of learning new platforms or new software is a recurring theme. In the late-1980s' reports, the advent of desktop publishing sent some interns either to tutorials or to workshops to learn how to do their jobs (Mason, 1987; Neild, 1990). Learning about computers, however, was often not seen as a problem but was welcomed as a way to advance or do more interesting work. For instance, one student wrote that, "I started with a general interest in writing and, as I worked in industry, developed an interest in computers" (Silletto, 1987, p. 7). Another mentioned that "[m]y enthusiasm and willingness to learn about computers enabled me to secure the internship in spite of my relative inexperience in that technical area" (Puterbaugh, 1988, p. 2).

Two other common references to electronic literacy involved issues of access and knowledge of system setup. In some of the earlier reports (pre-1990), there were several discussions of lack of access to computers. One intern found herself working away from the main desktop publishing system and then spending long stretches of time at a shared Macintosh to complete projects (Neild, 1990), while another complained several times about having to seek out an available computer because she did not have one of her own (Larsen, 1991). Access to appropriate software sometimes called for creative problem solving, as in the case of one intern who had to hand draw a number of "screen shots" because the system they were using would not take pictures of the screen—pictures that were deemed too important to leave out of the manuals because of the visual learning orientation of their users (Needham, 1993). Finally, some interns discussed becoming the "technical experts" of their offices. Probably the most telling example was one student who, when she arrived at her internship, discovered that she would be solely responsible for the setup of the desktop publishing system she would be using (Nedderman, 1992).

As far as socialization in the workplace is concerned, however, one report presents an interesting twist on how electronic media affect teamwork and collaborative effort. In this internship, the student was employed by a national brewing company as part of an effort to document a computer system in a recently completed facility. Beginning with the first day of his employment, the company made it very clear that the work environment at the plant was based upon the concept of teamwork. As he explained, "As a technical communicator, I worked as part of a team, working closely with every member of the department to obtain and verify sources. I also regularly participated in team meetings in order to seek group input into the procedures I was writing" (Needham, 1993, p. 3).

Although such collaboration might be common in many workplaces, the effect in this case was interesting because the writer had to become involved with the workers for at least two reasons. First, the workers were for the most part complete novices to computers: "[F]or many of them, this was the first job in which they needed to use computers to complete their work" (Needham, 1993, p. 13). He also discovered that much of the knowledge about the computer system was "in the minds" of the workers, and thus he needed to work closely with them to capture the procedures as these users actually perceived them. This close relationship became crucial to his work because, as he later discovered, some of the workers were skeptical of his role in the team. He was seen as an "outsider" who was working on what looked to them to be an academic thesis (p. 21). Hence, trust in the intern was a must.

Second, the intern knew that this was a short-term job. Once he was done with his sixteen weeks, the job of a writer at the plant would be phased out and probably handed over to consulting firms. Therefore, he decided to bring some of the workers into the development stage of the documentation. To accomplish this, he taught some of the workers rudimentary word-processing tasks that would allow them to make updates to the manuals. In addition, he held sessions where he and the workers discussed the features of the manuals and how these features were "tailored to their information needs and individual learning styles" (p. 24).

This example demonstrates how the computer, as an independent publishing unit, allows writers to bring audiences more directly into the actual writing/document-production process. If the manuals produced for this brewery had been sent out to be published, and if the workers had seen the writing as something more removed from their experience, I am sure that they would have been less likely to engage with the team concept as it pertained to the documentation process. Here the workers became part of the writing process and saw themselves, possibly, as producers of texts. I think we can also assume that the quality of the product was enhanced, at least where audience adaptation is concerned.

Writing for the Computer: User Advocacy, Politics, and Authority

During the past decade, writing for the computer industry has been a predominant source of employment for technical writers, and the MTSC internships are no exception. Many of the internships took place within large and small computer software or hardware companies, and even those that were located in "noncomputer" industries often involved writing instructions or reference information for computers. Obviously, most of these internships focused on the creation of print-based user manuals. However, embedded in this high-pressure, constantly changing environment of computer hardware- and software-documentation development is a subtle (and sometimes not so subtle) struggle for identity and power. Probably the most common example of power struggle comes in the context of user testing. At least ten of the internship reports mention some form of user testing of documents (usually at the end of the production process), and a few discuss rather openly the struggle that went on between the writers and managers or developers over the issue of testing the quality of manuals.

The strongest complaints about the reluctance to user test were voiced by one intern who worked for a large aircraft manufacturer. His task was to rewrite a computer database manual for software that aided employees in their training. Repeatedly, the intern asked to evaluate the manual during the production process, but he was consistently denied the time to do so, as management deemed testing too expensive. This intern went so far as to include an iterative testing design which he had developed for the project report, but that recommendation was ultimately rejected by his supervisor. At the end of his internshipo report, he explains that after the final manual went to press, they discovered several problems with the document that resulted in a complete reprinting of the manual. As the intern claims, this costly mistake would most likely have been avoided by some early evaluation; he advocated a test before the next version of the training manual:

> In my final letter to the project leader, I argued for the ne-
> cessity of repeated, preproduction document testing as a
> method of avoiding these various problems in the future. . . .
> I explained that evaluating the document after it has been in
> use for a month or more could improve subsequent versions
> of the Manual. The project leader dismissed the subject with
> a silent response, thus adding to my general frustration with
> the project. To the best of my knowledge, an evaluation of
> the Manual has yet to be performed. (Lukachko, 1991, p. 25)

Here we see a writer who clearly plays the role of user advocate: someone who wants to see users succeed and who wants
the company's product to succeed. However, silenced by a lack
of acknowledgment of his expertise, the intern was left more or
less powerless.

In another case, an intern wrote a reference manual for a complex set of telephone services. These instructions were not for end-
users, but rather were for system administrators and therefore
often entailed complicated procedures. For instance, this intern
described one problem the system administrators dealt with:

> If I'm in Seattle, in an office that uses a 1/1A version switch,
> and I want to forward calls to the Omaha office, which has a
> DMS100 switch, and my branch has features a, b, and c and
> uses AT&T phones, while the Omaha branch has x, y, and z
> with North Telecom phones, what type of call forwarding do
> I need? (Endicott, 1994, p. 13)

This company handled most questions through calls to service
representatives who were subject to heavy work loads. Therefore,
the manual was supposed to alleviate the need for phone support
(a common goal of computer-related companies, to say the least).
In this instance, the intern did manage to carry out some user
testing, but only because of his own initiative. Unlike the intern
working for the aircraft manufacturer, this intern's primary employer was an independent consulting firm which supported the
testing in its own facility.

One simple test was carried out, but the circumstances were
minimal at best: "My test subjects were not [our client's] system
administrators, so the test was far from ideal. But it was the best

we could manage" (p. 19). The tests did reveal several deficiencies in the manual, which included at least one substantial change to abbreviations used throughout the document and several clarifications of graphics. However, in the end the intern saw little benefit from the user tests as far as his relationship with the client was concerned. He laments in his report:

> I believe we produced a useful, informative, instructionally sound manual. But I don't think that's why our client was pleased—he was pleased because the manual looked good, and it made him [*sic*] look good to his colleagues. (p. 19)

While the two preceding examples do not necessarily depict anything outside the everyday experience of most technical writers (meeting deadlines, dealing with budgetary and other managerial constraints, having clients interested merely in the product), they do perhaps ring too true of the value that technical writers hold inside the social structure of industry. The role of the technical writer in the computer industry is constantly that of an underdog—one who must argue consistently for his or her point of view, but then have the argument (whether it is strong or not) discounted offhand merely because what she or he has to say is seen to be of little consequence. Not unlike an assembly line worker, the technical writer helps in the forward movement of the product, but the knowledge of the writer, particularly the knowledge the writer has of end-users or consumers, is sometimes ignored in the process or the product.

Writing through the Computer:
The Medium and Collaboration

As we move away from what Jay Bolter (1991) has termed "the late age of print" and into an era where the computer itself becomes the "text," professional communicators will be expected more frequently to write through the computer. Electronic mail, hypertexts, online documentation, and multimedia presentations or training materials will be common "texts" for the professional communicator. This is already the case for many writers. As far as the internship reports of the MTSC program are concerned, however, there is as yet little discussion of online projects as a communication site because the phenomenon is so new. For example, one report mentions developing a style sheet for online reports at an aerospace organization (Collins, 1992). But the exploration was considered highly experimental in the organization. Another intern (who has just completed an internship with a large software manufacturer) has indicated to me that he will be reporting on some user testing of online documentation. In addition, several interns who are currently employed are working online in one fashion or another, and these reports will be forthcoming.

Fortunately, one intern did have a substantial experience writing through the computer. I would like, then, to conclude my discussion of intern scenarios by concentrating on this student's experience because, although she is the only one reporting about writing primarily online, she does discuss a couple of issues that are representative of the challenges professional writers face (and will be facing) as we shift to a new medium.

This intern was hired to develop a large online help system for users of a popular word-processing software package. Her particular role was to update the current "draft" of the help system to operate under a new version of the software which had recently been released. She researched, wrote, and revised the hypertext itself. As part of the writing and revising, she coded the text to create the online program, ran the authoring programs to create it, and tested it for technical accuracy and completeness (Bates, 1992). Her writing process involved activities both inside and outside the traditional realm of professional writers. In itself, the process of developing this hypertext system would be interesting to analyze. But I'd like to focus here on her discussions of (1) the impact of the medium, and (2) the role of collaboration in the development of online texts.

In the analysis of her internship, Bates openly reflects the sentiments of several researchers when she says:

> Moving from print-based documentation to on-line docu-
> mentation necessarily involves a shift in a writer's thinking.
> . . . At first it was difficult for me to "let go" of my linear
> writing and thinking. I'd write about a topic, view it on-line,
> and discover that I'd repeated information between topics or
> pages that made navigating through the hypertext repetitive.
> Using the product on-line provided me with a whole new
> perspective. (p. 24)

To aid in this new thinking/writing process, she worked with
the other writers to develop a style sheet which would "ensure
consistency between topics and pages" (p. 24). They quickly discovered, however, that the style sheet was constantly outdated
because of the large number of modules in the hypertext. "Each
change and additional on-line function made the existing style
sheet obsolete" (p. 25). Thus, the change of medium affected not
only the individual writer's processes, but it also affected the traditional concept of the style sheet as something that provides consistency for a collaborative project. In other words, instead of being a static foundation for the text-production process, the electronic style sheet became more an integral part of the process—
being reshaped as the project proceeded.

In her internship report, this writer also mentions the importance of developing strategies for collaboration. In its conclusion,
she writes, "Collaborative strategies were vital to the success of
the [online] project" (p. 27). As an explanation of this statement,
she notes that it was imperative for group members to constantly
share sections of the hypertext that contained similar information
to "save time and increase consistency" (p. 27). Also, they kept
track of critical information, like lists of "buttons" that were a
part of the hypertext screens, by posting them on walls around
the office. This informal storyboard technique enabled the writers to stay in touch and, once again, attempted to promote consistency. Finally, she suggests that oral communication, especially
formal meetings, should have been a more central strategy:

> We tried to spread information through memos, but it be-
> came difficult. . . . Frequent meetings might have been a help-
> ful strategy [to allow] members to receive the same informa-
> tion at the same time. (p. 27)

Internships, Computers, and Professional Communication: Our Job Ahead

The internship stories that I have summarized above are, I think, interesting in themselves. As we watch our students enter the workplace, it is encouraging to see them confront their work with such diligence and even courage. We should feel good that they seem, for the most part, to achieve goals that they set for themselves. At the same time, though, these stories are cautionary. What, for instance, should we do in the classroom to better prepare them for the workplace? What is the role of theory, history, or reflection in our curricula? If, indeed, our students may have to argue for status and authority, how might we provide them with the best rhetorical tools to do so? These are, of course, large questions, but below I offer a few thoughts on how we might proceed.

Encourage Collaboration through/with the Computer

Although advocacy for collaboration and teamwork has been extremely visible in both research and the popular press, it has been slow in making an impact on the professional writing classroom. We often engage in peer editing and some group work, but we should make a concerted effort to make these activities central to each professional communication class—be it writing, editing, or designing. As the internship experiences demonstrate, collaboration during the production process is a necessary and even helpful activity. I agree that it can be difficult to achieve success in the classroom with collaboration, particularly when we must assign individual grades or if the outcome of teaching evaluations might be compromised by what students perceive as difficult learning experiences. Collaborate, though, we must.

Constantly Develop Industry Connections

Organizations such as the Council for Programs in Technical and Scientific Communication (CPTSC) have for years advocated the need for ongoing relations between industry and academe. The relationship between electronic literacy and internships makes these connections even more important. For instance, we all know how difficult it can be to obtain, or even just have access to, the kind of expensive computer equipment that some industries use on a daily basis. For this reason if no other, we should be able to tap into industry resources to help prepare our students. In another vein, however, we in the academy should be as visible as possible to industry so that industry personnel become aware of our needs. As I have said elsewhere (Johnson, 1992), the connection with industry is a two-way street, but unfortunately, it often is limited to a one-way flow.

Teach Theory and History

The need for theory and history of technical communication in our curricula might not be apparent in the experiences discussed here, but it certainly surfaces in several critical areas. For instance, the user-documentation writers, if they are ever able to implement usability in their companies, must know of the theoretical implications of user testing and data analysis. Also, some knowledge of the history of user-document testing (and the failures of untested systems) would be helpful in arguing for usability.

Finally, we should continue to use the experiences of our interns to help build understandings of industry communications and of our field in general. Various programs have different ways of keeping track of these experiences, and even if they are not formal reports like those used in the Miami program, tales from the crossing such as these could add enlightening and significant stories to the lore of our profession. That lore should be documented and archived for future students and teachers of professional communication.

References

Bates, C.E. (1992). Writing for the on-line medium: An internship with Comware Incorporated. Internship Report: Miami University, Oxford, OH.

Bolter, J.D. (1991). *Writing space: The computer, hypertext, and the history of writing*. Hillsdale, NJ: Erlbaum.

Bosley, D. (1988). Writing internships: Building bridges between academia and business. *Journal of Business and Technical Communication, 2*(1), 103–13.

Coggin, W.O. (Ed.). (1989). *Establishing and supervising internships*. Association of Teachers of Technical Writing, Anthology No. 9. Lubbock, TX: Association of Teachers of Technical Writing.

Collins, D.B. (1992). Internship as a technical publications editor at NASA Langley Research Center. Internship Report: Miami University, Oxford, OH.

Endicott, J. (1994). Problem-solving models in theory and practice: A case study of the development of a Centrex Plus owner's manual for US West Communications. Internship Report: Miami University, Oxford, OH.

Johnson, R.R. (1992). Refiguring academic-industry relations: Technical communications on a two-way street. In *Proceedings of the 1992 Conference on Programs of Technical and Scientific Communication* (pp. 7–13).

Larsen, R.L. (1991). An internship with the Civil Engineering Dynamics Division of MTS Systems Corporation (Minneapolis, MN). Internship Report: Miami University, Oxford, OH.

Little, S.B. (1993). The technical communication internship: An application of experiential learning theory. *Journal of Business and Technical Communication, 7*(4), 423–51.

Lukachko, C.M. (1991). An internship with General Electric Aircraft Engines (Cincinnati, OH). Internship Report: Miami University, Oxford, OH.

Mason, M.L. (1987). An internship with Oak Ridge Associated Universities. Internship Report: Miami University, Oxford, OH.

Nedderman, K. (1992). An internship as a technical communicator at Texas Process Equipment Company. Internship Report: Miami University, Oxford, OH.

Needham, R.K. (1993). Developing minimal manuals for a team of users: An internship at Miller Brewing Company (Trenton, OH). Internship Report: Miami University, Oxford, OH.

Neild, J.A. (1990). An internship with the Office of Cancer Communications in the National Cancer Institute. Internship Report: Miami University, Oxford, OH.

Puterbaugh, C.C. (1988). An internship with the Management Systems Division of the Procter & Gamble Company. Internship Report: Miami University, Oxford, OH.

Regulations governing internships: For employers of MTSC interns. (N.d.). Master's Degree Program in Technical and Scientific Communication, Department of English, Miami University, Oxford, OH.

Silletto, C.L. (1987). An internship with AT&T Information Systems (Denver, CO). Internship Report: Miami University, Oxford, OH.

Storms, C.G. (1984). Programs in technical communication. *Technical Communication, 31*(4), 13–20.

Tuman, M.C. (1992). *WordPerfect: Literacy in the computer age.* Pittsburgh: Pittsburgh University Press.

Part Four

Approaches to the Study of Electronic Literacy in Workplace Settings

Chapter 13

Theorizing E-mail for the Practice, Instruction, and Study of Literacy

Cynthia L. Selfe
Michigan Technological University

This chapter theorizes electronic mail as a social formation, acknowledging hopes for its ability to democratize, equalize, and enrich communication at the same time as it probes the identities of these electronic spaces as sites of literacy. Using examples of electronic mail use, this chapter argues that political, historical, and cultural forces constitute these spaces—which represent postmodern discursive formations in dynamic cultural landscapes. For educators this means that electronic mail has the potential to become a liberatory and critical practice.

In the October 1993 issue of *College English,* Gail E. Hawisher and Charles Moran offered English teachers the "beginnings of a rhetoric and a pedagogy" for including electronic mail in their professional "field of vision," pointing out that electronic mail has become "a medium for the exchange of the written language" and, thus, "a proper subject for study" for literacy educators and scholars in the "field of composition theory" (p. 629). Building on this work, professionals in English composition studies will continue the process of learning about electronic mail as a setting for human communication and literacy activity, tracing the ways in which this particular landscape affects—and is affected by—the readers and writers who inhabit and create it. This chapter suggests that the complementary activity of theorizing the landscape of electronic mail as a site of culturally determined language activity is an equally important effort—and one inseparable, at a fundamental level, from rhetorical and pedagogical explorations.

E-mail—as a technology that supports an increasingly broad range of literacy activities and communicative exchanges—exists within a complex web of social, economic, and ideological formations and systems (see Hansen, this volume). For literacy educators this means that they must recognize e-mail as an artifact invested with the interests and the ideologies of its designers, marketers, owners, and users rather than seeing it as a neutral tool. Examining e-mail through the lens of theory can help reveal the extent, and the nature, of these interests and the various ways in which they influence and are influenced by culture. Lacking this perspective, we would have a difficult time constructing a robust understanding of how this new technology functions.

Among the important questions that such theorizing activity can help our profession frame and address are:

- What is the cultural, political, ideological, and technological landscape within which e-mail exists? What are the relationships between e-mail and the ongoing social projects that serve as landmarks within this landscape: the belief in technological progress, the growth of the American economy, the expansion of global capitalism and democracy, and the improvement of the American educational system? Who benefits from the tendential force of this complex set of relationships?

- How are literate behaviors enacted within the various sites of e-mail systems? What are the relationships between electronic literacies—which include, as Hawisher and Moran (1993) suggest, a knowledge of e-mail systems—and changing concepts of subjectivity and agency, especially as these concepts figure centrally in the education of a literate citizenry?

- Given the recognition that e-mail systems are so complexly articulated with cultural, political, and ideological formations, what can teachers and students hope to accomplish in terms of political agency and social change within these sites?

The Promise and Potential of E-mail

Electronic mail, or e-mail, refers to the exchange of messages within a system of networked computers—either a local-area network (LAN) comprised of machines in one relatively small geographical location or a wide-area network (WAN) comprised of machines in several such locations. The term "e-mail"—generally used to refer to electronic messages—is difficult to consider in isolation from the systems of hardware and software that support the exchange of such communications. The vast majority of e-mail traffic takes place on the Internet, a global complex of more than 5,000 WANs, twenty-six countries, and several million users on more than 300,000 computers in several thousand educational institutions, businesses, and public agencies around the world (Cerf, 1991, p. 80). Supporting e-mail traffic in the coming decade—at least in the United States—will be the National Information Infrastructure (NII), a complex of telecommunication and computer-support systems, and the National Research and Education Network (NREN), an electronic highway over which e-mail, as well as other kinds of information, will travel.

Discussions of electronic mail, like Hawisher and Moran's (1993) exploration in *College English,* have inspired some hope among educators that e-mail environments might offer enhanced possibilities for literacy education and literacy activity. E-mail's potential as a landscape for literacy education is suggested by two primary sources of observations: first, involvement in, and observations of, e-mail exchanges themselves; and second, studies of related electronic communication environments—among them, online conferences, synchronous and asynchronous discussions, and telecommunication exchanges.

These studies and discussions suggest that online writing spaces have the potential of supporting increasingly open discursive exchanges characterized by the democratic consideration of—and the free participation in—public concerns and issues. Among the claims and hopes that educators have identified for such spaces are that they can

- support increasingly democratic, pluralistic, and egalitarian communication (Faigley, 1990; Lanham, 1989; Bump, 1990; Selfe, 1990; Schuler, 1994);

- support the open discussion of, research on, and education about civic issues that face our culture (Gore, 1992 and 1993; Telecommunications Policy Roundtable, 1994; Schuler, 1994);

- allow more people to access information and to communicate about issues and topics, including those who find traditional face-to-face exchanges less than amenable and those whose exchanges are constrained by time and/or distance (Gore, 1992 and 1993; Hiltz, 1986; Spitzer, 1989; Bump, 1990; Schuler, 1994);

- support increasingly rich possibilities for collaborative communication (Bump, 1990; Shriner & Rice, 1989; Eldred, 1989; Hiltz & Turoff, 1993) and for discursively based collective action on progressive political projects and research efforts (Clement, 1994; Gore, 1992 and 1993; Schuler, 1994; Zuboff, 1988);

- support discursive forums that serve to flatten more traditionally constructed hierarchies in businesses, organizations, and governments by connecting individuals directly to decision makers and to the information used in making decisions (Dubrovsky, Kiesler, & Sethna, 1991; Schuler, 1994; Clement, 1994; Zuboff, 1988); and

- eliminate or modify many of the nonverbal paralinguistic cues (e.g., clothing, status, race, age, gender) which contribute to the differential exercise of power in face-to-face communications (Kiesler, Siegel, & McGuire, 1984; Sproull & Kiesler, 1991a, 1991b).

Taken as a collection, these claims about, and hopes for, online communications express some of the real—and the ideal (Hawisher & Selfe, 1991)—characteristics of electronic exchanges such as e-mail. Interestingly, they also resonate with a set of goals— ideals, really—for global and national computer projects like the NREN and the NII (Gore, 1991; 1993).

The national communicative space to be supported by the NII is currently under discussion by a number of groups, including representatives of business, industry, government, and public organizations. And although these groups, and the individuals within them, differ widely in their makeup and goals, they generally share the Clinton administration's vision of the NII and the NREN as democratic, public utilities that will serve a range of communication purposes and have a broadly positive economic impact. For example, the Telecommunications Policy Roundtable, a coalition of more than seventy public interest organizations hoping to influence the design of the NII, have articulated the following goals for the system (Telecommunications Policy Roundtable, 1994):

- **Universal access:** All people should have affordable access to the . . . NII. Fundamental to life, liberty, and the pursuit of happiness in the Information Age is access to video, audio, and data networks that provide a broad range of news, public affairs, education, health, and government information and services. . . . Information that is essential in order to fully participate in a democratic society should be provided free.

- **Freedom to communicate:** The NII should enable all people to effectively exercise their fundamental right to communicate. Freedom of speech should be protected and fostered by the new information infrastructure, guaranteeing the right of every person to communicate easily, affordably, and effectively.

- **Vital civic sector:** The NII must have a vital civic sector at its core . . . which enables the meaningful participation of all segments of our pluralistic society.

- **Diverse and competitive marketplace:** The NII should ensure competition among ideas and information providers. The NII must be designed to foster a healthy marketplace of ideas, where a full range of viewpoints is expressed and robust debate is stimulated.

- **Equitable workplace:** New technologies should be used to enhance the quality of work and to promote equity in the workplace. . . . Workers should share the benefits of increased productivity that these technologies make possible.

- **Privacy:** Privacy should be carefully protected and extended.
- **Democratic policymaking:** The public should be fully involved in policymaking for the NII. (pp. 107–108)

The goals that Vice President Gore (1993) has articulated for the NII are related closely to those outlined by the Telecommunications Policy Roundtable—although the vice president's goals are set within a framework of economic benefits. In a speech that Gore presented to the National Press Club on December 21, 1993, he noted five primary principles for the design of the NII—that it should

- **encourage private investment:** The Clinton Administration believes . . . our role is to encourage the building of the national information infrastructure by the private sector as rapidly as possible.

- **promote and protect competition:** We should . . . act to avoid information bottlenecks that would limit consumer choice or limit the ability of new information providers to reach customers.

- **provide open access to the network:** We need to ensure the NII, just like the PC, is open and accessible to everyone with a good idea who has a product they want to sell.

- **avoid creating a society of information "haves" and "have-nots":** The most important step we can take to ensure universal service is to adopt policies that result in lower prices for everyone. . . . The less-fortunate sectors of the population must have access to a minimal level of information services through subsidies or other forms of public interest tithe.

- **encourage flexibility of use:** . . . flexibility and adaptability are essential if we are to develop policies that will stand the test of time. Technology is advancing so rapidly, the structure of the industry is changing so quickly, that we must have policies broad enough to accommodate change.

The Cultural, Political, Technological, and Ideological Landscape of E-mail Systems

These discussions of the NREN and the NII suggest a broadly held set of beliefs about technology, characterized most commonly by the notion that computer technologies have the potential—on both micropolitical and macropolitical levels—to support, and even bring about, important sociopolitical change within our culture: expanding avenues of democratic opportunity for individuals regardless of distinctions of race, socioeconomic status, disability, or gender; increasing the equity of both participation and reward within our social system; and equalizing some of the existing power differentials within our culture.

These beliefs, however, have been contested by technology critics and social theorists who make a strong case for understanding computer systems, such as e-mail, as operating within, and indeed often partially comprising, a set of tendential forces in our culture that favor the status quo rather than substantive change. These scholars would argue that computer systems in general have contributed not to social and cultural change, but, rather, to the reproduction of dominant social, economic, political, and ideological tendencies and formations—among them the competitive formations associated with capitalism and the oppressive formations associated with racism and sexism. Tracing the themes of these discussions can be useful to a theorizing of e-mail systems.

Technology and the Conditions of Capitalism

Certainly one of the most consistent relationships that critics have identified has to do with the role that technologies, like e-mail, play in helping to structure social and material relations along the axis of capitalism (cf., Braverman, 1974; Feenberg, 1991; Winner, 1986; Ohmann, 1985; Olson, 1987). In general, these authors argue that technology, when employed within the system of capitalism, serves not only to help achieve the *ends* of capitalism (e.g., to increase efficiency, productivity, and profits) but also to help establish *means* by which capitalism reproduces itself within our culture. Technology, in other words, helps to reproduce capitalism by supporting the particular social formations that allow capitalism to flourish (e.g., the centralization of power, the centralization of control over capital and the means of production, and the distancing of workers from the products of their labor).

In this context, the computer is considered to be not only a tool, used by humans to accomplish work of some kind in an efficient manner, but also—and perhaps more important—as a political technology that effectively structures social relations according to particular patterns associated with capitalism. Thus, it continues to benefit particular groups in our culture (e.g., those who are advantaged in terms of socioeconomic status, the educated, those working in white-collar jobs) by reestablishing their dominance. Langdon Winner (1986), drawing on the work of Marx and Wittgenstein, maintains that computer technology serves as a political tool that humans employ in the "ongoing process of world-making" (p. 17) to shape "social labor arrangements, make and consume products, and adapt their behavior to the material conditions they encounter in their natural and artificial environment" (p. 15).

Winner and others explore the ways in which technology not only contributes to the goals of "efficiency and productivity" (p. 19) that are characteristic of capitalism, but also embodies and reproduces the "specific forms of power and authority" (p. 19) that constitute capitalism as a social formation. As Winner continues to build the case, he argues that technologies "are ways of building order in our world . . . [and that] societies choose structures for technologies that influence how people are going to work, communicate, travel, consume" (pp. 28–29). Winner contends that adopting technology accepts "conditions for human relationships that have a distinctive political cast" (pp. 28–29).

In part, the activity of "world-making" is accomplished through the process of design—the values of capitalism are designed into computers through their features. For example, the expense and the complexity designed into major computer systems and other technologies serve, at least in part, to encourage centralized power and control over these systems, as scholars like Braverman (1974), Winner (1986), Olson (1987), and Ohmann (1985) have pointed out. These factors result in computer systems that are too expensive, too complicated, and too sophisticated to entrust to individual users—users who might make changes to these systems that adversely affect the work of other people. Because these design features encourage the centralized control of large computer systems, they serve, as well, to distance people from the products they create through their labor on computers and from important decision-making power over computers. Although individuals use computers to accomplish the specific work-related tasks assigned to them, they are frequently barred from making important decisions about how the technology is used, what technology is purchased, how technological systems are organized, or how technology is programmed.

An academic example can help reveal this process. Mainframe computers are generally purchased by the central administration of universities to be used as centralized recordkeeping devices that improve the efficiency and effectiveness of the university at large—to assist in the management of accounting, enrollment, and academic administrative tasks. These machines are designed to be so powerful and sophisticated that they must be maintained by a relatively elite group of specialists—programmers, technicians, systems administrators—who maximize efficient use and operation of the computer system and who limit access to mainframe machines to avoid problems that might hinder the achievement of these goals.

To support these centralized systems and to protect them, the administration also purchases and networks a large number of personal workstations that ensure clerical workers, faculty, and students limited access to the central computer system so these individuals can accomplish their work. Given the ways in which these workstations are labeled (e.g., *personal* computer) and assigned (e.g., to individuals on their desks), they give individuals the *impression* that the individuals have control over the technology being used. In actuality, however, individual users have only limited control. Frequently, for example, users cannot choose the software to be used on these machines because software packages must be standardized across the university to allow for exchanges of information and ensure compatibility with the centralized system. Nor do most individuals have the expertise needed to repair, maintain, or program these machines; to customize or change existing software packages; or to configure systems in ways that make them suitable to individual work styles. These personal workstations, moreover, allow individuals access only to certain parts of the central computer system and only to a limited use of that system: for authorized activities that increase the efficiency of the institution—checking enrollments, logging purchases on computerized accounting systems, conducting computer-supported research, registering for classes, accessing information on students, conducting research. To complete this cycle of control, authorized uses of technology are often monitored through the computer system itself—through a system of passwords, monitoring programs, and surveillance by systems administrators—to curtail the use of computer systems in ways that support the goals of individuals or groups outside the administrative ranks.

E-mail systems follow a similar trend—increasingly sophisticated designs lead to the increased equipment costs, and, thus, to increasingly centralized control and hierarchical decision making. In such systems, individuals' control over technology and their access to technology is related generally to socioeconomic status and class. E-mail, for example, while accessible to many individuals on the Internet (e.g., through a personal computer and modem or through a personal workstation), is also removed from popular control in other important ways. The cost of access to an Internet node, for instance, which at Michigan Tech costs $110,000 annually, represents one such limitation. Such nodes depend on sophisticated computer equipment, which must be purchased, configured, maintained, and repaired by experts and technical specialists. Further, these expensive node licenses are funded primarily by the government, by large corporations with access to large amounts of capital, or by educational institutions—often those that do research for the military-industrial complex and the government. The cost of the Internet means that smaller organizations without large amounts of capital may find it difficult to compete. One recent report indicates that three out of four private liberal arts colleges lacked access both to sophisticated computers and to the Internet in 1992—primarily because they could not afford such access (Wilson, 1993). Thomas DeLoughry (1994) adds that "[h]istorically black colleges, institutions serving American Indians, and those with low-income populations" (p. 19) have also gotten a late start in the costly business of getting Internet access.

Nor, as we have pointed out, does simple access to e-mail systems equate with control over technology. Although individuals who have access to e-mail on the Internet can decide some things (e.g., who to send e-mail to, who to include on listservs, or which mail to read and which to discard), they frequently have no control over decision making about the complex systems themselves (e.g., how much access to the Internet costs, where Internet nodes are located, who should design the Internet system, what features should characterize this system, what kinds of e-mail or systems activity should be encouraged or discouraged).

Despite these problems, the complex relationship between technology and capitalism persists because it is based on beliefs that appeal, in a commonsensical way, to a large number of people. Most Americans believe our country should, and must, invest in increasingly complex technologies in order to improve our performance, productivity, and national competitiveness on a continuing basis. Connected with this assumption is the belief that improved products mean increased corporate success for businesses, improved wages for workers, and an improved lifestyle for most Americans. Such beliefs rest at the heart of the reasoning Vice President Gore employs in support of the NREN and the Information Infrastructure and Technology Act :

> The Information Infrastructure bill and the rest of this package of legislation will improve the long-term health of the American economy and help ensure that our children have a higher standard of living than our generation had. It will improve American competitiveness and produce millions of jobs by revitalizing our research and technology base. (Gore, 1992, p. 27)

> By funding the development of new computer technology, this bill will improve the competitiveness of American industry, improve the education and training of American workers, and create entirely new industries. (Gore, 1992, p. 28)

> Federal policies can make a difference in several key areas of the computer revolution. The U.S. Defense Advanced Research Projects Agency (DARPA), the National Aeronautics and Space Administration, the National Science Foundation, and the Department of Energy have all spent millions of dollars. . . . [W]ithout federal seed money . . . American firms would not now dominate the world market for supercomputers. (Gore, 1991, p. 152)

> This kind of growth will create thousands of jobs in the communications industry. But the biggest impact may be in other industrial sectors where those technologies will help American companies compete better and smarter in the global economy. (Gore, 1993)

The vision outlined by these comments comprise what Lyotard (1984) might call a grand narrative of technological progress set within a capitalist frame. The plot of this narrative follows along these general lines: The expansion of the NII and the creation of the NREN—both examples of advanced technologies informed by the insights of science and engineering—will be good for our country and all of its citizens. These technological projects contribute in major ways to our country's progress as a nation. Building such systems will help reverse our flagging economy by creating jobs and expanding the computer industry. The systems themselves will increase our competitiveness, allow us to open new markets for American goods, and help us educate American students to function productively in a highly technological world. Given the cost of these systems, they must be funded, developed, and maintained centrally and in certain secure locations by experts who know how to use them efficiently and effectively.

It is within the articulated ideological relationships revealed by this narrative—where a belief in technological progress, a value on national competitiveness, and the recognition of economic security that is afforded by a healthy capitalist culture are connected—that the identity of computer technology is primarily constituted and reproduced in our culture. There are also, however, additional articulations—between technological progress, access to information, and educational opportunity, for example—that help frame ongoing discussions of computer systems supporting e-mail.

Technology, Information Access, and Educational Opportunity

The relationships among technology, information, and education form a second important set of connections to examine from
a theoretical perspective. In particular, it is illuminating to explore
how these particular social formations are linked by a common
set of cultural beliefs: among them, the belief that public education must introduce students to new communication technology
so that they can learn to access the new kinds of information and
the increased amounts of information available through these
systems; the belief that students exposed to these new communication technologies will be able to function more effectively as
literate citizens in a technological world; the belief that technology will help students learn more efficiently and effectively; and
the belief that learning about technology will allow students to
take advantage of increased opportunities for economic advancement. These beliefs—based on the commonsensical assumption
that success in educational settings will lead to success in professional settings—help establish a strong cultural association between the project of technological advancement and the projects
of improving public education, increasing economic opportunity,
and contributing to social progress.

The potency of these beliefs—enriched by their direct ties to
capitalism—is revealed most clearly when we examine them
within the context of the educational project. Public education in
this country is generally envisioned as a system that prepares individuals to take their place in a democratic society as productive
and literate citizens who have some understanding of democratic
government, some exposure to intellectual issues, and some preparation for making a living in a trade or profession. This belief in a
citizenry broadly educated to take its place in a democratic system is a potent and persistent vision, and one that shapes the current discussions of both the NREN and the NII. In the vice
president's speeches about these projects, he notes that these technologies are designed to provide individuals access to increasing
amounts of information so that they can make "incredibly accurate and efficient decisions" (1991, p. 150) as literate and responsible citizens—an argument that has resonance with other claims

made about the democratizing influence of e-mail and networked conversations (cf., Dubrovsky, Kiesler, & Sethna, 1991; Sproull & Kiesler, 1991a, 1991b; Lanham, 1989).

The act of equating information with knowledge, however, as Winner (1986) points out, "mistakes sheer supply of information with an educated ability to gain knowledge and act effectively based on that knowledge" (pp. 108–109). He continues:

> Surely there is no automatic, positive link between knowledge and power, especially if that means power in a social or political sense. At times, knowledge brings merely an enlightened impotence or paralysis. One may know exactly what to do but lack the wherewithal to act. (p. 109)

In part, this linking of information and knowledge is based on a "functionalist perspective" of literacy (Knoblauch, 1990, p. 76) that remains a strong, informing influence on our cultural understanding of educational projects and focuses on

> the efficient transmission of useful messages in a value-neutral medium. Basic skill and technical-writing programs in schools, many on-the-job training programs in business and industry, and the training programs of the United States military—all typically find their rationalization in the argument for functional literacy, in each case presuming that the ultimate value of language lies in its utilitarian capacity to pass information back and forth for economic or other material gain. (p. 76)

As critical pedagogists point out, however, access to information—whether through computers or other means—does not ensure either literacy or knowledge (cf., Knoblauch, 1990; Livingstone, 1987a; Shor, 1987). The "several million" users (Cerf, 1991) who use Internet-based e-mail systems, for example, have access to the texts of almost every public speech that the president and the vice president have made over the last two years; access to information issued by national, state, and local officials (including offices in the White House); access to policy discussions about a range of topics linked to governmental decision making; and access to the information provided by 3,000–5,000 news groups specializing in various topics (Abbott, 1994). There is no indication, however, that such access has resulted in increased democratic involvement by individual citizens, especially those from lower socioeconomic classes.

In part, the vice president's hopes for technology as a source of information and education have appealed to people because those hopes are based on the popular beliefs that technology can be used within both formal and informal educational systems to increase the general efficiency and effectiveness of educational practice and, thus, to increase the literacy of citizens and their general opportunities for success. This piece of common sense is nested in a larger and related set of beliefs about education in general: that our system of public education provides individuals from all social backgrounds equal access to basic educational opportunities in a democratic fashion; that a system of public education equalizes socioeconomic differences and encourages a classless society; and that all individuals who work hard in schools have access to upward social mobility in our culture (Livingstone, 1987b, p. 133).

The validity of these beliefs, of course, continues to be questioned both by sociologists and educators (cf., Giroux, 1992; Knoblauch, 1990; Livingstone, 1987a; Ohmann, 1985; Shor, 1987). These scholars have noted that schooling—and literacy education—is both a vehicle for the transmission of ideology and a medium within which the transmission of such belief systems takes place. As such, the educational system serves to reproduce the general outlines of existing social formations such as class structure and socioeconomic status, rather than supporting a restructuring of this system. In Ira Shor's words, schooling is a social "device through which a corporate society reproduces its class-based order . . . recreates a stratified society by socializing each new generation into its place in the established order" (Shor, 1987, p. 2).

Within this system, as many technology critics have indicated, the introduction and use of computer technologies seem to magnify and focus the effects of schooling—especially for students who belong to nondominant groups in our culture: those who are not white, not male, not English speaking, and not middle class. Richard Ohmann (1985) describes this relationship in the following terms:

Graduates of MIT will get the challenging jobs; community college grads will be the technicians; those who do no more than acquire basic skills and computer literacy in high school will probably find their way to electronic workstations at McDonald's. I see every reason to expect that the computer revolution, like other revolutions from the top down, will indeed expand the minds and the freedom of an elite, meanwhile facilitating the degradation of labor and the stratification of the workforce that have been the hallmarks of monopoly capitalism. (p. 683)

Mary Louise Gomez (1991) and Emily Jessup (1991) corroborate this view, pointing out that the democratization promised by the computer revolution in the early 1980s resulted only in continued inequities oriented along the related axes of socioeconomic status, class-based privilege, race, and gender. Summarizing the findings of a study by Cole and Griffin (1987), Gomez notes the following:

- More computers are being placed in the hands of middle- and upper-class children than poor children;

- When computers are placed in the schools of poor children, they are used for rote drill and practice instead of the "cognitive enrichment" that they provide for middle- and upper-class students; and

- Female students have less involvement than male students with computers in schools, irrespective of class and ethnicity. (p. 321)

By the end of the 1980s, as this information suggests, computers were present in every school, but they were being used in ways that sustained rather than challenged existing social inequities. Charles Piller (1992), in an article in *MacWorld*, notes that this trend has continued into the decade of the 1990s, making minority populations and lower socioeconomic populations America's fastest growing "technological underclass" (p. 218). Minority students, then, are the least likely during public schooling to gain skills that will serve them well in a world increasingly dependent on technology.

Nor are these effects limited to socioeconomic status and race. Emily Jessup (1991) points to a "gender gap" (p. 338) that exists in educational computing. Citing numerous research studies about computer support (cf., Gerver, 1989; Hawkins, 1985; Becker, 1987), Jessup notes that in programs at all levels of education,

> women tend to be strongly underrepresented. The extent of their underrepresentation varies from sector to sector and to some extent from country to country, but the fact of it is so ubiquitous that the evidence tends to become monotonous. (p. 336)

Computers serve as a discursive medium within which gender values are communicated and emphasized. Faigley (1992), Regan (1993), and Romano (1993), for example, have noted evidence of "sexist, racist, and homophobic" (Faigley, 1992) commentary in synchronous computer-based conversations.

The Potential of E-mail as a Social Formation

Although the trends for computer technology in general seem clearly established, it may be too early to tell whether the particular technologies associated with e-mail will exhibit a similar alignment along these same axes of capitalism, class-based privilege, race, and gender, or exhibit a similar role in the related project of education (or in the workplace, as studies in this volume suggest). There is, however, little evidence to think that they will fail to be so aligned—at least to some degree.

Especially within school systems, for example, uneven access to networks already exists in a pattern that reflects the gap between the "haves" and the "have-nots" (Gore, 1993). According to the current administration's estimates in 1992, only 14 percent of public schools had access to networks that could support broad-based e-mail applications in even one classroom, and only 22 percent of schools had access to one modem. Given this situation, although groups like the Telecommunications Policy Roundtable (1994) call for "universal access," even the vice president notes that access for "almost everyone" (Gore, 1993) is a more realistic goal.

Additional evidence suggests the alignment of e-mail along the related axes we have identified for computer technology in general. E-mail systems, for example, like most computer systems, support a privileging of the English language and, thus, exert a subtle but continuous colonial gesture toward the growing numbers of students in our school systems who speak English as a second, third, or fourth language. Large-scale, networked-based e-mail systems link computers through a common exchange standard called American Standard Code for Information Interchange (ASCII) that does not adequately support languages other than English. ASCII—because it was originally based on a 7-bit code—can handle, as Charles Petzold (1993) points out, only "26 lowercase letters, 26 uppercase letters, 10 numbers, and 33 symbols and punctuation marks" unless it is extended by 8-bit byte computer systems that allow it to handle 128 additional characters. Even with these additional characters, ASCII's alphabetic limitations preclude the full and adequate representation of Greek, Hebrew, Cyrillic, and Han characters (pp. 374–375).

In a recent article about Unicode—a proposed international replacement for ASCII—Petzold (1993) explores some of the implications of relying solely on ASCII:

> . . . there's a big problem with ASCII and that problem is indicated by the first word of the acronym. ASCII is truly an *American* standard, but there's a whole wide world outside our borders where ASCII is simply inadequate. It isn't even good enough for countries that share our language, for where is the British pound sign in ASCII? . . . ASCII . . . is not only inadequate for the written languages of much of the world, but also for many people who live right in my own neighborhood. (p. 375)

What remains most interesting about this situation—especially given that teachers, scholars, and computer designers generally acknowledge the limitations of ASCII—is that the change to a more broadly accommodating system has been so slow, even though the technological means for representing other alphabetic systems (e.g., the memory, the programming mechanics, the computer hardware) have been available for some time now. To change ASCII, however, is to work against a complex set of tendential forces encouraging inertia—existing software, hardware, documentation, and programming approaches. It also requires that individuals and groups in the computer industry abandon English as the *natural* language of computer technology. Such changes do not happen easily or quickly.

E-mail also shows signs of continued alignment along the axes of gender privilege. Pamela Takayoshi (1994), for example, has recently surveyed women on five electronic mailing lists and found that participants have experienced inadequate institutional support when they tried to gain access to e-mail systems, had difficulties in coping with masculinist models of teaching e-mail systems within professional development situations, and encountered direct harassment once they got into e-mail lists. In a related publication, Julian Dibble (1993) has written evocatively of a "rape in cyberspace," describing a *virtual* (hence, existing only within the memory of a computer), but nonetheless violent, sexual attack that occurred in LamdaMOO, a real-time conversational space on the Internet.

E-mail and Literacy Education

The recognition that e-mail systems are articulated in such complex ways with/in existing cultural, political, educational, and ideological formations should not lead to the conclusion that these structures constitute a seamless or totalizing system (de Certeau, 1984; Deleuze & Guattari, 1987; Laclau & Mouffe, 1985). Nor should the cautions of technology critics suggest that computers play *only* a conservative role in reproducing dominant social structures. Models of social systems that focus only on "ideology and domination as the homogenous and all-powerful determinant of culture and institutional practice," as Carl Herndl (1993, p. 352) points out, are limited both theoretically and practically in that they fail to account for the struggles, resistances, and changes that characterize the lives of real people.

In this sense, the project of theorizing e-mail remains radically incomplete until we also acknowledge how humans enact agency and resistance within this landscape, even while operating within existing fields of institutional forces and social constraints. A part of this task involves explaining why individuals and ensembled groups of individuals already use e-mail as a self-selected site for literacy practices. From these explanations, we can also extrapolate the potential of e-mail as a site for teaching and studying literacy in more formal ways.

E-mail as a Forum for the Practice of Literacy

One of the most salient characteristics of e-mail is that it represents a *self-selected site for the practice of literacy*—one of the few text literacy[1] environments in our culture whose use is expanding rather than shrinking, one of the few spaces that so strongly encourages participatory literacy in the form of writing,[2] and one of the few literacy environments that has not received the formal attention of English teachers. The scope of literacy practices that goes on within these environments is both extensive and vigorous. Within the Internet alone, to give an example from 1993, more than 1,776,000 computers serve as hosts, approximately 1,040,000 messages a month are written and sent through the major gateways, and approximately 80,000 users a day read some 35,000 articles posted on news services (Internet Growth Rates, 1993).

Despite these figures, teachers of English, as a profession, have not yet recognized the potency of these literacy sites—a fact that is not entirely surprising. Networked environments for communication have their origins on the margins of academic cultures (Fjermedal, 1986; Levy, 1984) and have been, until recently, the domain of technically oriented computer scientists and a youthful generation of adventurous explorers and hackers. Partially, but not entirely, as a result of these historical conditions, e-mail literacy has not yet assumed the same status that other forms of written literacy enjoy in either English education programs or in English departments. In part, this situation persists, as Nancy Kaplan (1991) points out, because our profession is so ideologically invested in the tradition of print. Concepts of tenure and promotion, authorship, and copyright, for example, rest securely on the foundations of printed texts. English teachers may be slow to recognize the power of the literacy practiced within the landscape of e-mail because they are only beginning to control and profit from these electronic activities on a large scale.

If these spaces remain relatively unrecognized by the formal establishment of literacy educators, however, they are nonetheless vigorous sites of literacy *practice* that focus on reading and writing as a forum of communication with other humans, as a forum for communication at work, and as a forum of public problem solving or exploration. Within these environments—through a reading of their own e-mail, the e-mail of others, or the conversations of group listserv exchanges—individuals have numerous informal opportunities to gauge both the extent and the limitation of their own discursive activity and to compare their own literate behaviors with the practices of others. The importance of these characteristics rests on a related understanding of *agency* and *resistance,* especially as these concepts are enacted discursively. These two terms, as Carl Herndl (1993) points out, have been used by theorists to describe how humans react against social reproduction and relations of dominance in their daily lives. *Agency* refers to the power of humans to influence and change the environments they inhabit and construct through their discursive practices. *Resistance* refers to the ways in which humans deny the power of dominant social formations. Drawing on the structuration theory of Anthony Giddens, Herndl (1993) explains these two concepts in the following way:

> Agents have both a "practical" knowledge of how things work which remains tacit and an explicit and more limited "discursive" knowledge of social practice which they can articulate. . . . Resistance becomes possible when agents recognize the recursive relationship between themselves as social agents and the structural properties of the social practices in which they participate. . . . [A]gents monitor their action reflexively. This makes it possible . . . to change the conditions of their action. (p. 353)

E-mail, in this context, can be understood, in part, as a discursive forum within which individuals and groups can struggle to articulate their own differing understandings and representations of social structures—and within which there exists the possibility of some common recognition of the need to change or alter these formations. This particular characteristic of e-mail is multiplied by the numbers and diversity of participants. Within the landscape of e-mail, for instance, African American, Hispanic American, and Native American tribal groups are now linked by e-mail—as are women's groups that focus on a variety of topics from child rearing to science policy to investment strategies. Similarly, e-mail groups composed of seniors, individuals with disabilities, gays and lesbians, and other political minorities have taken up locations in this discursive landscape. These groups and individuals exchange language in the same environment that supports the discussions of individuals who can be characterized as belonging to majority or dominant factions within our culture.

The importance of this mix of discourses—especially in relation to discursive agency and resistance—can be best understood from the perspective Antonio Gramsci (1971) provides on hegemony. Hegemony refers to the differential power relationships between dominant and nondominant groups in our culture. As Gramsci points out, hegemony is consensual and established around a set of commonly held values and beliefs inscribed in language and communicated constantly through discourse. Dominant groups in our culture, groups that profit from a particular hegemony, capitalize on these commonly held beliefs to maintain hegemonic relations—often exploiting language to this end in ways that mask, but not entirely hide, such relationships. To maintain the consent necessary for a hegemonic relationship to continue, however, dominant groups must be sensitive to nondominant groups calling for change or reform and must alter the language that they use to represent their consideration of these nondominant claims.

Evidence of hegemonic accommodation, for example, can be found in Vice President Gore's (1991; 1993) descriptions of the principles undergirding the NII and the NREN. These principles (encouraging private investment, promoting competition, providing open access, avoiding a society of information "haves" and "have-nots," and encouraging flexibility) show a keen awareness of the concerns of both dominant and nondominant groups in our culture. On the one hand, the discourse used to describe these principles stresses free enterprise, competition, economic development, and sophisticated research. On the other hand, this discourse concedes the importance of governmental intervention and support that provides access to every citizen regardless of ability to pay for this privilege. Despite the vice president's (1991) claim that these technologies will lead to "dramatic changes in civilization," the information system supports the status quo in terms of hegemonic relationships.

Hegemonic relationships, however, can also undergo change, when, as Gramsci (1971) notes, a critical mass of individuals and groups recognizes a set of related reasons to be dissatisfied with the current political and ideological system. When enough individuals or groups voice such "general, deep-rooted dissatisfaction" and identify routes through which to exert "individual and collective will" (Villanueva, 1992, pp. 22–23), they can resist current power relationships and work to establish a new hegemony that more satisfactorily addresses their concerns. The danger to such counter-hegemonic efforts is that dominant groups accommodate their discourse to the concerns and, thus, weaken or divert the impetus for significant social change. Villanueva (1992) notes this reaction to the civil rights movement in the sixties and seventies and to the women's movement more recently—when more radical positions were accommodated by dominant groups, but fundamental social restructuring failed to occur. The efforts both to maintain and also to dismantle hegemonic positions are carried out through discourse (Gramsci, 1991; Laclau & Mouffe 1985; Villanueva, 1992) and constitute an ongoing "war of position" (Villanueva, 1992, p. 32).

From this perspective, e-mail can be understood as a political space as well as a discursive space, a space within which the war of positions is waged through language and dialectic. This landscape provides individuals and groups access to a range of dominant and nondominant discourses, each of which represents social formations and cultural problems in different discursive terms and from different points of view. From the position of dominant groups, e-mail provides one more site within which to identify, and accommodate to, the concerns of nondominant groups. For nondominant groups, e-mail is a particularly potent site for discursive exchange because it ameliorates some of the geographic barriers that hinder collective action, providing direct access to individuals and other groups who share dissatisfactions, concerns, and solutions. In this way, e-mail also serves as a possible site for individual agency, resistance, and collective action based on the rhetorical articulation of shared ideological positions.

An interesting example of counter-hegemony involves the development of community networks and freenets. The focus for these networks, as Schuler (1994) describes, is on political involvement and participation

> [in order] to advance social goals such as building community awareness, encouraging involvement in local decision making, or developing economic opportunities in disadvantaged communities. (p. 39)

Freenets and the discourses on them have emerged, in part, as responses to the increasing legislation and rising costs associated with access to larger WANs—both the education/business/government-sponsored entities such as BITNET and Internet, or their public equivalents, such as CompuServe and Prodigy.[3] In addition, freenets allow a level of local control over discourses and an access to electronic landscapes, not always available on more complex and centrally controlled WANs. Access to freenets, and the information on them, is typically open to the public—although each of these networks has had to accommodate the social formations within which they exist. Community Memory, in Berkeley, for example, places terminals in laundromats and public libraries and is controlled by no central authority of any kind. It depends, however, on coin-operated terminals that charge users twenty-five cents to post entries and a dollar to start a new discussion forum. The Cleveland Free-Net has over 35,000 registered users and over 10,000 logins per day; it depends, however, on the storage capabilities of a large computer, centrally located and controlled through Case Western University (Schuler, 1994).

E-mail as a Site for the Teaching of Literacy

The self-sponsored literacy practices that individuals engage in on e-mail can help us extrapolate some sense of the possibilities e-mail poses for more formal literacy *education*. The theoretical perspective here is drawn primarily from liberatory pedagogy and composition studies. It poses as advantages the multiplicity of individuals, groups, and discursive viewpoints that characterize the space of e-mail, and the self-selected and self-sponsored literacy practices that occur within this landscape.

In 1994, Abbott identified more than 8,000 different groups on the Internet that occupy this electronic landscape: groups formed around national allegiances (e.g., Native Americans, Greeks, Algerians, Croatians, Brazilians, Cubans, Russians, Ecuadorians, Estonians, Romanians, Hungarians); literary works (e.g., Chicano literature, Hebrew literature, Islamic literature, Latin American literature, Greek literature, German literature); religious topics (e.g., Coptic Orthodoxy, Old Testament, New Testament, Eastern Orthodoxy, Christianity, Buddhism, Baha'i, Pagan, Quakers); political interests (e.g., immigration, human rights, policymaking, government information, disabilities, national security, communism, feminism, family studies, gay and lesbian topics, hazardous-waste management); and current events (e.g., the Bosnian conflict, Somalia, Grochz Kapusta, earthquakes, cyberspace, and nuclear war). The breadth of groups represented in these conversations means that the discourses circulating within the Internet frequently exhibit unconventional characteristics—a general lack of concern about spelling, the creation of new genres (e.g., logon and logoff notes, MOO and MUD scripts, and cross-posting requests), and new discursive conventions (e.g., emoticons, shortcut acronyms like BTW for "by the way" or IMHO for "in my humble opinion," and elaborate signature blocks consisting of quotations from favorite authors or graphic representations).

This discursive multiplicity, in part, means that e-mail systems constitute meeting grounds for different groups and different discourses—what Gloria Anzaldúa (1987) and Henry Giroux (1992) call "borderlands" and what Mary Louise Pratt (1991) calls "linguistic contact zones." These terms are used to designate "social spaces where cultures meet, clash, and grapple with each other, often in contexts of highly asymmetric relations of power, such as colonialism, slavery, or their aftermaths as they are lived out in many parts of the world today" (p. 34). The multiple discursive representations within these spaces present an interested version of reality. When these versions are juxtaposed, they place *difference* in a center-stage position and create the opportunity to focus on its various sources—economic, class-based, ideological, cultural, racial, gender-based.

These naturally potent, multilayered discourse environments may provide spaces that focus the attention of both faculty and students on the literacy practices of different groups. The aim of such study is congruent with projects described by liberatory and critical pedagogists (cf., Giroux, 1992; Apple, 1986; Cooper & Holzman, 1989; Shor, 1987) who focus on differences and contradictions that individuals and groups bring to classrooms in their written and spoken language. Through an examination of these differences that take place within particular social, cultural, economic, and historical contexts, liberatory educators aim to help their students to identify new discursive formations and positions that extend the discourses of possibility and to create potential for positive cultural, political, social, personal, or economic change.

Given that e-mail spaces often involve self-sponsored and self-selected writing, teachers may be able to use the messages composed for these sites to overcome a historical reliance on teacher-based assignments. Traditional teacher-based assignments, as composition scholars (cf., Cooper & Holzman, 1989; Knoblauch & Brannon, 1993; Lunsford, Moglen, & Slevin, 1990) have pointed out, frequently distance students from the self-sponsored writing that they would naturally choose to engage in, place artificial constraints on students' intellectual explorations, isolate students from the social contexts of language use and the responsibilities and richness associated with these contexts, and often result in inauthentic uses of language. Students write best, these scholars point out, when their writing grows out of authentic social and individual needs and situations (Cooper & Holzman, 1989).

E-mail messages, used within these contexts, may have several advantages as a focus for literacy instruction. They are often self-selected and self-sponsored. They exist in written form, already transcribed and available for students' critical and systematic examination of language practices. Individual messages, moreover, can be examined contextually, their effectiveness situated within larger written conversations and social situations, which are also inscribed in writing and available for examination. Such conversations, unlike formal teacher feedback or written peer commentary, involve naturally occurring responses to an individual's language use and, thus, provide powerfully convincing evidence of both the necessity for and the effectiveness of various rhetorically based decisions about language use. These conversations among, and within, e-mail groups can allow teachers and students to focus on the differences that characterize language in all its uses: different groups and the discourses they employ; the varying interpretations and representations of social formations through language; different arguments, approaches, and claims and how these work with different audiences; different ideological assumptions; and different motivations for writing and communicating.

The challenge for literacy educators who want to work with students' e-mail writing is to avoid turning the space of e-mail into the same artificial, teacher-centered, teacher-controlled environment that the traditional classroom has become. As Foucault (1979, p. 333) points out, the classroom and the prison already serve related functions as disciplinary technologies in our culture, and teachers habitually assume positions of control over the language practices of students in their classes. In this sense, it would be altogether too easy for teachers to enter the space of e-mail and assume a controlling or surveillance function over student writing that would eliminate much of the joy and freedom that now characterizes the practice of literacy in that space. Colonizing the landscape of e-mail in the name of education, however, would not accomplish the goals of expanding the discursive landscape of students in productive directions or of acquainting them with a sense of discursive agency. To accomplish the delicate balancing act of encouraging students to write from their own needs and teaching them various strategies of being systematically reflexive about their own writing and that of others, teachers will have to work much more closely with students as learning partners in the Freirian sense (1970). In this role, teachers will need to turn to students as learners themselves, to find out what students hope to accomplish with various pieces of writing as they are situated in particular electronic discussions, to listen as students identify why they make the rhetorical decisions they do, to help students identify those writing skills and techniques they want to focus on, and to consult with students as they compare their personal experiences and discourses with those of others.

Finally, in terms of literacy instruction, the space of e-mail provides one additional and important possibility—providing a space within which teachers and students can make a critical study of the effects technology has on literate exchanges. As Andrew Feenberg (1991) points out, our culture will begin to apply computer technologies toward more productive and democratic ends only when we can gain a critical perspective on our current uses of these machines. To accomplish this goal, Feenberg suggests, we need to teach people to "re-contextualize" (p. 191) technology—a process that involves tracing the existing naturalized relationships between technology and social, political, and cultural formations related to capitalism and refocusing our attention on the human interests which capitalism suppresses.

One way literacy educators can help accomplish this task is to educate students in the practice of foregrounding humans in their relations with machines—especially within the context of literacy practices. Educators, for example, can involve students in comparing their literacy practices within computer environments to their literacy practices in other print-based environments, with the goal of identifying how technology affects the communication practices of individual writers and groups of writers. These comparisons could focus on the ways in which access to technology affects literacy production (e.g., the location of computer access for writers with differing hierarchical status within an organization, the measure of safety with which computer access is available to writers of different genders, the cost of computer access for writers with differing economic status) or the ways in which the features of technology affect the literacy practices of writers (e.g., the linguistic effects of spell checkers and style checkers on prose, the physical effects of screen design on the ways individuals read and comprehend a text, or the psychological effects of e-mail on individual correspondents).

E-mail as a Site for the Study of Literacy

Using a perspective offered by theory, we can also extrapolate some sense of the possibilities e-mail poses as a forum for the study of the multiplied and fragmented discourses that characterize the electronic age (Faigley, 1992; Lyotard, 1984; Poster, 1990), especially as these discourses reveal their association with interested social formations and dominant groups in our culture. Such study—as postmodern theory and theories of radical democratic action suggest—can lead not only toward a useful "critique of contemporary culture" (Faigley, 1992, p. 212), but also toward the possibility of identifying "discursive conditions for the emergence of collective action" that will serve the continuing goal of "struggling against inequalities and challenging relations of subordination" (Laclau & Mouffe, 1985, p. 153).

The postmodern theory of Fredric Jameson (1991) can provide a context within which to understand both the importance and the difficulty associated with this scholarly and political effort. Jameson—using as points of departure the work of Max Horkheimer and Theodor Adorno (1991), Jean Baudrillard (1983), Ernesto Laclau and Chantal Mouffe (1985), and others—describes how the possibilities for collective action in a postmodern age are effectively limited by the multiplication and disintegration of social identities that accompany the global expansion of multinational capitalism. To counter this effect, Jameson suggests the strategy of demystifying certain discursive formations that naturalize this project—in particular, the rhetoric of "pluralism" (p. 320)—and seeking a way of establishing connections among postmodern subjects on the basis of more realistic perceptions of economic and social conditions.

The reasoning behind this effort is complex. Jameson (1991) begins by unmasking the "self-congratulatory rhetoric" (p. 320) associated with pluralism, revealing the multiplication of microgroups based on nonclass issues as a naturalized result of contemporary capitalism "in its third (or 'multinational') stage" (p. 319). Capitalism, as it expands globally, becomes "hungry and thirsty for . . . the endless production and proliferation of new groups and neoethnicities of all kinds" (p. 325). These groups function as "so many new markets for new products, so many new interpolations for the new advertising image itself" (p. 325). To rationalize this process, Jameson notes, an "ideology of groups" (p. 320) is constructed and framed in the rhetoric of pluralism. This ideology, in turn, serves two essentially reproductive purposes: to feed the appetite of global capitalism and, at the same time, to hold out false hope that our society has come to be based not on traditional class differences but on the increasingly democratic appreciation of various micropolitical groups. Through the process of naturalization that accompanies this ideology—which masks the authentic economic conditions of classes and diffuses the potential of collective action—the conditions for expansion of global capitalism are reproduced.

The fragmented space of the postmodern world, for Jameson, then, is a space of expanding production. The multiplication of subjectivities within this space serves to distract individuals and groups from recognizing the real economic and social conditions within which they function, and, more important perhaps, may prevent them from acting effectively with a sense of personal or collective agency. Individuals encountering the expanse and the effects of postmodernity—in images multiplied through MTV, in narratives replicated in movies, in proliferations of architectural space, in multiplicities characterizing the consumer culture—glimpse a world peopled by "multiplied bodies," a space "redolent of personal identities" (Jameson, 1991, p. 358) continually under production. Within this dizzyingly complex landscape, Jameson notes, we are often overcome with the "premonition that the more people we recognize, even within the mind, the more peculiarly precarious becomes the status of our own hitherto unique and 'incomparable' consciousness or 'self'" (p. 358).

If this postmodern vision of e-mail is disturbing, it is also a useful context for understanding several phenomena that currently characterize the growth of e-mail—the "prodigious enlargement" (Jameson, 1991, p. 354) of e-mail within territories claimed by the expansion of global capitalism; the explosion of self-established e-mail discussion groups, news groups, and bulletin boards; the eagerness of groups to colonize cyberspace by claiming members in other countries; and the common practice of cross-posting messages to multiply the reach of communication. This postmodern perspective also serves to contextualize the emergence of the multiple in community nets, the electronic ventriloquism associated with "Internet relay chats" (IRC), and the multiplication of personalities in MOOs and MUDs.

For some postmodern scholars, however, the terrifying space of the postmodern also provides an arena for rediscovering the changing nature of discursive agency and the potency of collective, class-based action. Faigley (1992), Laclau and Mouffe (1985), and Lyotard (1984), for example, see a solution as well as a problem in the postmodern multiplication of voices, subjectivities, and discursiveness. As Lyotard points out, when discourses are multiplied, as they are in the postmodern era, when they are produced by an increasingly wide range of individuals and micropolitical groups, they have the effect of supplanting and enfeebling the grand narratives that have wielded such power within the space of modernity—among them, master narratives of science, progress, and democracy. Thus, the power of the micronarratives characteristic of postmodernism are more localized in nature and constituted by the ensembled knowledge of fewer individuals. As a result, privileged discursive positions are "no longer particularly determinant" and cease to be "functional in perpetuating and reproducing" the ideological systems that they represent (Jameson, 1991, p. 398).

Postmodern spaces like e-mail, then, in multiplying discourses, also multiply opportunities for agency and resistance. Within such spaces, individuals and groups represent reality and social formations in discursive terms meaningful to them. At the same time, these agents and ensembles of agents can identify those representations, concerns, and needs that they have in common with—and in opposition to—other individuals and groups. Within these spaces, finally, there exists the possibility of exercising collective action that grows out of the mutual recognition and understanding of economic and social conditions. These possibilities, of course, are difficult to realize: they are masked by ideology; they are infrequent and momentary; they stand in opposition to tendential social forces; and they may seem contradictory to different liberatory goals. For these reasons, the formal study of such processes is all the more important, especially for scholars involved in the examination of literacy practices. Observing the discourses in e-mail spaces, as Faigley (1992) points out, will help us come to a better understanding of how postmodernity has reconstituted the possibilities of agency and collective action and how we can change conditions to improve the world in which we live.

Conclusion

This chapter has attempted to use perspectives afforded by various social theories to begin describing the landscape of e-mail, especially as this space is constituted by political, economic, historical, and cultural forces. The project of theorizing e-mail, however, involves processes of illumination and complication that are as complexly recursive and dynamic as technology itself. And so this beginning is only one beginning.

As e-mail continues to change—as it aligns with different social formations in dynamic cultural landscapes, as the political positions and concerns of groups inhabiting this space change, as the space of e-mail itself expands and is legislated, as the technology that supports these communicative exchanges is altered—the nature of theorizing and the results of theoretical analyses will change as well. Changing right along with these formations will be our ability to perceive, reflect on, and interpret the discursive practices that happen within and around e-mail. Projects like this are never done; they're just under way.

Notes

1. I use the term "text" here in a limited way to refer to written (or typed) language only, rather than to the entire range of visual, social, and oral "texts" that permeate our culture.

2. Participants on electronic listservs—which I have included here as part of an e-mail environment—can, and often do, "lurk." That is, participants may choose to read the conversation without contributing written responses to it. The lure of electronic conversation, however, is a strong one, and as far as I can tell from my own experiences and observations on the nets, the majority of participants are active writers as well as readers—although they may not do both consistently on all lists that they belong to. Many e-mail users, for example, choose to lurk on some lists—perhaps because they feel less comfortable with the topic, or because they do not yet "know" the other participants, or because they are unfamiliar with the etiquette of the group, or because they simply do not have time to both read and write. On other lists, however, these same individuals may write frequently. Lurking can also be a temporary phenomenon. Some participants, for example, have spates of

lurking—often due to time constraints, or to topics that are less interesting or more threatening, or to the amount of writing they are doing on other lists.

It is indicative, I believe, that the term "lurking" retains a slightly negative connotation, although the onus on lurking may be lessening as more people are active on more lists. There is still a general feeling in networked conversations that participants should—in some way and at some appropriate time relatively soon after joining any given list—let the group of participants know that a new member is "listening" and may want to contribute. Often, this is accomplished with a short message of introduction—"Hi, my name is Cindy Selfe, and I just joined this list. Does anyone know how to. . . ." It is interesting that these introductory messages often contain a question—the speech act I recognize in such messages indicates that the "newbie" (newcomer to the list) has an appropriate interest in the group's discussion, comes willing to listen, and has no immediately hostile intentions toward the group. Such an interpretation, however, may be naive in its assumptions.

3. The refinement and use of packet-charging technologies and the increasing exploitation of large-scale commercial networks that appeal to the public have resulted in rising costs for consumers. Figures published in a 1992 *New York Times* article indicate that commercial public networks such as Prodigy and CompuServe charge approximately $50.00 for starter kits on their systems, between $8.00 and $15.00 for basic use each month, and some additional per-message or per-minute charges as well. The capital stake that commercial groups have in promoting these electronic systems to citizens is not a small one: information-as-commodity is big business—approximately 3.4 million people (1.75 million on Prodigy and 1.69 million on CompuServe) subscribe to commercial networks at the rates we have mentioned (Grimes, 1992, pp. 13–15).

References

Abbott, T. (1994). *"Internet World"'s on Internet '94*. Westport, CT: Mecklermedia.

Anzaldúa, G. (1987). *Borderlands: La frontera, the new mestiza*. San Francisco: Aunt Lute.

Apple, M.W. (1986). *Teachers and texts: A political economy of class and gender relations in higher education*. New York: Routledge & Kegan Paul.

Baudrillard, J. (1983). *Simulations*. (P. Foss, P. Patton, & P. Beitchman, Trans.). New York: Semiotext(e).

Becker, H.J. (1987). Using computers for instruction. *BYTE*, 149–162.

Braverman, H. (1974). *Labor and monopoly capital: The degradation of work in the twentieth century.* New York: Monthly Review Press.

Bump, J. (1990). Radical changes in class discussion using networked computers. *Computers and the Humanities, 24,* 49–65.

Cerf, V.G. (1991). Networks. *Scientific American,* 72–81.

Clement, A. (1994, January). Computing at work: Empowering action by "low-level users." *Communications of the ACM, 37*(1), 53–63.

Cole, M., & Griffin, P. (1987). *Contextual factors in education: Improving science and mathematics education for minorities and women.* Madison, WI: Wisconsin Center for Educational Research, University of Wisconsin.

Cooper, M.M., & Holzman, M. (1989). *Writing as social action.* Portsmouth, NH: Boynton/Cook-Heinemann.

de Certeau, M. (1984). *The practice of everyday life* (S. Randall, Trans.). Berkeley: University of California Press.

Deleuze, G., & Guattari, F. (1987). *A thousand plateaus: Capitalism and schizophrenia* (B. Massumi, Trans.). Minneapolis: University of Minnesota Press.

DeLoughry, T.J. (1994, February 23). Unconnected. *The Chronicle of Higher Education, 40*(25), A19–A20.

Dibble, J. (1993, December 21). A rape in cyberspace or how an evil clown, a Haitian trickster spirit, two wizards, and a cast of dozens turned a database into a society. *Village Voice,* 36–41.

Dubrovsky, V.J., Kiesler, S., & Sethna, B.N. (1991). The equalization phenomenon: Status effects in computer-mediated and face-to-face decision-making groups. *Human-Computer Interaction, 6,* 119–146.

Eldred, J. (1989). Computers, composition, and the social view. In G.E. Hawisher & C.L. Selfe (Eds.), *Critical perspectives on computers and composition instruction* (pp. 201–218). New York: Teachers College Press.

Faigley, L. (1990). Subverting the electronic notebook: Teaching writing using networked computers. In D.A. Daiker & M. Morenberg (Eds.), *The writing teacher as researcher: Essays in the theory and practice of class-based research* (pp. 290–311). Portsmouth, NH: Boynton/Cook-Heinemann.

Faigley, L. (1992). *Fragments of rationality: Postmodernity and the subject of composition.* Pittsburgh: University of Pittsburgh Press.

Feenberg, A. (1991). *Critical theory of technology.* New York: Oxford University Press.

Fjermedal, G. (1986). *The tomorrow makers: A brave new world of living-brain machines.* New York: Random House.

Foucault, M. (1979). *Discipline and punish: The birth of the prison.* New York: Vintage.

Freire, P. (1970). *Pedagogy of the oppressed.* (M.B. Ramos, Trans.). New York: Continuum.

Gerver, E. (1989). Computers and gender. In T. Forester (Ed.), *Computers in the human context: Information technology, productivity, and people* (pp. 481–501). Cambridge, MA: MIT Press.

Giroux, H.A. (1983). *Theory and resistance in education: A pedagogy for the opposition.* South Hadley, MA: Bergin & Garvey.

Giroux, H.A. (1992). *Border crossings: Cultural workers and the politics of education.* New York: Routledge, Chapman and Hall.

Giroux, H.A., & Freire, P. (1987). Series introduction. In D.W. Livingstone (Ed.), *Critical pedagogy and cultural power* (pp. xi–xvi). South Hadley, MA: Bergin & Garvey.

Gomez, M.L. (1991). The equitable teaching of composition. In G.E. Hawisher & C.L. Selfe (Eds.), *Evolving perspectives on computers and composition studies: Questions for the 1990s* (pp. 318–335). Urbana, IL: The National Council of Teachers of English; Houghton, MI: *Computers and Composition.*

Gore, A. (1991). Infrastructure for the global village. *Scientific American, 265*(3), 150–153.

Gore, A. (1992). The information infrastructure and technology act. *EDUCOM Review, 27*(5), 27–29.

Gore, A. (1993, December 21). Remarks to the National Press Club. Washington, DC.

Gramsci, A. (1971). *Selections from the prison notebooks* (Q. Hoare & G.N. Smith, Trans.). New York: International Publishers.

Grimes, W. (1992, December 1). Computer as a cultural tool. *New York Times,* C13–15.

Hawisher, G.E., & Moran, C. (1993). Electronic mail and the writing instructor. *College English, 55*(6), 627–643.

Hawisher, G.E., & Selfe, C.L. (1991). The rhetoric of technology and the electronic writing class. *College Composition and Communication, 42*(1), 55–65.

Hawkins, J. (1985). Computers and girls: Rethinking the issues. *Sex Roles, 13,* 165–180.

Herndl, C.G. (1993). Teaching discourse and reproducing culture: A critique of research and pedagogy in professional and non-academic writing. *College Composition and Communication, 44*(3), 349–363.

Hiltz, S.R. (1986). The "virtual classroom": Using computer-mediated communication for university teaching. *Journal of Communication, 36*(2), 95–104.

Hiltz, S.R., & Turoff, M. (1993). *The network nation: Human communication via computer.* Rev. ed. Cambridge, MA: MIT Press.

Horkheimer, M., & Adorno, T. (1991). *Dialectic of enlightenment.* (J. Cumming, Trans.). New York: Continuum.

Internet growth rates. (1993, December 22). E-mail cross-posting.

Jameson, F. (1991). *Postmodernism or the cultural logic of late capitalism.* Durham, NC: Duke University Press.

Jessup, E. (1991). Feminism and computers in composition instruction. In G.E. Hawisher & C.L. Selfe (Eds.), *Evolving perspectives on computers and composition studies: Questions for the 1990s* (pp. 336–355). Urbana, IL: National Council of Teachers of English; Houghton, MI: *Computers and Composition.*

Kaplan, N. (1991). Ideology, technology, and the future of writing instruction. In G.E. Hawisher & C.L. Selfe (Eds.), *Evolving perspectives on computers and composition: Questions for the 1990s* (pp. 11–42). Urbana, IL: National Council of Teachers of English; Houghton, MI: *Computers and Composition.*

Kiesler, S., Siegel, J., & McGuire, T.W. (1984). Social psychological aspects of computer-mediated communication. *American Psychologist, 39*(10), 1123–1134.

Knoblauch, C.H. (1990). Literacy and the practice of education. In A. Lunsford, H. Moglen, & J. Slevin (Eds.), *The right to literacy* (pp. 74–80). New York: Modern Language Association of America.

Knoblauch, C.H., & Brannon, L. (1993). *Critical teaching and the idea of literacy.* Portsmouth, NH: Boynton/Cook-Heinemann.

Laclau, E., & Mouffe, C. (1985). *Hegemony and socialist strategy: Towards a radical democratic politics.* London: Verso.

Lanham, R. (1989). The electronic word: Literary study and the digital revolution. *New Literary History, 20*(2), 265–290.

Levy, S. (1984). *Hackers: Heroes of the computer revolution.* New York: Dell.

Livingstone, D.W. (Ed.). (1987a). *Critical pedagogy and cultural power.* South Hadley, MA: Bergin & Garvey.

Livingstone, D.W. (1987b). Upgrading and opportunities. In D.W. Livingstone (Ed.), *Critical pedagogy and cultural power* (pp. 125–136). South Hadley, MA: Bergin & Garvey.

Lunsford, A., Moglen, H., & Slevin, J. (Eds.). (1990). *The right to literacy.* New York: Modern Language Association of America.

Lyotard, J.-F. (1984). *The postmodern condition: A report on knowledge.* (G. Bennington & B. Massumi, Trans.). Minneapolis: University of Minnesota Press.

Ohmann, R. (1985). Literacy, technology, and monopoly capitalism. *College English, 47*(7), 675–689.

Olson, C.P. (1987). Who computes? In D.W. Livingstone (Ed.), *Critical pedagogy and cultural power* (pp. 179–204). South Hadley, MA: Bergin & Garvey.

Piller, C. (1992), Separate realities: The creation of the technological underclass in America's public schools. *MacWorld,* 218–230.

Petzold, C. (1993, October 26). Move over, ASCII! Unicode is here! *PC, 12*(18), 374–376.

Poster, M. (1990). *The mode of information: Poststructuralism and social context.* Chicago: University of Chicago Press.

Postman, N. (1992). *Technopoly: The surrender of culture to technology.* New York: Vintage.

Pratt, M.L. (1991). Arts of the contact zone. *Profession '91,* 33–40.

Regan, A. (1993). 'Type normal like the rest of us': Writing, power, and homophobia in the networked composition classroom. *Computers and Composition, 10*(4), 11–23.

Romano, S. (1993). The egalitarianism narrative: Whose story? Which yardstick. *Computers and Composition, 10*(3), 5–28.

Schuler, D. (1994, January). Community networks: Building a new participatory medium. *Communications of the ACM, 37*(1) 39–51.

Selfe, C.L. (1990). Technology in the English classroom: Computers through the lens of feminist theory. In C. Handa (Ed.), *Computers and* community: Teaching composition in the twenty-first century (pp. 118–139). Portsmouth, NH: Boynton/Cook-Heinemann.

Selfe, C.L., & Hilligoss, S. (Eds.). (1994). *Literacy and computers: The complications of teaching and learning with technology.* New York: Modern Language Association of America.

Selfe, C.L., & Meyer, P.R. (1991). Testing claims for on-line conferences. *Written Communication, 8*(2), 163–192.

Sheingold, K., Martin, L.M.W., & Endreweit, M.W. (1987). Preparing urban teachers for the technological future. In R.D. Pea & K. Sheingold (Eds.), *Mirrors of the mind: Patterns of experience in educational computing* (pp. 67–85). Norwood, NJ: Ablex.

Shor, I. (1987). *Critical teaching and everyday life.* Chicago: University of Chicago Press.

Shriner, D.K., & Rice, W.C. (1989). Computer conferencing and collaborative learning: A discourse community at work. *College Composition and Communication, 40*(4), 472–478.

Spitzer, M. (1989). Computer conferencing: An emerging technology. In G.E. Hawisher & C.L. Selfe (Eds.), *Critical Perspectives in Computers and Composition Instruction* (pp. 187–200). New York: Teachers College Press.

Sproull, L., & Kiesler, S. (1986). Reducing social context cues: Electronic mail in organization communication. *Management Science, 32*(11), 1492–1512.

Sproull, L., & Kiesler, S. (1991a). Computers, networks and work. *Scientific American, 265*(3), 116–123.

Sproull, L., & Kiesler, S. (1991b). *Connections: New ways of working within the networked organization.* Cambridge, MA: MIT Press.

Takayoshi, P. (1994). Building new networks from the old: Women's experiences with electronic communications. *Computers and Composition, 11*(1), 21–35.

Telecommunications Policy Roundtable (1994, January). Renewing the commitment to a public interest telecommunications policy. *Communications of the ACM, 37*(1), 106–108.

Villanueva, V., Jr. (1992). Hegemony from an organically grown traditional intellectual. *Pre/Text, 13*(1/2), 18–34.

Wilson, D.L. (1993, December 15). Private liberal-arts colleges found to lag in Internet access and sophisticated computers. *The Chronicle of Higher Education, 40*(17), A17.

Winner, L. (1986). *The whale and the reactor: A search for limits in an age of high technology.* Chicago: University of Chicago Press.

Zuboff, S. (1988). *In the age of the smart machine: The future of work and power.* New York: Basic Books.

Chapter 14

Working across Methodological Interfaces: The Study of Computers and Writing in the Workplace

James E. Porter
Purdue University

Patricia Sullivan
Purdue University

This chapter explores the assumptions—personal, disciplinary, and transdisciplinary—that drive the study of computers and writing in the workplace. The authors use the strategy of multiple mapping (a technique from postmodern geography) to expose a variety of possible researcher roles and disciplinary frameworks, with the aim of promoting a more critically reflective research praxis.

> When research comes to study the very realm within which it operates, the results which it obtains can be immediately reinvested in scientific work as instruments of reflexive knowledge or the conditions and the social limits of this work, which is one of the principle weapons of epistemological vigilance.
>
> (Bourdieu, 1988, p. 15)

Some material in the section on the Max study was borrowed from Sullivan, P.A., & Porter, J.E. (1993a). On theory, practice, and method: Toward a heuristic research methodology for professional writing. In R. Spilka (Ed.), *Writing in the workplace: New research perspectives* (pp. 220–237). Carbondale: Southern Illinois University Press.

In this chapter, we hope to be methodologically reflective and "epistemologically vigilant" as we examine issues in the study of computers in the workplace. We are especially interested in considering various methodological *frames* we use as researchers (and as readers of research) and in noting the strengths and limitations of those frames.

In the study of computer use in the workplace or in the classroom, our thinking is guided by discussions in several different fields. We can call on professional writing, computers and composition, organizational communication, technology transfer in sociology and communication, usability studies in human factors and computing, interface studies in computer support for collaborative work, technology theories in literary and communication studies, and other likely subjects. We argue in this chapter that as we read or do research, we must be aware (1) of the ways that we frame (and are framed in) our specific studies and (2) of the possible disciplinary positions we could take for that research—within frames of ideology, method, theory, and practice.

In the past, researchers could perhaps confidently ground their studies by simply announcing the method used—a "case study," for example, or a "survey," or an "ethnography"—in conjunction with a certain unique site. But because we are conscious of multiple disciplines' traditions of method, and because we are aware of the contingency of our findings and the ideology of site selection, we cannot let ourselves be comfortable with announcing *a* method or site any more. We have to build method and critique sites. We have to situate each investigation: Why undertake this study at this time? How does it contribute to current issues? What frame(s) of understanding are we bringing to the study?

Obviously, we see methodology not as Method—that is, not in the modern sense, as rigid structures to be applied without critique to a set of writing phenomena. Rather, we see methodology in a postmodern sense as local, contingent, malleable, and heuristic, and we see research generating situated knowledge—or rather a kind of pragmatic know-how (vs. know-that) kind of knowledge (see Sullivan & Porter, 1993a, for a fuller discussion).

We begin the discussion in this chapter with (1) a brief description of the postmodern mapping methodology that is our chief analytic tool. We then turn to (2) a discussion of three of our research experiences. In the first, we were researchers doing a case study; in the second, we were corporate consultants doing a qualitative meta-analysis; in the third, we were corporate consultants developing a database of research findings. We hope to show how our position in each experience—the critical frame we took and the role that was assigned (or that we assigned ourselves)—was both methodologically empowering and methodologically blinding (we must admit). Each of those frames is further critiqued as we then move to (3) consider some of the methodological frames we see as operating in the three fields in which this volume is most directly involved—professional writing, rhetorical theory, and computers and composition. We conclude (4) by suggesting a postmodern rhetorical methodology for the study of computer use in the classroom and in the workplace.

Methodology: Postmodern Mapping

First, a word about methodology. Our own method in this chapter is a spatial/visual kind of postmodern geography. We use postmodern mapping methods similar to those used by Pierre Bourdieu in *Homo Academicus* (1988) and Edward Soja in *Postmodern Geographies* (1989). Mapping is one tactic for constructing positionings of research that are reflexive—a key to developing postmodern understandings of research (see Foucault, 1984; Barton & Barton, 1993). We ourselves have used this method of mapping relationships and positions visually and spatially in several works (Sullivan & Porter, 1993a; 1993b). We have a number of sound theoretical reasons to support our mapping—but we also both like to draw pictures. It helps our thinking.

Maps may be constructed out of observations that support categories of interest, as Bourdieu did in *Homo Academicus.* In that work, he developed comparative mappings of the French faculty (see p. 50, for example) in order to argue that in the social structures of the 1968 French academic world, one can find the sources of their professional categories. His maps were critical to teasing out the distinctions made in the study about the varied types of power at work, and they were constructed statistically out of the data supporting the oppositions he developed among academic capital, cultural capital, and intellectual capital. These maps became reflexive because the project was centered on Bourdieu's own environment and positioned him within the frame. They helped him establish that turn to the self-portrait.

In a sense, Bourdieu was anticipating the moves of current cultural geographers, such as Soja (1989), who create geographical renderings of communities that include competing pictures of social and physical space. In his treatment of Los Angeles, for example, Soja builds a space for Los Angeles by treating the space historically, by contrasting cultural factors of the 1960s and 1980s while simultaneously presenting competing maps that depict employment, employment shifts, plant closings, changes in aerospace employment, electronics firms, corporate and banking headquarters, residences for engineers, residences of blue-collar and executive workers, and distribution of ethnic residents. He then undercuts the medley of maps by showing how a totalizing vision of the space is impossible given the various paradoxes at work in the mappings. Although he does not add himself to the picture (even though he is a Los Angeles-area resident and urban planner), Soja reasserts the importance of social space.

We are fascinated by such mappings and see them as a way to position research studies in the field and to thereby guide methodological reflections. A map can be judged, we think, on what it allows, what it blocks, what else might be pictured, and how it freezes time.

The mappings that follow depict three experiences from our own work with computers in workplace situations. By describing these situations and by mapping our current reflections on them, we show both how our collective research informs a better understanding of issues surrounding computers and writing in the workplace and also how it blinds researchers to important considerations. Later, by mapping the participants in the three experiences into disciplinary frames, we can begin to discuss how particular research experiences fit into (and challenge, and poke holes in) the collective research we are completing in this area. In our first experience, Max plays several roles (writer, designer, usability tester, student) and has trouble negotiating them well enough to see the bigger picture; in other words, he is, like us, blind to his frame. In the second and third experiences, a number of framing problems emerge: First, the testers in ABC's Usability Department resist seeing their methods *as* methods. Second, we, as the researchers and consultants in the project, are not successful in helping the testers see their methodological blind spots. Third, we as the researchers-turned-developers produce too academic a concept for the database. Fourth, we as the developers cannot manage to overcome platform delivery problems inherent in the project.

Experience #1: The Max Study

For eighteen months in 1989 and 1990, we conducted a case study of a professional writing student, who designed, drafted, revised, tested, and continued to revise a tutorial orienting students to Aldus PageMaker 3.01 (Porter & Sullivan, 1994; Sullivan & Porter, 1993a; 1990a; 1990b). "Max" (the writer) began his project as a student in Jim's advanced technical writing class, where we were gathering information for a study into how students in Jim's class incorporated feedback from readers about instructional texts they were writing (Porter, 1989; Sullivan & Porter, 1990a). We became more interested in Max after this course, as his class experience became more distant, because his investment in that piece of writing was intense and because he was interested in testing the usability of the document he was creating.

In one phase, we detailed how Max ran five usability tests; we looked at his interactions with users (all of them women) and how he changed the tutorial after their sessions. We observed that this writer's rhetorical orientation—his implicit theory of how tutorials should operate—served as a terministic screen that filtered his notion of what the users were doing and what their actions meant.

In our study of Max's usability test, we observed that he slotted the users' actions and comments into the framework he already held: "Max's view of documentation and his use of the user test information reflected his systems orientation and his bias toward content and correctness criteria" (Sullivan & Porter, 1990a,

p. 34). Max's theory was that content not only mattered most but also was discretely separated from and prior to writing:

> Writing, to Max, was a means of packaging content, for which reason it may be important. But Max did not have anything like a social constructionist notion of writing. To Max, writing did not influence or interact with "content"; it simply transmitted it. In other words, Max held to an information transfer model (see Driskill, 1989, pp. 127–128). (Sullivan & Porter, 1993a, p. 227)

Max further evidenced values in keeping with an engineering systems orientation:

> [G]ood documentation is comprehensive, covering all the necessary material and providing a complete and accurate description of a procedure. Users must be told everything to do; [Max's] tutorial provides lock-step directions for performing the tasks and either the users get it "right" or they get it "wrong." (Sullivan & Porter, 1990a, p. 34)

We found Max's rhetorical theory consonant with his systems approach, an approach that predictably led him to add to the content or fix the style whenever he encountered user problems. He did not consider making global changes in the structuring of system information (as the system was a given in his orientation), nor did he entertain changes to the design of the document (as the design had been fixed to accommodate a logical presentation of the system). His allegiance to the system superseded his commitment to users.

We do not think Max's actions uncommon ones among documentation writers: his interpretive screen highlighted such problems as missing information, poorly understood terms, and stylistic blunders at the same time as it filtered out such problems as users' needs for other tasks to be included in the tutorial or better conceptual models of the software. Our sense of Max's encounters with users was this:

> We could say that Max was not "attuned" enough to practice (see Phelps, 1988, pp. 220–223, on attunement), not sensitive enough to his data, to his observations of users. We could also say that he was not conscious enough of his own theory.

We would say that he expressed no awareness of it at all: it was simply a given of the setting. (Sullivan & Porter, 1993a, pp. 227–228)

As we examine this user-testing phase of the Max study from our current interest in clarifying the framing of the work, we see two ways the writer could have worked out of the difficulty. Max's blind spot was that he viewed practice—in this case, what users actually did with his tutorial—as simply providing information, data. The more productive use of practice here would have been to see it as dialectically challenging theory, to regard the data of the user test as resistant to the dominant assumptions Max was bringing to the setting (see de Certeau, 1984, on the resistant nature of practice). The other way Max might have helped himself is by calling upon multiple theories. To admit that there are multiple theories is, in the first instance, to notice the inadequacy of Theory conceived as a single and universal unifying structure.

Figure 1 depicts our current understanding of the last phase of the Max study, in which Max was studying the users of his tutorial as a prelude to making final changes to that document. Simultaneously, we were studying Max studying the users' use of the tutorial.

The text is made dominant in our map because it dominated Max's concerns. Although Max could have been focusing primarily on the users or on their interaction with computers, he focused almost exclusively on the text he had produced, trying to judge its success. Likewise, we could have focused on the users, the interaction between users and computers, or the text. Further, we could have focused on Max, on our relationship to this phase of the study, or on the relationship of this picture to the ones we could have drawn of earlier phases in the study. We chose to focus on Max (Sullivan & Porter, 1990a) and his interaction with the event of users trying to negotiate a print tutorial and a computer to create a document. We could have put this event in the context of earlier classroom behavior (Sullivan & Porter, 1990b), in the context of the history of the document's development, or in the context of the users' backgrounds and reasons for cooperating with the study. We could also have focused on our own reasons for singling out this event in the history of Max's involvement

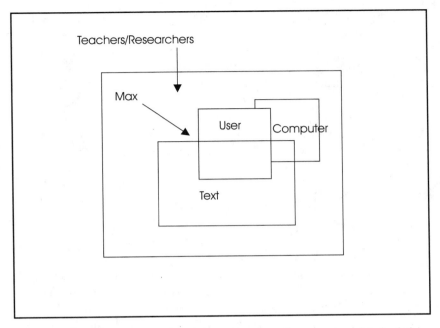

Figure 1. Study of Max obtaining user feedback about tutorial.

with this document. We could have focused on the gender issue: To what degree were Max's responses to the users responses to them as women? Would he have treated their responses more seriously if they had been men? In short, the study could support other depictions.

Although our Max study (and we have determined that there is no single "Max study" here) looks at a student, we find our study typical of workplace studies of documentation in its placement of the computer as fixed entity in the frame. Although the document Max is testing is produced to help students use the computer to learn how to lay out text and graphics in a computer context, the computer is the most remote consideration. Max hardly ever concerns himself with how users and computers work together; he does not focus on computer-use habits. When he does focus on the computer, he usually comments that a user doesn't understand some aspect of the operating system. Because he accepts the system as prior and correct in his commentary, the user is labeled as "in error" in such cases. So, the computer has a kind of background force (as tool or as wizard) but no interactive identity (as assistant or as partner).

This view of the role of the computer might explain why workplace researchers in professional writing have, for the most part, *not* much considered the role of technology in defining workplace writing (a point we discuss in more detail in a later section of this chapter): the computer is simply a given, a neutral platform, a necessary infrastructure supporting writing activities but not fundamentally influencing or constituting those activities.

Experience #2: The Meta-Analysis Project

From 1990–1993, we conducted two projects as freelance consultants for ABC's usability department. In the first project, which we call the Meta-Analysis Project, we analyzed over sixty usability reports produced by members of the department over an eighteen-month period, conducted interviews with members of the group, and ran a follow-up survey. In this project, we were situated as *reviewers and meta-analysts* of the group's collective work.

The aim of the Meta-Analysis Project was to recommend ways the group could better manage and use its research data. We were brought in to help ABC determine what their four years of work in testing the usability of software had accomplished. "What have we learned?" was management's central question. To accomplish this task, we read the reports produced over eighteen months, looking for commonalities in their methods, their subjects, their topical concerns, their analytic strategies, their reports' themes, and so on. We also interviewed all the members of the department in order to discern their positions vis-à-vis the work, their opinions of what they had learned, and their needs for codifying that knowledge. After codifying some of our findings (using techniques for qualitative meta-analysis), we followed those interviews with a survey about synthesizing usability findings. Our six months of research resulted in a report detailing the reports' common themes and a recommendation that the department build a database for report findings.

We focused in our research on identifying themes that cut across products because the working classification of studies in the department was along the lines of product. If you asked the testers about what they did, testers always talked from the perspective of *particular products* (i.e., software applications) and occasionally interface components—but unless specifically prompted, they seldom talked about issues that cut across products (e.g., problems users have with online help or problems new users have with computers). We saw our task, in part, as one that identified those cross-product themes as a way to help the testers think more synthetically of the knowledge they were gaining. In our report, therefore, we talked about the knowledges the department was displaying in their reports about (1) specific products, (2) product types (themes across particular products), (3) users, and (4) methods for testing usability of computer products. We claimed that the first knowledge was overt and featured while the second, third, and fourth were present-but-buried. Those other knowledges tended to be talked about in the hall—"Inexperienced users tend to have trouble with this type of action," or "We know X about feedback that users need," or "Use Y test to get at your question"— but were not featured in the reports (though they could normally be found in the reports if you dug for them).

Figure 2 depicts the relationships we uncovered as we proceeded through the project. Because we did not use only the reports in our work, but supplemented them with interviews that probed how the testers saw the report fitting into the task of improving usability, how they did their studies, and what they thought was important about what they were learning, we were able to build a setting for those reports.

As we proceeded deeper into the project, as we reflected on the project, and as we learned more from its results and from the people in the department, our mapping of the context for their reports became more complex. As Figure 2 tries to illustrate, the reports are a juncture available for the discussion of concerns arising out of the central event of the department, the usability session. These reports are the site for working out questions such as: How do the testers synthesize their knowledge of the product with the responses users have in their usability sessions? How do the usability sessions affect the conceptions developers have of the product?

Thus, we have situated the report as one potential center for Figure 2 (the other is the usability session), and foreground it,

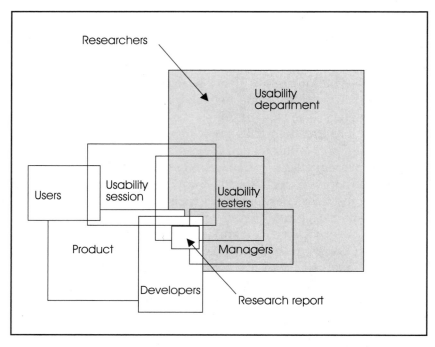

Figure 2. ABC software, Phase 1 (research).

because we realized that the usability reports were situated in a complex network of relations that revolved around the usability session but which involved product developers, managers, testers, and the usability participants themselves. The usability sessions provide the events that drive the department, while the reports are tremendously important as a trace of significant events, of a community of previously disparate groups that existed momentarily for a specified purpose and which then disintegrated. As a result of our study, we claim the reports are the stability of the department. We acknowledge that other renderings of these relationships are possible. If someone else valued the usability testers as the center—as the embodiment, because of their multiple experiences of usability events, of usability knowledge in the group—a different drawing would emerge. Alternative pictures could also accompany centering the activities on the product being developed or on the usability session. Interestingly enough, we doubt that anyone in the department would center the knowledge-making action of their work on the users who participate in the usability sessions; those users act primarily as enablers.

Experience #3: The Database Project

A second project we did for ABC, which we call the Database Project, extended from the first. Together with a third co-consultant, we developed an online usability database for storing significant test findings. Our aim was to help the group build its base of usability knowledge by making test results more readily accessible to group members working on new projects (and also to other departments in the company seeking usability input). Our role in this project was somewhat different. Rather than acting as reviewers/researchers, we were creating a product for use by the group. In this project, then, we were more *writers/designers,* who ourselves also had to be *usability testers* to understand the group's needs.

As a way to get the database started, the consulting team developed the database entries for all past reports, with the task being moved to the usability testers as the consulting team's work was completed. Although the database was completed (for a brief moment), the department testers were never convinced to enter their new reports into the database. Thus, after six months, the database was not current enough to justify its day-to-day use; it became a historical artifact in the form we developed it. But the central idea of the project—to put findings online—did not die; instead, it pushed the department to put all reports online and to begin to put report excerpts online for the whole company.

Why did this project evolve along different lines after our involvement with it ceased? There are many reasons, some related to the database platform, some to the testers' habits, some to the work-load/reward system in the department, some to a difference in conception of its worth/use, and so on. A short answer is that the database as we conceived of it did not automate an action that testers currently did by hand, and so using it was not a natural move for them.

In large part, the problems with the database can be traced to its platform for delivery. Instead of having the database loaded onto the machines testers used for their written work (Windows™ workstations), the database was housed in a special machine (a freestanding Macintosh workstation on a cart). This meant that a person had to go and locate the designated machine (it could be in one of ten or twelve offices), perhaps wait until another person finished using it, push the cart to his or her office, plug it in, and try to remember how to use it. We did some training and provided brief written instructions for use, but most of the researchers had little understanding of searching for material in the ways that librarians (and academics) would, and so the instructions got separated from the machine very quickly.

We had been excited about the prospects of this database because we thought that it could ease a number of difficulties for the testers. It could, for example, help the testers quickly decide whether any previous studies were relevant to a current request for testing; it could help testers link present findings to past findings; it could help researchers locate reports with similar methods to the ones they were contemplating; and so on. Management was excited because the database had a section that tried to track the impact of studies (i.e., how many of the suggested changes were made) and because part of the database could be loaded onto a central server for the company to see (which was a way to advertise the success of the group). A number of the testers were enthusiastic because they wanted an easier way to get at reports, findings, and methods.

The varied sources of that excitement contributed another kind of problem to the project—too many focuses. It is true that databases support alternative focuses in theory (they actually are the best method for flexibly arranging nonnumerical information for future retrieval). But in this case, some of the information required by the database to make it meet some of the needs was not part of the group's established report writing procedures—and we found changing those procedures to go beyond the scope of the project. The most notable example was tracking the impact of the study by listing how many of a report's recommendations were adopted. That tracking required data which were not in the original report, which could not be gathered for several weeks after the report was published, and which were not gathered consistently by the department for some very good reasons. Understandably, testers were going to resist constructing database entries that could not be completed until they did follow-up several weeks after writing the report. They were more likely to write database entries when those entries could be written simultaneously with the report and could be taken (almost verbatim) from the report; such entries, however, could not meet the varied goals for the database.

In part because the department head who had initiated the project departed, and in part because none of the three of us was actually a member of the department (and willing to do the work to adapt the database to the emerging needs), the difficulties with the database we designed were never solved. But the project idea did evolve. Today it consists of putting report excerpts online for the company. It now focuses on dissemination of results (one of the department head's goals) rather than helping the testers (as we intended) or tracking department success (another of the department head's goals). A prime departmental goal is to make usability information available instantaneously (and online), which they think particularly helpful to those employees at remote locations.

Figure 3 depicts our relationship with ABC in the Database Project as it unfolded over the year or so we participated in it. We see ourselves as outsiders to the department and the company, which gave us the distance to be successful with the meta-analysis and the distance to be out of touch in the Database Project. To our way of thinking, the reports continued to dominate the knowledge-making relationships, with the database seen as having more to do with those outside the department and less to do with the testers and their report-creating processes. As is obvious from our discussion above, Figure 3 reflects our understanding of how the project evolved and is not our ideal. Had the project turned out as we had hoped, the testers would have had a closer relationship with the online database, making the database less the province of the company.

If Figure 3 were drawn from the perspective of another group touched by the Database Project, we expect the relationships depicted would change. Few in the department were interested in

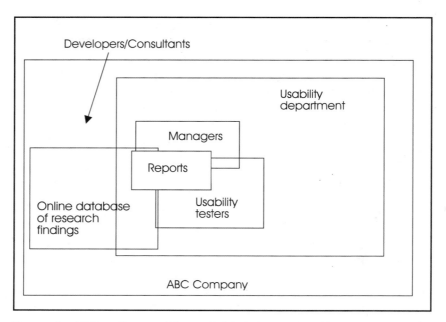

Figure 3. ABC software, Phase 2 (database development).

using the database to stimulate research; few thought it important to their mission beyond its ability to make some usability information available to the company. We recognize that because we could not deliver a product that integrated itself easily into the testers' writing processes, we could not effect the change we wanted in their writing habits. The computer proved to be a mighty foe in this case. It showed us how technological habits of writing resist changes that are not well integrated with those habits. Early on in the project, we recognized that the platform problem would be an obstacle to the database having the effect we wanted, but we did not have the power or authority or financial support to change the platform. We suggested the importance of coordinating the database design with training in the use of the database and in rethinking report writing processes, but the department, for various reasons, was not interested in rethinking their report writing procedures. Even though we were experienced writing teachers, we did not realize how hard it would be to influence these writing processes. Perhaps because we didn't provide the package on a platform that would make it easy for them to fit into current procedures, we could not overcome our positions as consultants (outsiders who are temporarily involved; transients to be survived).

Toward a Postmodern Method of Reflective Mapping

Our experiences point to how important it is for researchers in computers and writing to situate themselves in relation to their own sites of study and to reflect on their potential positionings within those sites: in other words, to understand your standpoint, including the limits of your own field or disciplinary frame. Two other points we want to make about the mapping strategies we have used above: (1) No two maps are alike. When you begin to configure the complexity of relations in any study, and when you position yourself in the study, you see that there are various roles for researchers and participants, multiple alignments, all sorts of preferences and blind spots. It seems like a mess. (2) We do not conclude from the apparent mess that "no two research projects are alike, that all research studies are distinct"—or that methodology is impossible or invalid. The power of the mapping strategy is in showing that by mapping, you can get a better handle on a messy picture. (Chaos theory is, after all, a theory about how chaos works.) Postmodern research may be messy-modal rather than multimodal, but we think there can be such a thing as a postmodern methodology that is not self-contradictory and that is still capable of generating local knowledge (in Geertz's sense of the term).

We now want to consider positioning our methodological frames for each of the three experiences in terms of several fields' views of research. Figure 4 depicts various methodological positions that we see operating in a number of fields interested in the study of computers and writing in the workplace (including rhetoric/composition, professional writing, and computer and composition), and it positions the three research experiences discussed above within its grid. This grid operates partly by identifying a range of positions along a theory-practice continuum (an argument we developed in Sullivan & Porter, 1993a).

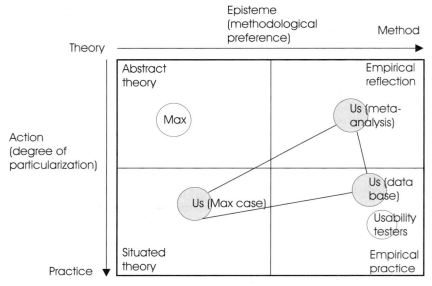

Figure 4. Methodological frames.

This map operates on two axes: the theory-to-practice axis (depicted vertically) and the theory-to-method axis (depicted horizontally). The vertical axis locates knowledge according to degree of particularity: Is general knowledge or Theory possible across situations? If you think so, then you tend toward the abstract or general grid. The horizontal axis is the one of methodological preference: in rhetoric/composition, we see this as the continuum between those who prefer theoretical/empirical approaches versus those who prefer empirical approaches to generating knowledge.

Loosely construed, the axes construct four quadrants for characterizing methodology. If we identified the most extreme positions, the four corners of the square, we might distinguish them thusly:

- abstract theory, which focuses on abstract relationships and identities and does not situate its thoughts in particulars (believed or observed); the position of ahistorical metanarrative

- empirical reflection, which focuses on abstract discussions of method and does not situate its thoughts in particulars

- situated theory, which focuses on relationships and identities that are grounded in particular situations but does not suggest those relationships are part of a larger metanarrative

- empirical practice, which focuses on observed behavior in particular situations but does not theorize those observations in any abstract way; acceptance of methods as established and fixed

Obviously, the most extreme positions (the corners) are the clearest, cleanest, neatest, and most difficult to locate in the specter of published research. Nobody actually lives there. Simultaneously, the center of the square is the richest, most contradictory, most contingent, and most difficult to maintain position. (Is this the position of *praxis*—the point of balance between theory and practice that Carolyn Miller [1989] talks about?) If we mapped actual scholars, researchers, and writers onto this map, few would fall in corners or in the center. Yet we do see tendencies in researchers to privilege certain frames.

As we map the three experiences we discussed earlier onto this grid of theory, practice, and method, we see Max as occupying the "abstract theory" quadrant. He wanted to believe in the importance of observing the particular behaviors of the users he studied—yet he deflected the data of their "practices," by interpreting all of their actions in terms of an overall Theory of Text, System, and User which he was not willing to surrender or revise. In his theory, the system is a given, and the trick to writing documentation is to produce a piece of documentation that will help the ignorant user *understand* (notice: not "use") the system. In Max's defense, we have to acknowledge that the role of technical writers in most companies is probably firmly established along these same lines. How often do technical writers actually have the political power to suggest changes in system design? Frequently, they are working in a realm where engineers and systems designers rule absolutely.

We see the members of the usability department at ABC as occupying the "empirical practice" quadrant. They, for the most part, do not believe that developing knowledge across tests is part of their mission; they see their job as answering the client's questions now and quickly. In their frame, knowledge is specific to the product, to the client's needs, and to the particular test. Thus, they see little value in studying findings from other tests, even though they would allow that extending findings across tests would improve the scientific value of their work.

We see ourselves as occupying different positions in the three different studies—which leads us to suspect that we are somewhat nomadic in our approach to research. In the Max study, our critique of Max took the form of our wishing he would pay more attention to users. "Listen to these people," we wanted to tell him, but we didn't; we wanted him to take a situated approach to his theory. In our work on the Meta-Analysis Project, we took the position of empirically reflective researchers examining the methodological assumptions of a group of research practitioners. To some extent, our problems with the Database Project may have been due to our maintaining this reflective role despite the fact that our assigned role in the second project was fundamentally different. We suspect that our being methodologically over-reflective prevented us from designing the database in a more practice-oriented way that the department would have found more palatable.

We are suggesting, too—in case it is not obvious by now—that researchers in rhetoric/composition, professional writing, and computers and writing also have their preferred quadrants. In fact, disciplines and subdisciplines tend to occupy some sectors and not others. Much of the research and the teaching/learning accounts in rhetoric/composition, for example, fit into empirical practice, while much of the theoretical work fits into abstract theory. Workplace research in professional writing locates most of its work in practice, with situated theory and empirical practice gathering most of the work. *Computers and Composition* publishes primarily about practice, with theory of texts/hypertexts fitting into the abstract theory sector. Research into the use of computers in the workplace fits primarily into empirical practice.

We see these methodological preferences linking up with "site preferences." Figure 5—our last visual, we promise—maps different research sites on the same frame. From left to right, the grid distinguishes between studies that are highly conscious of the role of technology ("technology rich") versus those that dismiss the role of technology or which do not study environments

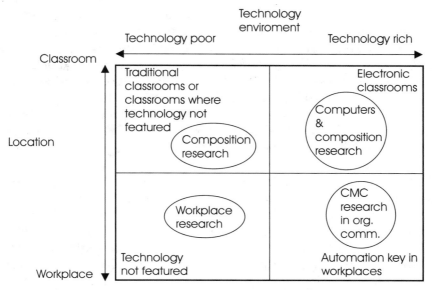

Figure 5. Research site frames.

where that role is very obvious. (Though we would contend that technology *does* inform composition instruction even in the traditional classroom—it's just that when machines aren't actually in the classroom, the presence of the "print paradigm" is not so obvious.) From top to bottom, the grid represents studies which focus on classroom activities versus research in the workplace.

While we see some complexity with the way we might map researchers on our *methodological* frames grid (because no one actually occupies the extreme corners), it is striking to us how widely research fields differ in their preferences for sites. Computers and composition researchers examine the effects of computer technologies on writing—and hardly anybody else does. Between 1990 and 1992, *Computers and Composition*—the primary journal for the computers and composition community—published fifty-two articles on computers and writing, 100 percent of its total, not surprisingly. What is surprising is that during that same time, *College Composition and Communication* published only two articles on computers and writing (2.4 percent of its total), *College English* published four (3.9 percent), *Research in the Teaching of English* published three (6.5 percent), and *Written Communication* published nine (17.6 percent) (Sullivan, 1993). (We see this same pattern of segregation in published collections, discussed below.) In other words, we see some evidence of a fairly exclusive segregation about who covers what sites. It may well be that these research communities are defining themselves, de facto, according to sites—but this is the question we wish to raise and, if we decide that this is true, challenge the segregation. This sort of segregation is particularly problematic for the study of the topic which defines this collection, as there seems to be no research field taking responsibility, yet, for the study of computers and writing in the workplace.

Research in computers and composition by and large occupies the upper-right quadrant: it is classroom-based and technology-based, as we see in articles published in *Computers and Composition* and in numerous collections (e.g., Hawisher & Selfe, 1991; Selfe & Hilligoss, 1994). This may be due in large part to the fact that many people in the computers and composition community are first-year composition teachers and administrators in charge of computer labs. They tend to have a very situated view methodologically, which fits with their situated view of technology. The strength of this research approach is its situated and thoughtful approach to technology. However, we do not see much evidence of attention to workplace writing practices. The preferred site of study for computers and composition research is the computer classroom. While there is considerable need to study the first-year classroom, exclusive focus on a single dominant site limits the field's potential for effecting change outside the writing classroom. We see it this way: The workplace is the primary writing site our students will inhabit, and the computer is one *lingua franca* that links the classroom and the workplace. Computers give us a way to cut across the dominant binary in place here—classroom versus workplace—providing a means for researchers to change workplace writing practice. We think computers and composition researchers' critical and thoughtful approach to writing technologies should extend to all the sites where technology is used in the production of writing.

Professional writing researchers, by contrast, have paid close attention to workplace writing practices—but, interestingly, without much attention to the technologies that support workplace writing. In the several major collections focusing on workplace studies in professional writing, few contributors focus on computers. We identified four major collections of workplace research in professional writing: Odell and Goswami (1985), Kogen (1989), Blyler and Thralls (1993), and Spilka (1993). Of a total of sixty-one chapters in these four collections, only three chapters focus predominantly on computer technologies in the workplace. Workplace studies in professional writing also underestimate the importance of the classroom as a workplace research site. There are frequent *discussions* of the classroom in professional writing research, but few classroom *studies*. The distinction here is key. Workplace research too often assumes that knowledge about the workplace should feed classroom practice, but not vice versa. The classroom perhaps is the best site for effecting fundamental changes in the nature of workplace literacy; it certainly provides an opportunity for experimentation, for testing new possibilities (whereas workplace action can be constrained by "the way things have always been done").

Rhetoric theorists/historians and composition researchers have tended either to ignore the workplace as unimportant (as simply an "applied" location for rhetoric theory) or to view it with suspicion (as Big Business or The Capitalist Enterprise). The tendency is to view electronic technologies as neutral or transparent—that is, as not having a significant effect on discursive practices but being, at best, a simple channel for discursive practices. Some who have noticed the technology have cast it in an evil light, seeing computers only as tools for a capitalist bureaucracy (Ohmann, 1985). We notice that recent major collections by rhetorical theorists contain no focused discussion of the role of computer writing technology: of a total of thirty-nine chapters in the Enos and Brown (1993), Harkin and Schilb (1991), and Gere (1993) collections, not one of the chapters focuses predominantly on the role of computer technology. Though we feel that computer writing technology is an incredibly important influence on "defining the new rhetorics" of postmodernism, most postmodern rhetoric theorists apparently disagree. Though not a collection, Lester Faigley's (1992) *Fragments of Rationality* is one significant exception that we hope signals a change.

A fourth group of researchers not directly "in" the general composition community provides yet another position on these issues. Researchers like Zuboff (1988) and Sproull and Kiesler (1991) take what we would call a CMC perspective toward the use of computers in the workplace (Porter, 1993). This perspective is defined by its predominant focus on the modes of technology used for *communication* in business, but its focus is by and large not *writing*. While this research perspective tends to be situated in some respects (especially sensitive to the role of technology, broadly construed), it interprets workplace practices in terms of an overall communication theory applied to specific media choices (e.g., e-mail versus telephone). CMC research favors oral over print media and tends not to take a developed rhetorical view which acknowledges writing itself as a distinct kind of technology with its own rhetorical nature.

Conclusion

We hope that the methodological mapping strategy we are offering here suggests some fruitful possibilities for researchers who are extending the research on computers and writing in the workplace.

First, clearly, this mapping technique has the heuristic intent of encouraging researchers to "situate" their studies according to two interrelated frames:

- Researchers can plot the relationships within specific studies (as we do in Figures 1, 2, and 3), situating themselves in relation to participants in the study and to the numerous possible focuses of a given study. As we have discussed, it is often difficult—and maybe impossible—for researchers to do this while they are engaged in data collection. As we noticed in the Database Project, we were not able to understand our situated role in the project until we were well into the project. Perhaps such reflection must necessarily occur sometime later—but that is not to dismiss its value as a practical knowledge that can be deployed in future projects. Plus, the mapping is intended to distinguish a project, to identify the particular roles for participants and researchers, the social elements involved, the textual dynamics—in short, to complicate the usual view that research involves two parties, observer and participant. (This is particularly important to feminist researchers and others who want to draw participants into researcher roles and to draw research into emancipatory frames.)

- Researchers can plot their research position relative to other researchers in a field or in several fields (as we do in Figures 4 and 5). Mapping is a way to identify preferences, tendencies, and, of course, blind spots. Such a mapping exercise can serve to critique fields' interests and locations ("perhaps we are doing too much work on X"; "perhaps we are doing too many studies only situated in the workplace"). It can also serve to suggest places for new researchers to locate: the blind spots and gaps in a research field's work offer an opportunity for the new researcher to make a significant contribution.

How are the two frames interrelated? What makes our approach postmodern is that the interpretation of findings moves between the two frames—the study frame and the field frame: one frame identifies the relations *within* a study; the other frame identifies the relations *between* a study and other work in a field; and the two frames destabilize each other.

Second, we hope to open up spaces for productive links between three camps which we feel have not sufficiently appreciated one another: computers and composition, professional writing, and rhetorical theory/history. We want our strategy to reveal several distinct blind spots that we believe offer fields an opportunity for future work:

- For general rhetoric/composition research, we want to open the possibility of more study of writing technologies and of workplace literacies.

- For professional writing research, we want to open the possibility of more study of the role of writing technologies in defining workplace literacies.

- For computers and composition research, we want to open the possibility of more study of the use of writing technologies in the workplace.

For the study of computers and writing in the workplace, and more generally, we see the parameters of "literacy" as too limited in each of these three fields—and we would like to encourage a kind of cross-fertilization between the fields of both methods and sites in an effort to enrich notions of literacy. Also, in particular, we want to challenge the separation of "workplace" and "classroom" studies—a binary we find ethically problematic as well as methodologically limiting.

Third, and finally, we hope to promote a postmodern approach to research methodology. We see the beginnings of such a methodology in the work of cultural anthropologists who take a reflective-situated view (Geertz, 1983; Bourdieu, 1977); in the work of computer theorists and human factors specialists who are developing a situated view (Bødker, 1991; Ehn, 1988; Greenbaum & Kyng, 1991; Suchman, 1987; Winograd & Flores, 1986); and in the work of feminist methodologists (Lather, 1991; Roman, 1992; Stanley, 1990).

What does a postmodern methodology look like? First, it promotes researcher-situated reflexivity—addressing especially the issue of the researcher's standpoint relative to (as well as relationship with) research sites and participants. Second, it recognizes the distinct and situated nature of any observation; it is especially sensitive to "local conditions" (such as particular forms of computer technology in use). Third, it is conscious of the role of power, politics, and ideology in any setting, starting perhaps with the possibility of the researcher's power over participants; institutional hierarchies that may perhaps impact researcher role or participant behavior; gender factors that may influence how a researcher participates in a study; etc. Fourth, it is especially reflective of the shifting relationships through the course of a study: researchers' perspectives probably never remain consistent throughout a study, and researcher roles may change from study to study. We think that the old categories for studies—case study, ethnography, experiment, meta-analysis—are probably not adequate for foregrounding relations within any particular study.

(They have the tendency to favor commonalities across, rather than differences between, studies.)

What we are advocating here is a research *praxis,* a perspective that sees research as a kind of reflection-in-action (Schön, 1983). We think empirical research can generate useful local knowledge as long as it exercises a kind of postmodern critical-reflective *praxis.* We find James Sosnoski's (1991) distinction between modern Theory and postmodern *theorizing* helpful to understanding this position: *Theory* is the "modernist notion of an explanatory metacommentary . . . [or] paradigmatic explanations of natural phenomena," and postmodern *theorizing* is reflection/action that is "not 'meta' to other discourses" (p. 199). Obviously we are doing, and encouraging, a lot of theoretical reflecting in this chapter—but the kind of theorizing we are advocating is postmodern in the sense that the maps we draw are not meta-maps, but rather, heuristic ones. As we approach the study of computers and writing in the workplace, we are urging researchers *not* to look for the One, Holy, and Perfect Methodological Interface, but to embrace working across methodological interfaces.

References

Barton, B.F., & Barton, M.S. (1993). Ideology and the map: Toward a postmodern visual design practice. In N.R. Blyler & C. Thralls (Eds.), *Professional communication: The social perspective* (pp. 49–78). Newbury Park, CA: Sage.

Blyler, N.R., & Thralls, C. (Eds.). (1993). *Professional communication: The social perspective.* Newbury Park, CA: Sage.

Bødker, S. (1991). *Through the interface: A human activity approach to user interface design.* Hillsdale, NJ: Erlbaum.

Bourdieu, P. (1977). *Outline of a theory of practice.* (R. Nice, Trans.). New York: Cambridge University Press.

Bourdieu, P. (1988). *Homo academicus.* (P. Collier, Trans.). Stanford, CA: Stanford University Press.

de Certeau, M. (1984). *The practice of everyday life.* (S. Randall, Trans.). Berkeley: University of California Press.

Driskill, L. (1989). Understanding the writing context in organizations. In M. Kogen (Ed.), *Writing in the business professions* (pp. 125–145). Urbana, IL: National Council of Teachers of English and Association for Business Communication.

Ehn, P. (1988). *Work-oriented design of computer artifacts.* Stockholm: Arbetslivscentrum.

Enos, T., & Brown, S.C. (Eds.). (1993). *Defining the new rhetorics.* Newbury Park, CA: Sage.

Faigley, L. (1992). *Fragments of rationality: Postmodernity and the subject of composition.* Pittsburgh: University of Pittsburgh Press.

Foucault, M. (1984). Space, knowledge, and power. In Paul Rabinow (Ed.), *The Foucault reader* (pp. 239–256). New York: Pantheon.

Geertz, C. (1983). *Local knowledge: Further essays in interpretive anthropology.* New York: Basic Books.

Gere, A.R. (Ed.). (1993). *Into the field: Sites of composition studies.* New York: Modern Language Association of America.

Greenbaum, J., & Kyng, M. (1991). *Design at work: Cooperative design of computer systems.* Hillsdale, NJ: Erlbaum.

Harkin, P., & Schilb, J. (Eds.). (1991). *Contending with words: Composition and rhetoric in a postmodern age.* New York: Modern Language Association of America.

Hawisher, G.E., & Selfe, C.L. (Eds.). (1991). *Evolving perspectives on computers and composition studies: Questions for the 1990s.* Urbana, IL: National Council of Teachers of English; Houghton, MI: *Computers and Composition.*

Kogen, M. (Ed.). (1989). *Writing in the business professions.* Urbana, IL: National Council of Teachers of English and Association for Business Communication.

Lather, P. (1991). *Getting smart: Feminist research and pedagogy with/in the postmodern.* London: Routledge.

Lyon, A. (1992). Interdisciplinarity: Giving up territory. *College English, 54,* 681–693.

Miller, C.R. (1989). What's practical about technical writing? In B.E. Fearing & W.K. Sparrow (Eds.), *Technical writing: Theory and practice* (pp. 14–24). New York: Modern Language Association of America.

Odell, L., & Goswami, D. (Eds.). (1985). *Writing in nonacademic settings.* New York: Guilford.

Ohmann, R. (1985). Literacy, technology, and monopoly capital. *College English, 47*, 675–689.

Phelps, L.W. (1988). *Composition as a human science: Contributions to the self-understanding of a discipline.* New York: Oxford University Press.

Phelps, L.W. (1991). Practical wisdom and the geography of knowledge in composition. *College English, 53*, 863–885.

Porter, J.E. (1989). Assessing readers' use of computer documentation: A pilot study. *Technical Communication, 36*, 422–423.

Porter, J.E. (1993, May). *Rhetorics of electronic writing.* Paper presented at the Ninth Conference on Computers and Writing, Ann Arbor, MI.

Porter, J.E., & Sullivan, P.A. (1994). Repetition and the rhetoric of visual design. In B. Johnstone (Ed.), *Repetition in discourse: Interdisciplinary perspectives, volume 2* (pp. 114–129). Norwood, NJ: Ablex.

Roman, L.G. (1992). The political significance of other ways of narrating ethnography: A feminist-materialist approach. In M.D. LeCompte, W.L. Millroy, & J. Preissle (Eds.), *The handbook of qualitative research in education* (pp. 555–594). San Diego: Academic Press.

Schön, D.A. (1983). *The reflective practitioner: How professionals think in action.* New York: Basic Books.

Selfe, C.L., & Hilligoss, S. (1994). *Literacy and computers: The complications of teaching and learning with technology.* New York: Modern Language Association of America.

Soja, E. (1989). *Postmodern geographies: The reassertion of space in critical social theory.* London: Verso.

Sosnoski, J.J. (1991). Postmodern teachers in their postmodern classrooms: Socrates begone! In P. Harkin & J. Schilb (Eds.), *Contending with words: Composition and rhetoric in a postmodern age* (pp. 198–219). New York: Modern Language Association of America.

Spilka, R. (Ed.). (1993). *Writing in the workplace: New research perspectives.* Carbondale: Southern Illinois University Press.

Sproull, L., & Kiesler, S. (1991). *Connections: New ways of working in the networked organization.* Cambridge, MA: MIT Press.

Stanley, L. (Ed.). (1990). *Feminist praxis: Research, theory, and epistemology in feminist sociology.* London: Routledge.

Suchman, L. (1987). *Plans and situated actions: The problem of human-machine communication.* New York: Cambridge University Press.

Sullivan, P. (1991). Taking control of the page: Electronic writing and word publishing. In G.E. Hawisher & C.L. Selfe (Eds.), *Evolving perspectives on computers and composition studies: Questions for the 1990s* (pp. 43–64). Urbana, IL: National Council of Teachers of English; Houghton, MI: *Computers and Composition*.

Sullivan, P. (1993, May). *Uses of method in computers and composition studies.* Paper presented at the Ninth Conference on Computers and Writing, Ann Arbor, MI.

Sullivan, P.A., & Porter, J.E. (1990a). How do writers view usability information? A case study of a developing documentation writer. *Asterisk (Journal of Computer Documentation), 14,* 29–35.

Sullivan, P.A., & Porter, J.E. (1990b). User testing: The heuristic advantages at the draft stage. *Technical Communication, 37,* 78–80.

Sullivan, P.A., & Porter, J.E. (1993a). On theory, practice, and method: Toward a heuristic research methodology for professional writing. In R. Spilka (Ed.), *Writing in the workplace: New research perspectives* (pp. 220–237). Carbondale: Southern Illinois University Press.

Sullivan, P.A., & Porter, J.E. (1993b). Remapping curricular geography: Professional writing in/and English. *Journal of Business and Technical Communication, 7,* 389–422.

Winograd, T., & Flores, F. (1986). *Understanding computers and cognition: A new foundation for design.* Norwood, NJ: Ablex.

Zuboff, S. (1988). *In the age of the smart machine: The future of work and power.* New York: Basic Books.

Editors

Patricia Sullivan is associate professor of English and director of the technical writing program at Purdue University, where she also teaches in the rhetoric graduate program. Her writing intersects research methodology, computers and composition, and professional and technical writing; her consulting examines the usability of various computer products. She has twice won National Council of Teachers of English awards for best publication in technical and scientific communication. A former Chair of the NCTE Committee on Technical and Scientific Communication and a member of the Committee on Instructional Technology, she is completing *Writing Technologies and Critical Research Practices* (co-authored with James E. Porter).

Jennie Dautermann is assistant professor of technical communication and rhetoric at Miami University, Oxford, Ohio, where she specializes in qualitative research methods and writing across the disciplines. She was recently named a finalist in the NCTE promising researcher competition for her study of the collaborative writing of hospital nurses. She has published in the areas of computer pedagogy, software usability, professional communication, and discourse analysis.

Contributors

Nancy Allen is assistant professor of English at Eastern Michigan University, where she teaches professional communication courses and coordinates a Macintosh classroom. Her published work reflects her interests in business and technical communication, humor as discourse, collaborative writing, and teaching.

David K. Farkas is associate professor in the Department of Technical Communication at the University of Washington and holds a Ph.D. in English from the University of Minnesota. He has a longstanding interest in online editing software and supervised the development of a prototype online editing tool in 1987.

Craig J. Hansen is assistant professor and co-chair of the Department of Writing at Metropolitan State University in St. Paul, Minnesota. He has published a variety of works in the areas of business communication, technical communication, computers and composition, and the use of communication technologies in the workplace.

Powell G. Henderson, a computer programmer and systems analyst by trade, is currently chief of the Base Services Branch of White Sands Missile Range, New Mexico. He recently received his M.A. in technical and professional communication from New Mexico State University.

Tharon W. Howard is assistant professor at Clemson University, where he teaches in the graduate program in professional communication and directs the department's usability testing facility and a document design lab. He has served as Chair of the NCTE Instructional Technology Committee and recently completed for publication a book on the *Rhetoric of Electronic Com-*

munities. He is currently investigating efforts to introduce electronic networking technologies to K–12 teachers.

Hachiro Isoda received his Ph.D. in electrical engineering from Meiji University. He joined the Central Research Institute of Electric Power Industry (CRIEPI) in 1970 and has been engaged in research on power systems control and planning and human factors concerning nuclear plant maintenance. He is currently deputy director of the Nuclear Information Center of CRIEPI.

Robert R. Johnson is assistant professor at Miami University in Oxford, Ohio, where he teaches technical communication and rhetoric. His research interests include usability, the history of technical communication and rhetoric, and issues of democracy and communication. He is currently working on a book-length study that investigates applications of rhetorical theory to technology.

Johndan Johnson-Eilola works in the rhetoric and composition program at Purdue University, where he teaches graduate and undergraduate courses in professional communication, documentation, and computers and composition. He has published on computers and communication in numerous journals and edited collections. He is currently completing *Nostalgic Angels: Rearticulating Hypertext Writing,* a book on the social and political aspects of hypertext.

Susan B. Jones is a senior technical writer at MIT in the central computing group, Information Systems. She enjoys working and debating with her colleagues in the network applications development group. Although she sometimes feels quixotic, she continues to believe that there is a place for usability testing in this "post-usability" age.

Marvin C. McCallum is a senior scientist at the Battelle Seattle Research Center. His applied research has focused on the determination of user requirements for various types of developing systems and the design and evaluation of complex systems. His human factors support of design and evaluation has been applied to automobile controls, navigation displays, nuclear power plant displays, decision support systems, and documentation software. He has published the results of his research in more than fifty book chapters, journal articles, and technical reports.

Barbara Mirel is assistant professor in technical and professional communication in the School for New Learning at De Paul University, where she also directs the curriculum-wide writing-assessment program. She teaches courses in workplace writing, research methodology, and documentation, including courses conducted electronically on the Internet. She is a book review editor for *IEEE Transactions on Professional Communication,* national secretary of the ACM-Special Interest Group on Documentation (SIGDOC), and the new article editor for the *Journal of Computer Documentation.* Published widely in technical communication journals and edited books, her research has highlighted the uses of database technologies at work, instructions for complex tasks and problem solving, and the ways that context affects usability.

Jennifer Morgan is a principal research scientist at Battelle Seattle Research Center. Her experience includes more than fifteen years in software engineering and software development project management and four years in avionics hardware prototype development. She is experienced in designing and developing software systems for a wide variety of traditional computer mainframes, minicomputers, and microcomputers; in addition, her experience as part of a team developing state-of-the-art navigation hardware has given her a unique ability to integrate both hardware and software solutions. She has done development work in several computer languages on a variety of platforms.

Steven E. Poltrock holds a Ph.D. in cognitive psychology from the University of Washington. He conducted research in perception, cognition, and mathematical psychology at the University of Denver and Bell Laboratories. Now at Boeing, he leads a research project dealing with collaborative authoring.

James E. Porter is associate professor and director of business writing at Purdue University, where he teaches in the rhetoric Ph.D. program. His research focuses on issues of ethics and audience in professional writing and electronic discourse. Author of *Audience and Rhetoric: An Archeological Composition of the Discourse Community,* he is currently completing *Rhetorical Ethics and Internetworked Writing* and *Writing Technologies and Critical Research Practices* (co-authored with Patricia Sullivan).

Robert M. Schumacher Jr. is currently a network services engineer in the Customer Interface Systems and Human Factors Group at Ameritech in Hoffman Estates, Illinois. His current interests are in graphical- , character- , and phone-based user-interface standards and in human factors issues in electronic publishing. He was formerly employed by Covia Partnership and Bellcore, where he researched and designed phone-based interfaces. He is currently an associate editor of *Ergonomics in Design.* He received his B.A. in psychology and speech communication from Eastern Illinois University in 1981, and A.M. and Ph.D. in cognitive and experimental psychology from the University of Illinois at Urbana-Champaign in 1989. He is the former president of the Chicago Metropolitan Chapter of the Human Factors and Ergonomics Society.

Stuart A. Selber is assistant professor and Internet/multimedia specialist in the Department of Technical Communications at Clarkson University. He has published on the social and rhetorical dimensions of computing in technical communication journals and edited collections. He is currently an associate editor for communication technology issues for *IEEE Transactions on Professional Communication.*

Cynthia L. Selfe is professor and department chair of the Department of Humanities at Michigan Technological University. She co-founded and continues to co-edit *Computers and Composition.* She is co-editor of *Critical Perspectives on Computers and Composition Instruction,* the *CCCC Bibliography on Composition and Rhetoric* (1991–1993), and *Evolving Perspectives on Computers and Composition Studies* (all with Gail Hawisher); *Computers* *and Writing: Theory, Research, Practice* (with Deborah Holdstein); and *Literacy and Computers* (with Susan Hilligoss). She is currently completing *Historical Perspectives on Computers and Composition: The Growth and Emergence of a Field* (with Gail Hawisher, Paul LeBlanc, and Charles Moran).

Brenda R. Sims is associate professor and director of technical writing at the University of North Texas. She has also published articles in the *Technical Communication Quarterly,* the *Journal of Business Communication,* and the *Technical Writing Teacher.* She has a textbook, *Technical Writing for Readers and Writers,* forthcoming.

Douglas R. Wieringa is a research scientist at the Battelle Seattle Research Center. He has applied his education in technical communication to a variety of projects in addition to that described in this chapter, including developing standards for nuclear power plant procedures, producing a newsletter on industrial health and safety, investigating the usefulness of flowcharts as procedures, and writing and editing a variety of technical reports. He is a co-author of *Procedure Writing: Principles and Practices.*

Joseph Y. Yasutake has recently retired after a long career in human factors, training, and integrated logistics support. He has worked for the U.S. government and Lockheed and was most recently manager of human factors for the Electric Power Research Institute (EPRI).

Index

Abbott, T., 268, 279
Abstract theory, 310, 312
Access
  to information infrastructure, 210–211, 259, 260
  to technology, xxii, 227–230, 242
  unevenness of, 271–272
Accuracy
  of online editing, 162
  in procedure documentation, 143
Adorno, T., 283
Afternoon (Joyce), 126
Age cues, in e-mail, 48
Allen, M.W., xviii, xix
Allen, N., xxv
Allen, T.J., xix
Alred, G.J., 159
Amato, J., 127
Ameritech, 146–150
Anderson, P., 217
Anonymity, in e-mail, 48
Anzaldúa, G., 279
Apple, M.W., 280
Articulation theory, 131–133
Artificial intelligence, 206
ASCII (American Standard Code for Information Interchange), 228, 272–273
Aspects (Online editing tool), 160
Asterisks, in e-mail, 52
Athena Computing Environment, 26–27
Atkinson, D.L., xvii
Atlantic Monthly, 117
Authors
  and copyrights, 189
  dialogue with editors, 156–157, 167
  profit protection for, 186
  rights of, 185, 186–187

Automating technologies
  in corporate sites, 119
  distinctions of, 116
  vs. informating technologies, 121
  in World Wide Web, 120
Automation
  expense vs. benefits, 147
  simplicity/complexity of, 150–151
  worker displacement by, 129
  workplace resistance to, 305–306

Back pain, 162
Baecker, R.M., 174
Barabas, C., xiv
Barker, T.T., xvii, 203
Barley, S.R., xix
Barton, B.F., xiv, 96, 296
Barton, E., 217, 218
Barton, M.S., xiv, 96, 296
Bates, C.E., 247–248
Batson, T., xvii, 9, 232
Battelle Institute, 144, 147
Baudrillard, J., 283
Baylor College of Medicine, 134
Beard, J., 182, 184, 185, 194
Beason, G., xviii
Becker, H.J., xvii, 271
Bentham, J., 203
Bergstrom, M., 96
Bernhardt, S.A., xiv
Bertin, J., 96, 105
Biber, D., 57
Bing, G., 209
BITNET, 43, 278
Blumenthal, C., 191, 195, 196
Blyler, N.R., 315
Bødker, S., 319
Boehm-Davis, D., 95
Boeing corporation, 134–135, 159
Boilerplate techniques, 3, 7, 9